Lovecraft's Boyhood Cat

Ken Faig, Jr.

I, and probably many of my readers, find the name of Lovecraft's boyhood cat offensive. However, I do not think it is right to try to censor or bowdlerize history for the sake of our own sensibilities. If they wish, readers are welcome to substitute "Blackie" throughout for the actual name of Lovecraft's boyhood cat. I hope that very few of my readers will seek to deny that the gifted young boy loved his pet and mourned its disappearance in that dreadful year (1904), which also witnessed the death of his grandfather and the loss of his home at 454 Angell Street in Providence.

It is no secret that Lovecraft adored cats. He relished lots of epistolary attention on the cats kept by some of his correspondents, such as R. H. Barlow, Clark Ashton Smith, and E. Hoffmann Price. (He met Barlow's cats in person during his months-long visits to the Barlow home in 1934 and 1935.) After he and Annie Gamwell moved to 66 College Street in 1933, he delighted in the antics of the cats who loved to sun themselves on the roof of the neighboring shed, whom he dubbed the "Kappa Alpha Tau" fraternity. He customarily kept catnip in his pocket to delight feline acquaintances. Occasionally he would invite a neighboring feline into his own quarters for play. But after boyhood he never had a cat of his own.

Bobby Derie identified for me the first surviving epistolary reference to Nigger-Man. Writing from Grand View, Idaho, on 17 October 1895, Whipple V. Phillips told his grandson to "take care of Nig" (*LFF* 1046). This tells us that Nigger-Man was definitely in residence by that date, and furthermore that the short form of his name used by the family was Nig. It may have been Lovecraft's grandfather who was responsible for the naming of Nigger-Man.

Surprisingly, Lovecraft's own letters are fairly sparing in mentions of his own boyhood cat. However, he doted on his memories of his happy boyhood at 454 Angell Street and wrote to his aunt Annie Gamwell on 19 August 1921:

> I yet recall the happiness of Aug. 20, 1903, when I attained that age [thirteen]—the balmy evening in the yard at #454 under the trees with my telescope, seemingly secure in a prosperous environment, & fresh with the wonder of gazing up through space at other worlds. And my old nigger-man was leaping in & out of the shadowy bushes, occasionally deigning to let his Grandpa Theobald pick him up, put his green shining eye to the telescope, & show him the cryptical surfaces of remote planets—where for all we know the dominant denizens are lithe, quadrupedal, sable-furred gentlemen like Nigger-Man himself. (*LFF* 43)

He identified his boyhood cat by name as early as his letter to Edwin Baird dated 3 February 1924: "I can assure you that Nigger-Man is (or was, alas!) a glorious and purring reality!" (*Letters to Woodburn Harris and Others* 49). In fact, he had the habit of calling any black kitten "nigger-man." In a letter to Lillian D. Clark dated 20 July 1925 he called a black kitten whom he had encountered in a watchmaker's shop "the finest black kittie that I've seen since the days of my own nigger-man!" (*LFF* 316). Only a week later (27 July 1925) he again wrote to Mrs. Clark of the "loveliest little coal-black nigger-baby that ever purred or said 'meow' . . . Not a non-black hair on the little devil—& his face exactly like my vanished Nigger-Man's" (*LFF* 323–24).

When little Samuel Perkins arrived as a new member of the Kappa Alpha Tau fraternity in 1934, Lovecraft also described him as a "nigger-man."[1] (e.g., letter to Maurice W. Moe, 17 July 1934 [*Letters to Maurice W. Moe and Others* 351], letter to James F. Morton, 19 July 1934 [*Letters to James F. Morton* 354]. Lovecraft described another cat as "the furry incarnation of my old Nigger-Man of thirty years ago!" in his letter to Clifford M. Eddy, 26 January 1930 (*Miscellaneous Letters* 172).

---

1. Note that HPL did not use capital letters when he was using this term generically to refer to black cats.

THE LOVECRAFT ANNUAL

Edited by S. T. Joshi   No. 19 (2025)

Contents

Abbreviations used in the text and notes:

AT   *The Ancient Track* (Hippocampus Press, 2013)
CE   *Collected Essays* (Hippocampus Press, 2004–06; 5 vols.)
CF   *Collected Fiction* (Hippocampus Press, 2015–17; 4 vols.)
IAP   S. T. Joshi, *I Am Providence: The Life and Times of H. P. Love-craft* (Hippocampus Press, 2010; 2013 [paper])
LL   *Lovecraft's Library: A Catalogue,* 5th rev. ed. (Hippocampus Press, 2024)

Copyright © 2025 by Hippocampus Press
Published by Hippocampus Press, P.O. Box 641, New York, NY 10156
www.hippocampuspress.com

Cover illustration by Allen Koszowski. Hippocampus Press logo designed by Anastasia Damianakos. Cover design by Barbara Briggs Silbert.

Lovecraft material is used by permission of The Estate of H. P. Lovecraft; Lovecraft Holdings, LLC.

Lovecraft Annual is published once a year, in Fall. Articles and letters should be sent to the editor, S. T. Joshi, ℅ Hippocampus Press, and must be accompanied by a self-addressed stamped envelope if return is desired. All reviews are assigned. Literary rights for articles and reviews will reside with *Lovecraft Annual* for one year after publication, whereupon they will revert to their respective authors. Payment is in contributor's copies.

ISSN 1935-6102
ISBN 978-1-61498-476-4

Lovecraft specified Nigger-Man's own coloration in his letter to Helen V. Sully, 15 August 1935: "What keeps me alive is the ability to look back to the past & imagine I am still in 1902 or 1903. Of all my dreams, about 0.80 are of that period—with myself in short trousers & at the old house, with my mother, grandfather, black cat Nigger-Man, &c. still alive" (*Letters to Wilfred B. Talman* 429). Nigger-Man turned up in several letters which Lovecraft wrote near the end of his life. He wrote to Harry O. Fischer on 10 January 1937[2]:

> What a boy he was! I watched him grow from a tiny black handful to one of the most fascinating & understanding creatures I've ever seen. He used to talk in a genuine language of varied intonation—a special tone for every different meaning. There was even a special "prrr'p" for the smell of roast chestnuts, on which he doted.[3] He used to play ball with me—kicking a large rubber sphere back at me from half across the room with all four feet as he lay on the floor. And on summer evenings in the twilight he would prove his kinship to the elfin things of shadow by racing across the lawn on nameless errands, darting into the blackness of the shrubbery now & then, & occasionally leaping at me from ambush & then bounding away again into invisibility before I could catch him. (de Camp 40; *IAP* 97)

Then he wrote to Genevieve Sully on 7 February 1937: "I can well credit the acuteness of comprehension which you mention, for my old Nigger-Man of more than 30 years ago possessed something very similar. The phenomenon of the cream-bottle lid reminds me of Nigger-Man's instant responsiveness to the

---

2. Joshi and Schultz (*Letters to C. L. Moore and Others* 18) state that HPL probably wrote three letters to Harry Otto Fischer (1910–1986), of which they print fragments of one, which they date to late February 1937. The fragment they print (323–25) does not include the passage about Nigger-Man. De Camp presumably obtained access to the letter to Fischer of 10 January 1937 from a private source.

3. HPL also wrote to Lillian D. Clark on 29 November 1924 of a Thanksgiving dinner prepared by his wife which included "boiled & roasted chestnuts . . . which would have delighted the heart of my epicurean old Nigger-Man of 21 years ago!" [*LFF* 228].

phrase 'roast chestnuts,' which typified his ideal of epicurean delight" (*Letters to Wilfred B. Talman* 485).

Whether Nigger-Man's name was bestowed by Lovecraft himself or by another family member is unknown. We do know from what Lovecraft wrote to Fischer in 1937 that he first knew his pet as a kitten. While his mother Susie Lovecraft had returned to her parents' home at 454 Angell Street[4] in Providence to give birth to Howard in 1890, she and her husband resided in the Boston area after their marriage in 1889—first in Dorchester, and then in the vicinity of Auburndale,[5] where Winfield Lovecraft eventually acquired a lot for building. The young couple and their son are known to have vacationed in Dudley, Massachusetts, in 1892. But in April 1893, Winfield Lovecraft, who was suffering from tertiary syphilis, became delusional during a business trip to Chicago and was returned involuntarily to Providence and committed to Butler Hospital, where he died in 1898. If they were still living in Massachusetts at the time Winfield was returned to Providence, Susie and her son must soon have relocated to her parents' home. If a neighbor's cat had a litter of kittens at about the same time, it might have been the occasion for the Phillips family to adopt one of the kittens to help cheer young Howard during all the changes occasioned by his father's committal. So I agree with S. T. Joshi (*IAP* 97) that 1893 is a good probable date for the birth of Nigger-Man and his adoption by the Phillips family.

As for the name given the young feline, Nigger-Man was a black cat and named accordingly. *Felis niger* is Latin for black cat; *homo niger* for black man. Lovecraft wrote to Lillian D. Clark of another feline encounter on 20 August 1924: "a moment later another appear'd—this one jet black, like my old nigger-man" (*LFF* 150).

---

4. Numbered 194 Angell Street until renumbered as 454 Angell Street in 1896.

5. In correspondence, HPL claimed his parents had resided in the home of poet Louise Imogen Guiney (1861–1920) and her mother in Auburndale, but surviving correspondence of Miss Guiney from 1892 identifies her boarders as Germans.

Like many cat owners, Lovecraft was convinced of the superior intellect and abilities of his pet. Most cats like to bat at objects tossed before them, but it is certainly not impossible that Nigger-Man liked to kick a ball back at his master. As for communications via purring or various intonations of other noises like meows, who is to say? Boiled horsemeat had been sold in London for consumption by cats for many years, but cat food per se did not begin to be marketed until the mid-1870s. Nigger-Man was probably fed table scraps supplemented by occasional treats like roasted chestnuts. As a mature cat, he may well also have been expected to be a mouser, and to supplement his diet thereby. Even an immaculately kept three-story wooden house (built c. 1875) would probably have had colonizations by mice which needed to be controlled.

Nigger-Man apparently had freedom of the grounds at 454 Angell Street. There was an ample fenced yard and a carriage house among other places to explore. A line of low shrubs extended along the Angell Street frontage of the home. Whether there was a mud room through which Nigger-Man could have accessed the house, or even a small cat door, does not seem to be known. Perhaps an inconspicuous place might even have been found for a litter-box (e.g., in the basement), so that Nigger-Man did not have to venture outside in the coldest weather. Commercial cat litter had yet to be marketed, but any kind of loose soil could probably have been pressed into service. Cats instinctively use their back paws to cover their feces, even in the wild.

Sadly, Nigger-Man eventually disappeared. Lovecraft wrote to Duane Rimel on 13 May 1934: "I think I told you that disappearance was also the fate of my beloved old Nigger-Man" (*Letters to F. Lee Baldwin* 74). Lovecraft provided further details in his letter to J. Vernon Shea, 23 October 1931: "And *cats*—well, you're welcome to your own opinions, but I can tell you that if I had a real home the first thing I'd get would be a pair of coal-black, silky kittens with large yellow eyes! I still mourn my old Nigger-Man, who wandered into his native night in 1904" (*Letters to J. Vernon Shea* 74). Lovecraft wrote to Maurice W. Moe on 5 April 1931 concerning the disappearance of Nigger-Man:

"I had been vastly attached to my grandfather and to my birth-place, and when both—to say nothing of my beloved cat Nigger-Man—were swept away in the course of a few months, I was about ready to cash in myself" (*Letters to Maurice W. Moe and Others* 301).

Nigger-Man apparently disappeared not long after the death of Whipple Phillips in March 1904. Since the death of Whipple's wife in 1896, the marriage of Annie Phillips to Edward F. Gamwell in 1897, and the marriage of Lillie Phillips to Franklin C. Clark in 1902, Susie Lovecraft and her son had been increasingly alone with Whipple V. Phillips in his large house. There was only one live-in servant enumerated in the household in the 1900 U.S. census. Problems affecting the remaining property of Whipple's Owyhee Land and Irrigation Company in Idaho (including a burst dam) occurred in the same year as his death and probably only made the settlement of his estate more complex. In any case, the home at 454 Angell Street was sold in the spring or summer of 1904, and Susie and her son had to move to the ground-floor flat (numbered 598) at 598-600 Angell Street. Whether Susie and her son attempted to move the eleven-year-old Nigger-Man with them to 598 Angell Street is unknown. De Camp (40) speculates that the senior cat may have disliked the change and run away (perhaps seeking his old home). In the last analysis, we are only able to write for Nigger-Man's epitaph: dis-appeared 1904. He was probably about eleven years old at the time of his disappearance—a feline senior citizen, especially in the early twentieth century.

Lovecraft seldom discussed his boyhood cat in correspond-ence, preferring to concentrate on the living cats of his corre-spondents. However, in his story "The Rats in the Walls," published in *Weird Tales* in March 1924, he did use "Nigger-Man" as the name of the senior cat owned by the American heir who inherited and renovated Exham Priory (CF 1.381). Of course, "The Rats in the Walls" is not the only Lovecraft fiction featuring cats. Cats jump from the dark side of the moon to the dream world (where they are allied with the forces of good) in *The Dream-Quest of Unknown Kadath*. In "The Cats of Ulthar," the story is told why no man can kill a cat in Ulthar. There are undoubtedly other examples of cats in Lovecraft's fiction which might be cited.

Is there any further memorial for Lovecraft's boyhood cat Nigger-Man? I think there might be. A famous photograph was taken of 454 Angell Street and its inhabitants in (I think) the summer of 1895[6]:

Whipple V. Phillips is seated in front of the shrubbery on the Angell Street façade. His wife, Robie (Place) Phillips, is seated behind him (to his right) on the porch. She was probably already ailing and would die in January 1896. To Whipple's right, on the walkway, adorned in all her finery, is young Annie Phillips (1866–

---

6. The photograph (apparently taken from an album) was originally the property of family friend Nelson Rogers and passed from him to HPL collector Jack Grill (1903–1968). It was listed in the catalogue of Grill's collection (Owings-Binkin, item 534; see also plates between pp. 22–23) and acquired by Sean Donnelly. (The photograph is no longer owned by Donnelly.) I am grateful to David E. Schultz and Sean Donnelly for the images from the photograph reproduced in this paper. Blogger David Haden (Tentaclii) made a colorized version of the photograph for his blog.

1941), perhaps already dating Brown University graduate student and instructor Edward F. Gamwell. To Whipple's left is, I think, his eldest daughter Lillie Phillips (1856–1932). Here is an enlargement including the four persons captured in the photograph:

Clearly, Lillie is holding something dark-colored in her hands. Does she grasp the head with her left hand and support the torso with her right? Is there a tail dependent from the main body? Of course, it is difficult to tell, but would she hold a purse or a wrap with quite the same arrangements of her arms? On Lillie's right hand, which appears to cradle the posterior of what she is holding, I can distinguish her thumb and four fingers. On the other hand, her left hand appears very blurry and I am not sure I can distinguish any fingers—perhaps she moved during the exposure. Where the animal's head ought to be appears to be very flat and elongated. Perhaps Nigger-Man—disturbed by all the fuss—is pressing his face into Lillie's bosom and we see only his shoulders and the back of his head. However, David E. Schultz believes that Nigger-Man is in fact facing the photographer, with his head below Lillie's blurry left hand.

The reader must be the judge, but my opinion is that Lillie is holding the two-year-old Nigger-Man in her arms. Where were Susie and her son Howard when this photograph was taken? We do not know. If the photograph was taken in the summer of 1895, Howard was probably not yet five, too young for school; besides, it was summer. (He is not known to have attended school until he went to Slater Avenue School in 1898.) There does not seem to be any indication of anyone behind Robie Phillips on the porch. We can only say that Susie and her son were apparently otherwise engaged when the photograph was taken. Perhaps difficulty was anticipated in keeping Howard still for the necessary duration of the exposure, and some other activity found for him and his mother during the photographic session.

Of course, we are all mortal, and all the human beings depicted in the photograph are long gone—the last, Annie (Phillips) Gamwell, died in 1941. But it is amazing to think that another life—even more ephemeral than human beings—may have been captured in this 1895 photograph. The human beings depicted all rest in Swan Point Cemetery—as well as Winfield, Susie, and Howard Lovecraft. What became of the remains of Nigger-Man will undoubtedly remain unknown. If his remains were carted away with the trash, it may be possible that the skull of a certain black cat still rests in some long-disused Providence dump. If he fell victim to a predator, perhaps his skeletal remains rest in the predator's erstwhile den.

Some writers on racism in Lovecraft's work today would hold the three-year-old boy (or at least his family) fully accountable for the naming of his boyhood cat. That racism mars some of his published work and some of his posthumously published letters is an admitted fact. We need not, however, hate the man and his works (or cancel their memory) because of his defects. I think Nigger-Man has been the innocent victim of some of this discussion. I would rather leave him darting in and out of the shrubbery in the twilight at 454 Angell Street in the years 1893–1904. The joy he brought to the boy and the joy the boy brought to him remain. Whether he is depicted in the 1895 photograph of 454 Angell Street or not, he remains a part of the Lovecraft story. Like all pets, he taught his owner lessons of love and of loss—lessons which the boy took with him to help navigate the challenges of adult life.

View to the west of #454 (do we see a second fence or plant supports in a garden?). Angell Court was eventually built on some of the land in the background.

Shrubbery on Angell Street façade of #454 (with Annie E. Phillips) (note basement windows)

Carriage house to north of 454 Angell. Demolished 1931.[7] Driveway to Elmgrove Avenue separated by fence. Second story was living quarters for coachman and family.

---

7. Possibly to create parking spaces for medical offices at 454 Angell.

Acknowledgments

I thank David E. Schultz and Bobby Derie for assistance with references to Nigger-Man in Lovecraft's correspondence. Schultz, Sean Donnelly, and David Haden assisted me with the ca. 1895 photograph of 454 Angell Street. I remain solely responsible for all statements of fact and of opinion in the monograph.

Works Cited

de Camp, L. Sprague. *Lovecraft: A Biography*. Garden City, NY: Doubleday, 1975.

Lovecraft, H. P. *Letters to C. L. Moore and Others*. Ed. David E. Schultz and S. T. Joshi. New York: Hippocampus Press, 2017.

———. *Letters to F. Lee Baldwin, Duane W. Rimel, and Nils Frome*. Ed. David E. Schultz and S. T. Joshi. New York: Hippocampus Press, 2016.

———. *Letters to Family and Family Friends*. Ed. S. T. Joshi and David E. Schultz. New York: Hippocampus Press, 2020. [LFF]

———. *Letters to James F. Morton*. Ed. David E. Schultz and S. T. Joshi. New York: Hippocampus Press, 2011.

———. *Letters to J. Vernon Shea, Carl F. Strauch, and Lee McBride White*. Ed. S. T. Joshi and David E. Schultz. New York: Hippocampus Press, 2016.

———. *Letters to Maurice W. Moe and Others*. Ed. David E. Schultz and S. T. Joshi. New York: Hippocampus Press, 2018.

———. *Letters to Wilfred B. Talman and Helen V. and Genevieve Sully*. Ed. David E. Schultz and S. T. Joshi. New York: Hippocampus Press, 2019.

———. *Letters to Woodburn Harris and Others*. Ed. S. T. Joshi and David E. Schultz. New York: Hippocampus Press, 2022.

———. *Miscellaneous Letters*. Ed. David E. Schultz and S. T. Joshi. New York: Hippocampus Press, 2022.

Owings, Mark, and Irving Binkin. *A Catalog of Lovecraftiana: The Grill/Binkin Collection*. Baltimore: Mirage Press, 1975.

Letters to the *Providence Journal*

H. P. Lovecraft

Robert E. Lee

To the Editor of the Sunday Journal:

In the Journal of Jan. 24 I noticed a letter of Charles F. Janes relating to Roosevelt's proposed memorial to Gen. Robert E. Lee, in which several statements somewhat derogatory to the great Confederate leader's motives are made. Mr. Janes asserts that our President honors Gen. Lee only because he was an able warrior, insinuating that the cause for which he so valiantly labored and bravely suffered was wrong, indirectly accusing him of attempting to "destroy this Government of the people, by the people and for the people," and calling him a "foe of the country." This unjust treatment of Gen. Lee can be construed as nothing more than a survival of the rabid, unreasoning spirit which pervaded the North before, during and immediately after the Civil War. When Robert E. Lee became a General in the Confederate Army, he did so not as an enemy, but as a friend of the Republic. He saw that no peace could come to the Union if Southern affairs were to be managed by Northerners who had no definite ideas of the actual conditions in the South, and who derived their information as to slavery from false and exaggerated reports, or from hysterical effusions like "Uncle Tom's Cabin," which portrayed the darkest side of the situation. In other words, he clearly saw that his State had seceded only because the yoke of the Union born too heavily upon it, and that its secession was within the limits of constitutional right.

It was not without regret that Gen. Lee entered into battle against the flag under which he had once nobly fought; it was not that he loved the Union less, but Virginia more. Believing in the best of faith that he was benefiting the country by separating the two discordant sections, fighting up to the very last for the cause he knew to be right, yet supported only by a pitifully small band of hungry, sick and ragged heroes, Gen. Robert Edward Lee deserves not one word of censure from the American people, but volumes of praise and veneration. As Senator Hill of Georgia once truly said: "He was Caesar without his ambition. He was Cromwell without his bigotry. He was Napoleon without his selfishness. He was Washington without his reward."

H. P. LOVECRAFT.

Providence, Jan. 24.

General Lee and His Cause

To the Editor of the Sunday Journal:

Of the three letters regarding Gen. Robert E. Lee in the Journal of Feb. 7, each seems to present a different amount of condemnation of the great warrior. The article signed "Prescott," appears to be the most unjust, hence demands first attention. In the course of this letter, it is stated that Lee was "lured on by the ambition, not only of becoming victor in the finals, but the Washington of the South." That Lee was, in intent and purpose, the "Washington of the South," cannot be disputed by any intelligent observer, but to aver that the hope of victory and renown was, instead of honor and unswerving principle, the object which spurred him on, is most unfair to a man of such a type as Robert E. Lee represents.

The General was not ambitious; he was, instead, of a character unexcelled by that of any other American, save possibly Washington. Had he been less upright, had he possessed less Virginian honor, or had he felt less sincerity of purpose, he would not have remained loyal to his oppressed and troubled State, but would have accepted the tempting offer of Lincoln to command the Union forces in place of Gen. Winfield Scott. His glorious honor is shown by his words to Gen. Hampton in 1869, when he told the noted cavalry leader that he did nothing but his duty in fighting with the Confederacy, and that he would repeat this course if the same conditions existed. His was the truest patriotism, a rigid devotion to the state, which had been forced into battle by its oppressors.

That the United States Government declined to accept the citizenship of Lee after his surrender is a fact which must always throw a shadow on its reputation for justice and fairness, for after the war, the great commander realized his defeat, recognized the union, and said to his men, "Remember that we are one country now. Do not bring up your children in hostility to the Government of the United States. Bring them up to be Americans." In the face of such a magnanimous sentiment, is it not rather small and petty to suggest, as does the "Prescott" letter, that the erection of a Lee memorial be left to those on the Virginia side of the Potomac?

The letter of Charles F. Janes makes as its principal point an attempt to prove Gen. Lee a "foe of the country." Mr. Janes asserts that in telling how the brave military leader "entered into battle against the flag, under which he had once nobly fought." I admit that he was a "foe of that flag and the country which it represents." That he was a very reluctant foe of the American flag is a fact, which no one desires to controvert, but that that, or any one flag, could truly represent the divided country of 1861, is a point which requires thought. A country is, in the last analysis, essentially composed of nothing but its people, and when these become divided into two sections, who shall say which section is actually the true country, even though one retains the old name and flag?

When the war cloud first menaced America, the Southerners desired to retain the Union banner and simply fight for their rights, but as this would have been rebellion, they decided to adopt a more peaceful course, and secede, which they did, without the intention of war. The war was caused by attempts to force the seceded States back, for which there was no constitutional justification. Horace Greeley, himself a Northerner, said: "We hope never to live in a republic whereof one section is pinned to the residue by bayonets." Southern States were as much as if not more truly American than their Northern neighbors, hence Gen. Lee in fighting with the Confederacy, did not wage war against his country; but fought with one part of it against another part, for a cause which would have benefited both. That his section did not bear the old name, nor carry the old flag was no fault of his, for he and his men were all Americans, seeking their rights from those who would not grant then willingly.

The letter of Bertha G. Higgins contains an inquiry as to where in the United States Constitution will be found an admission of the right of a State to secede from the Union. The answer is in articles IX. and X. of the amendments. Article IX. reads: "The enumeration in the Constitution of certain rights shall not be construed to deny or disparage others retained by the people." The text of article X. is: "The powers not delegated to the United States by the Constitution, nor prohibited by it to the States, are reserved to the States respectively, or to the people." As there is nothing prohibitory of secession in the Constitution, these articles may be considered as tacit admissions of the rights of States to withdraw from the federation. They are from the first set of amendments, having been proposed in 1789. Without them, it is doubtful if some of the Southern States would have ratified the Constitution and entered the Union in the first place.

The moral right of secession is a different and more weighty matter than the legal right, but an impartial observer cannot fail to see that it was not without great deliberation, long suffering, and patient waiting that the eleven Confederate States exercised their constitutional prerogative and withdrew from the Union. The provocation was great, far greater than the average Northerner can imagine. It was not one act alone, but a series of persecution that forced the Southern States to a choice between withdrawal and ruin. The excessive tariff whereby the North waxed rich at the expense of the South, coupled with the unfair legislation against slavery, was more than enough to give a moral right to secession, even had no legal right resisted.

However, the outcome of the war has proved not only the futility of the Constitution, but the practical permanence of the

Union. Therefore the people of both sections should now be unanimous in attempting to make the Union one in spirit as well as fact, in attempting to dispel those last drops of bitterness against the Government which linger in so many Southern minds, and that remaining vestige of Northern prejudice which causes the average New Englander to applaud the Union side of the great civil struggle without more than a superficial glance at its causes, events, and effects. What could accomplish such a unification more than a memorial, erected by a reverent and united people, to Robert Edward Lee, the brave Confederate general, who labored so valiantly to benefit his country by division?

H. P. LOVECRAFT.

Providence, Feb. 10.

"The Clansman's" Other Side

To the Editor of the Sunday Journal:

The action of the Police Commission the court in permitting the presentation of the Rev. Thomas Dixon, Jr.'s, drama of reconstruction times, "The Clansman," during the week of Sept. 13, is a hopeful sign, inasmuch as it is indicative of the fact that, despite the protest of the negroes, the truth may be publicly shown and spoken. "Magna est veritas, et praevalebit." In the North, where only scattered portions of the black race are found, the play no doubt seems exaggerated, and the depths of African racial character portrayed in it seem almost incredible to those accustomed to the relatively superior negroes of the Northern States, but to condemn this drama as some have lately done is unfair.

"The Clansman" teaches us a lesson of which some are sadly in need, namely, that we must never, under any circumstances, at any time, or in any place, again allow the negro, with his dark ancestry of innumerable centuries of savagery, to become in any way a political power, or to hold any office whatsoever over persons of the superior Aryan race, and that never must the Ethiopian approach the Caucasian on the plane of absolute equality, lest, as is said by "Stoneman" in the play, the noble Anglo-Saxon population of this country degenerate into a puny breed of mulattoes. "Race prejudice" is often condemned, but is it not an essential instinct for the preservation of the purity and distinction of races, an instinct almost as important as that of self-preservation? To "uplift" the blacks in masses to our level is impossible. Ethnology, even more than history, shows us that the African has still far to progress in the upward trend of natural evolution before he can call the Aryan "brother." To study the negro in his native savage state is enough to disprove the oft-repeated platitude that slavery is the cause of the inferiority of the race in this country.

Another point of error in some denunciations of "The Clansman" regards the moral status of the Ku Klux Klan. The Klan was illegal, no one desires to controvert that point. But the "law" that it defied was but a travesty on justice, but a ruinous series of revengeful attacks on the decent people or the South by ignorant and malicious "carpet-baggers," "scalawags," and blacks. The Ku Klux Klan was composed of the noblest of young Southrons that the land could afford, an organization of Honor, Chivalry, Humanity, Mercy and Patriotism, to protect the weak, innocent and oppressed from unjust "law," and the more hideous and unspeakable terrors of the black peril. To deny that such a black peril existed, and would exist again if the negroes, once more came into power, is prejudiced folly. As a slave, the average negro was happy, contented and peaceable; free, the innate demon comes uppermost, especially if aided by unscrupulous whites who have interests of their own in the matter. To say that "The Clansman" arouses "hate" against the negro is untrue. "Hate" for a race as a race is unthinkable. The black at his normal level is a part of the perfect scheme of nature, harmonious and unobtrusive. "Hate" is due only to those of our own race who seek to disturb nature, and raise the African above, or depress him below his natural place. The black, according to everything that is right, should not be in America. Two distinct races can never peaceably inhabit the same continent, a fact that should have occurred to the slave traders when they unwittingly planted the seeds of African barbarism on the soil of our fair land. But that evil having been done, the only true way to escape from the difficulty would seem to be continued slavery, together with gradu-al emancipation, and colonization of large numbers of the black in Africa, the land from which they unwillingly came, and where they normally belong. Negro slavery was a poor system of labor, it is true, to exist in a civilized nation, but it was the only system by which the blacks could be held to their place among a superi-or race. While in individual cases negroes have risen high, it cannot be denied that the race is utterly unfit in the mass to hold power. Negro crime was unknown in slavery, but after a premature emancipation had loosed upon the South an enor-mous pack of dusky savages, with but a thin veneer of civiliza-tion to offset a world-old heredity or barbarism, led by crafty, evil-minded and grasping "white trash," who directed their ever-changing and childish minds into channels even more ruinous than those which they themselves would have followed if al-lowed to drift on alone, is it a wonder that the men of the South banded together in order to secure for themselves and their fam-ilies the protection that the United States Government refused them? As was written on the title page of the revised prescript of the Klan: "Damnant quod non intelligunt." Therefore, the Aryan who denounces the Ku Klux Klan and, incidentally, the play which truly shows its noble activity, shows himself to be no very staunch friend or his race, nor of his country.

H. P. LOVECRAFT.

Providence, Sept. 21.

Sources

Derie, Bobby. deepcuts.blog/2024/11/27/deeper-cut-h-p-lovecraft
-three-letters-to-the-editor-1909/

Lovecraft, H. P. "'The Clansman's' Other Side." *Providence Journal* (26 September 1909): 18.

———. "General Lee and His Cause." *Providence Journal* (14 February 1909): 18.

———. "Robert E. Lee." *Providence Journal* (31 January 1909): 17.

Visualizing Cthulhu: Art, Adaptation, and Lovecraft's "The Call of Cthulhu"

Dylan Henderson

I. Introduction: Cthulhu Still Lives

Images of Cthulhu abound. They are everywhere. For better or worse, Lovecraft's most famous creation, with its "pulpy, tentacled head," enormous "scaly body," and "rudimentary wings" (CF 2.24), is rapidly becoming every bit as iconic as Boris Karloff's monster, Bela Lugosi's Dracula, or Lon Chaney, Jr.'s Wolf Man. A complete list of Cthulhu's appearances in various media would be as tiresome as it would be unnecessary, but for those interested, Don G. Smith's encyclopedic *H. P. Lovecraft in Popular Culture* provides a starting point for future research.[1] Published in 2006 and already outdated, it examines how artists have adapted Cthulhu and Lovecraft's other fictional creations in various media, especially television and film, which are Smith's specialty. Perhaps even more so than filmmakers, illustrators have found Lovecraft's fiction to be a gold mine of inspiration: Smith's chapter on comic books and graphic novels contains thirty-five entries, some of which adapt more than one work. Despite the apparent enthusiasm for such projects, Smith himself considers them misguided, noting that "Lovecraft's greatest horrors (or monsters) do not adapt well to visual depictions, as most Lovecraft film adaptations prove. The payoffs, so

---

1. While Smith provides general readers with a comprehensive overview of Lovecraftian adaptations, the recent anthology *The Medial Afterlives of H. P. Lovecraft: Comic, Film, Podcast, TV, Games*, edited by Tim Lanzendörfer and Max José Dreysse Passos de Carvalho, takes a very different approach by offering scholars a more detailed examination of individual adaptations.

to speak, are always disappointing compared to what the reader might imagine based on Lovecraft's prose" (137).

Rebecca Janicker, writing a decade after Smith, disagrees. Basing her argument on illustrations contained in *The Lovecraft Anthology*, a two-volume collection of comic books published by Self Made Hero in 2011 and 2012, Janicker defends attempts to adapt or remediate Lovecraft's work—to translate, so to speak, his written descriptions into visual images. She realizes, of course, the unique difficulties that Lovecraft's approach to horror poses, noting that "even when dealing with ostensibly indescribable, perhaps fundamentally unknowable events that challenge the limits of human perception and understanding," comic books "do not—and they cannot, in a medium such as this—leave everything to the imagination" (484). The medium demands, in other words, that illustrators depict or attempt to depict what Lovecraft describes, even if Lovecraft's descriptions defy visualization. Despite the difficulties involved, Janicker insists that illustrators can, and have, successfully adapted Lovecraft's work to a visual medium, specifically the comic book or graphic novel: "Comics," she concludes, "as a distinctive arena for both preserving and enhancing elements of Lovecraft's fictional worlds, are especially suited to adaptations of Lovecraft's work" (485).

Since the publication of Janicker's essay in 2015, visual depictions of Lovecraft's creations, and of Cthulhu in particular, have continued to multiply. Indeed, the market for such illustrations seems inexhaustible. Since 2018, "The Call of Cthulhu" alone has given birth to at least two graphic novels and one illustrated edition, sired by artists Dave Shephard, Gary Gianni, and François Baranger. These three works, which retell Lovecraft's story in its entirety, may be the most exhaustive attempts at illustrating the narrative, but single images of the monster, usually depicting it as it emerges from its watery tomb, have appeared on books, shirts, games, and posters. An online search generates countless images, often created by amateur illustrators for no other reason than pure pleasure. Why, one might ask, are so many artists driven to depict Cthulhu, or if these artists are merely responding to demand, why are readers so eager for these depictions? The sheer number being produced may indicate a dissatisfaction with what others have accomplished, a desire felt by the artist, perhaps, to capture what has eluded everyone else. Do any of these images, as Janicker contends, enhance Lovecraft's narratives? Or are they, as Smith asserts, invariably disappointing? If, as I would argue, images of Cthulhu simultaneously tantalize and frustrate readers, what are they missing? And what can they teach us about adaptation, "The Call of Cthulhu," and Lovecraft's approach to visualization?

II. Context: Lovecraft and the Arts

Appropriately enough, Janicker begins her argument with a discussion of Lovecraft's lifelong interest in the visual arts and its presence in his fiction, a subject of increasing interest to scholars and, as we will see, of especial relevance to "The Call of Cthulhu." Although Janicker touches on Lovecraft's admiration for Henry Fuseli, Francisco Goya, Sidney Sime, Anthony Angarola, and Gustave Doré (all of whom Lovecraft cites in "Pickman's Model") as well as the role of art in several of Lovecraft's stories, the scope of this subject demands more space than a single essay or article has to give. After all, as Andrew Paul Wood has noted, examples of ekphrasis appear throughout Lovecraft's work, as do allusions to specific artists, a reflection of Lovecraft's knowledge of, and passion for, the visual arts. Indeed, Lovecraft mentions his favorite artists as often as he does his favorite writers: by my count, seven of his weird tales contain references to Edgar Allan Poe, four to Arthur Machen, two to Lord Dunsany, and one to Algernon Blackwood, while five refer to Doré, four to Sime, and three to Goya. Another five mention the "nightmare paintings" of Clark Ashton Smith (CF 3.40).[2] Adding to

---

2. The search function provided by *The H. P. Lovecraft Archive* made the following analysis of HPL's horror fiction possible: "Dagon," "The Transition of Juan Romero," "The Shunned House," "The Horror at Red Hook," "The Whisperer in Darkness," *At the Mountains of Madness*, and "The Thing on the Doorstep" allude to Poe; "The Horror at Red Hook," "The Call of Cthulhu," "The Dunwich Horror," and "The Whisperer in Darkness" to Machen; "The Nameless City" and *The Case of Charles Dexter Ward* to Dunsany. As for

this wealth of research material are the painters and sculptors who appear as characters in Lovecraft's fiction, especially Henry Anthony Wilcox, Richard Upton Pickman, and Robert Blake, and the discussions of art and aesthetics scattered throughout Lovecraft's voluminous correspondence. Drawing from this rich spring, Carl Sederholm, Vivian Ralickas, Andrew Paul Wood, and Steven J. Mariconda have all analyzed Lovecraft's use of the visual arts in his work, Mariconda contending that, in Lovecraft's fiction, art serves an epistemological purpose, overcoming "ever so slightly, the limitations of our five senses" and providing humanity with a perspective on reality hitherto denied (100). Suffice it to say that the seemingly narrow question this essay poses—what can we learn from recent attempts to adapt Lovecraft's written descriptions of Cthulhu to a visual medium?— touches on issues, such as Lovecraft's views on art, germane to a much broader conversation.

Missing from this ongoing debate, however, is a discussion of contemporary illustrations, a subject that Lovecraft often talked about in his letters and which relates directly to our inquiry. The topic furnished Lovecraft and many of his correspondents, whether fellow writers or devoted fans, with a never-ending source of controversy, prompting them to discuss the issue every time a story by someone in the Lovecraft Circle appeared in print accompanied by an illustration. Of course, the lurid covers Margaret Brundage created for *Weird Tales* also attracted attention, as did the discovery of new artists, such as Virgil Finlay. Curiously enough, Lovecraft seemed to find the subject of less interest than his correspondents or the readers of "The Eyrie" did, and he rarely wrote at length about the illustrations attached to his stories or the stories of his friends. Indeed, while

---

Blackwood, he provides "The Call of Cthulhu" with its epigraph. Doré, meanwhile, appears in "Dagon," "The Horror at Red Hook," "Pickman's Model," "The Whisperer in Darkness," and "The Horror in the Museum"; Sime in "The Call of Cthulhu," "Pickman's Model," "Medusa's Coil," and "The Horror in the Museum"; Goya in "The Hound," "Pickman's Model," and "Medusa's Coil"; and Smith in "The Call of Cthulhu," "Pickman's Model," "Medusa's Coil," *At the Mountains of Madness,* and "The Horror in the Museum."

Lovecraft would write page after page on a topic that intrigued him, showing little if any concern for length or even his own time, he rarely wrote more than a few lines about the illustrators working for *Weird Tales* and often simply repeated the same sentiments over and over, praising a few favorites, such as Finlay and Hugh Rankin, and condemning the others. In a representative letter written to William F. Anger in 1935, Lovecraft dismisses the illustration accompanying C. L. Moore's "Julhi," though he admits that "it would have to go a long way to take the cellar championship from some of the other 'art' work in the magazine," and suggests that "the best thing Wright could do is to cut out all illustrations—unless he can provide material equal to Rankin's better products" (*Letters to Robert Bloch and Others* 230).

Lovecraft's oft-stated preference for Rankin, whom he initially considered superior even to Finlay, demands a closer look, for most people, then and now, find the work of Brundage, Finlay, and J. Allen St. John far more impressive than Rankin's sometimes crude efforts. Finlay's first cover for *Weird Tales*, for instance, which graced the February 1937 issue and depicts a swordsman striking at a shambling corpse, elicited panegyrics from the magazine's readers, who praised its vivid realism (see figure 1). In the April issue of that year, one perceptive reader compared Finlay to Rankin, these being "the only two artists who seem capable of producing a truly weird effect in their illustrations," and pointed out that "Rankin relies on vague formlessness for his results, while Finlay does that which is infinitely harder: actually reveals his horrors clear-cut" (Jamison 506).

And yet, what Lovecraft appreciated about Rankin was the quality just mentioned: the "vague formlessness" of his work, which hinted at more than it revealed. In a letter written to Fritz Leiber in 1936, he insists that "weird illustrations" should be impressionistic: "No," he writes, "I don't think weird illustrations should be detailed. They should have the vagueness & suggestions of instability & mutation characteristic of true dreams. That is why, in W T, I have always preferred Hugh Rankin to others who are better draughtsmen" (*Letters to C. L. Moore and Others* 308). The suggestive, dreamlike quality of Rankin's work

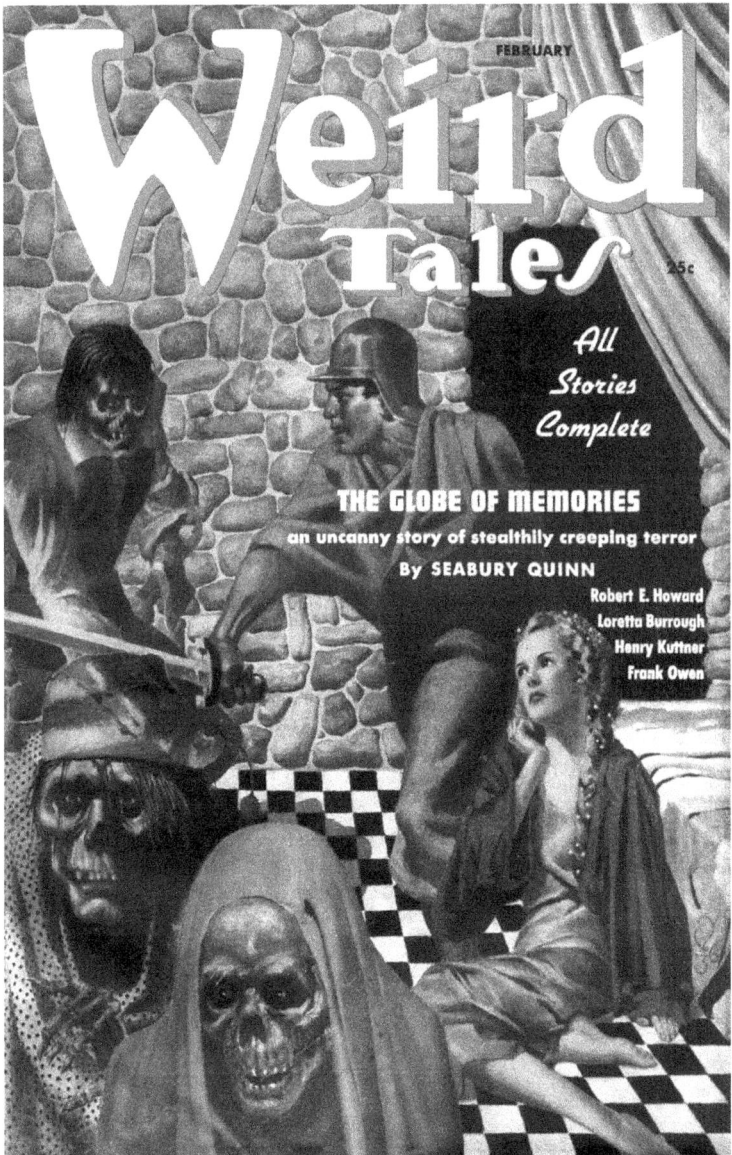

Fig. 1. Virgil Finlay. Cover. *Weird Tales* 29, No. 2 (February 1937).

is apparent in his illustration of "The Call of Cthulhu," which appeared in the February 1928 issue of *Weird Tales* (see figure 2). Sketched in charcoal on textured paper, the illustration, at first glance, depicts nothing more than a few nude shapes, which may or may not be fully human. A closer look reveals what may be a pillar, atop which sits what could only be a small statue of Cthulhu, but such a description fails to capture the true nature of the drawing or the experience of viewing it. Simultaneously distorted and indistinct, its subject matter lies hidden behind a dark fog, which the viewer's eye can only try to pierce. One might say that, instead of seeing, the viewer guesses at what he sees, in the process constructing more in his mind than what exists on the page. As we will see, that Lovecraft preferred this approach to the "clear-cut" realism practiced by Rankin's peers tells us something about the method that Lovecraft used in the story itself.

"The ring of worshipers moved in endless bacchanale between the ring of bodies and the ring of fire."

Fig. 2. Hugh Rankin. *Weird Tales* 11, No. 2 (February 1928): 159.

The idea for that story originated, quite fittingly, in an image. In 1920, six years before he wrote "The Call of Cthulhu," Lovecraft described the dream that would someday inspire the story: "I was in a museum of antiquities," he writes, "somewhere in Providence, talking with the curator, a very old and very learned man. I was trying to sell him an odd bas-relief which I had just modeled myself from clay" (*Miscellaneous Letters* 100). The curator, laughing, informs him that the museum only purchases ancient artifacts, but when Lovecraft replies that he created the image in his dreams, the old man becomes curious. In the dream, Lovecraft shows him the sculpture, but in his letter, he struggles to describe it, stating only that it "was of old Egyptian design" and "apparently [portrayed] priests of Ra in procession" (100). Easily overlooked, that word "apparently" suggests that Lovecraft saw the image depicted on the bas-relief, but even so, he could not state with conviction what it signified. The curator's response, however, indicates that he knows what Lovecraft does not. "Horror stricken," the old man demands to know who Lovecraft really is and then offers to buy the sculpture, though Lovecraft senses that he wishes to destroy it (100). In his letter, Lovecraft claims that the dream continued past that point, although he could not remember what followed. In any case, he created a plot germ from the fragment he did remember and added it to his commonplace book.[3] According to the diary

---

3. In his commonplace book, HPL attached the following note to his recollection of the dream: "Add good development and describe nature of bas-relief" (*CE* 5.220). The emphasis placed on the description may indicate that HPL's original conception of the story centered around the image itself. How HPL, through "good development," turned this simplistic narrative into something as complex as "The Call of Cthulhu" remains a mystery, and a testament to the human imagination, but scholars can still speculate. Perhaps the story, not unlike "Pickman's Model," originally ended with a revelation: a close look at the hitherto unseen bas-relief, which has caused the story's characters so much excitement and wonder. If so, the bas-relief would need to depict something truly outré, something completely outside the established artistic tradition, which has so many Gothic branches. Only something like Cthulhu would satisfy the plot's requirements, and yet HPL, once he had envisioned this radical departure from the ordinary, must have realized that a story about such a monster would be more

Lovecraft kept while living alone in New York, he returned to the story on 13 August 1925, providing it with a title and creating a synopsis or outline of the plot (CE 5.165). The story itself, however, would remain unwritten until the summer of 1926. S. T. Joshi contends that Lovecraft could not write such an ambitious story until he had returned to Providence and the frustration engendered by his experiences in New York had begun to dissolve (126), and while that is undoubtedly true, the story's long pregnancy suggests that the difficulties that Lovecraft, as a writer, had to overcome were considerable. At the heart of these problems lies the challenge of transforming something as vague and amorphous as a dream, which, in this case, consists of little more than a single image and the reaction it inspires, into a complete and satisfying narrative. Thus, how Lovecraft depicts that seminal image in the finished story is a question of the utmost importance.

III. Analysis: Visualizing Cthulhu

The following summary is needed not to acquaint readers with Lovecraft's most famous short story, but to draw attention to how readers encounter Cthulhu in the text. That story begins with a discovery: the first-person narrator, Francis Wayland Thurston, inherits the papers of his grand-uncle, Professor George Gammell Angell. While looking through this material, some of which pertains to a secretive cult his uncle had been researching, Thurston discovers a clay bas-relief, which defies description: "Above these apparent hieroglyphics was a figure of evidently pictorial intent, though its impressionistic execution forbade a very clear idea of its nature. It seemed to be a sort of monster or symbol representing a monster" (CF 2.23). Note that Thurston states repeatedly that he cannot understand what he sees, sowing doubt with words like "apparent," "intent," and

---

satisfying than a story about an image of such a monster. But what to do with the original bas-relief, which the artist had "fashioned [. . .] in his dreams" (CE 5.220)? HPL's solution places the monster at the center of the narrative yet retains the image. Indeed, as we will see, the story becomes a series of escalating encounters with additional images.

"impressionistic," and he even admits, when he uses the word "evidently," that he cannot say for certain that the image is of "pictorial intent." The design may not, in other words, be an attempt at mimesis or representation at all, its purpose being—like the accompanying hieroglyphs—linguistic rather than artistic. Struggling to convey something of its nature, Thurston describes it not as a "monster or a symbol representing a monster," but as a figure that "seemed to be a sort of monster or symbol representing a monster," the redundancy of his language (his use of the words "seemed to be" and "sort of") emphasizing just how difficult the image is to describe. In *Weird Realism: Lovecraft and Philosophy*, Graham Harman perceptively analyzes this very aspect of Lovecraft's writing style, concluding that "no other writer is so perplexed by the gap between objects and the power of language to describe them" (3). This perplexity, as we will see, reverberates throughout "The Call of Cthulhu," which is Lovecraft at his most elliptical and elusive. Indeed, the descriptions therein recall nothing so much as the effort, always futile, to describe something seen in a dream, a reflection perhaps of the story's odd genesis.

Echoes of Lovecraft's original dream also shape what follows. Thurston learns that a local artist, Henry Anthony Wilcox, created the bas-relief in his sleep and later showed it to Thurston's uncle, who began investigating the strange dreams haunting people around the globe, visions which ranged from "uneasy but formless nocturnal impressions" to an "acute fear of the gigantic nameless thing visible toward the last" (CF 2.28, 29). Lovecraft is playing with readers here: instead of developing the cryptic image he gave them earlier by adding more description, he is giving them less. He is stripping the image down, reducing it to impressions and allusions to a "nameless thing," two words that, when paired together, convey almost no information whatsoever. It is worth noting, in any case, that the sensitive, specifically artists and aesthetes, suffered the most during this pandemic, for they saw more than other people did, but then, for reasons unclear to Angell, the dreams abruptly ended. Having read the cuttings Angell collected on the matter, Thurston turns to the account of Inspector John Raymond Legrasse, who, after raiding

a murderous cult in Louisiana, had brought its idol to a conference that Angell attended. This small statue provides readers
with their second glimpse of Cthulhu:

> The figure, which was finally passed slowly from man to man for
> close and careful study, was between seven and eight inches in
> height, and of exquisitely artistic workmanship. It represented a
> monster of vaguely anthropoid outline, but with an octopus-like
> head whose face was a mass of feelers, a scaly, rubbery-looking
> body, prodigious claws on hind and fore feet, and long, narrow
> wings behind. This thing, which seemed instinct with a fear-
> some and unnatural malignancy, was of a somewhat bloated
> corpulence, and squatted evilly on a rectangular block or pedes-
> tal covered with undecipherable characters. (CF 2.31)

Yet again, instead of encountering Cthulhu in the narrative,
readers encounter a stylized representation of it, which may or
may not match the reality. At first glance, this second description, with its wealth of detail, appears to provide readers with a
concrete image, one that they can visualize in their minds, but a
closer examination suggests that, yet again, words cannot capture the true nature of this image. Note that the figure does *not*
have an "anthropoid outline," but a "vaguely anthropoid outline," and instead of an octopus head and a rubbery body, it has
an "octopus-like head" and a "rubbery-looking body." As Harman has observed, these distinctions matter, for if readers imagine a humanoid with a rubbery body and an octopus head, they
will not see what Angell, whose experience is being summarized
by his nephew, saw at that conference (24).

After this second description, readers encounter even more
images of Cthulhu, which hide and reveal at the same time. Professor Webb, for instance, another one of the attendees at the
conference, mentions a fetish that he saw in Greenland, which
"so far as he could tell [. . .] was a rough parallel in all essential
features of the bestial thing now lying before the meeting" (CF
2.33). Thurston himself sees the new statue that Wilcox has recently made, which makes him "shake with the potency of its
black suggestion" (CF 2.42). Again, these images, like the baf-
fling hieroglyphics that sometimes adorn them, seem to suggest

more than their actual shapes convey. Appropriately enough, it is an image that triggers the beginning of the end, though, to be more precise, what readers encounter is actually a written description of a photograph of a statue of Cthulhu—an image of an image. From this, Thurston learns of Gustaf Johansen, a Norwegian sailor, whose diary, summarized by Thurston, provides readers with their first and only glimpse of Cthulhu itself.

According to this diary, after a series of misadventures at sea, which coincide with the dream pandemic that so fascinated Angell, Johansen and his shipmates discover a new island in the Pacific. Much like the hieroglyphics that no one can read or the images that no one can describe or the name—"Cthulhu"—that no one can pronounce, the ruins they encounter defy any attempt at verbal description: "Without knowing what futurism is like," Thurston writes, "Johansen achieved something very close to it when he spoke of the city; for instead of describing any definite structure or building, he dwells only on broad impressions of vast angles and stone surfaces" (CF 2.51). While exploring this nightmarish place, with its "abnormal, non-Euclidean" (CF 2.51) geometry impossible to visualize, they open a vast door, from which Cthulhu finally emerges. From almost the beginning of the story, readers have been waiting for this moment, having been teased, again and again, with written descriptions of artistic representations. And yet, if Lovecraft has removed the second layer (the artistic representations of Cthulhu), the first remains, and language, like the visual arts, will prove unable to capture the monster's true nature. Indeed, Lovecraft does not even attempt to do so. His long-awaited description of Cthulhu, as seen by Johansen for the first time, provides readers with almost nothing that they can use to visualize the monster:

> The odour arising from the newly opened depths was intolerable, and at length the quick-eared Hawkins thought he heard a nasty, slopping sound down there. Everyone listened, and everyone was listening still when It lumbered slobberingly into sight and gropingly squeezed Its gelatinous green immensity through the black doorway into the tainted outside air of that poison city of madness. (CF 2.53)

Instead of a visual description, Lovecraft gives readers a smell, followed by a "nasty, slopping sound." What finally emerges is defined not by its *appearance*, but by its *actions*, not by nouns and adjectives, in other words, but by verbs and adverbs, words like "lumbered" and "squeezed," "flopped" and "hesitated," "slavered" and "gibbered" (CF 2.53–54). Even when Johansen, having boarded the ship, rams the pursuing creature, which had earlier "slid greasily into the water," Lovecraft refrains from providing readers with a visual image: "There was a bursting as of an exploding bladder, a slushy nastiness as of a cloven sunfish, a stench as of a thousand opened graves, and a sound that the chronicler would not put on paper" (CF 2.54). How fitting that this description ends not with a sight, but with a sound that the writer will not record.

IV. Conclusion: The Call of the Artist

While this bald summary cannot capture the experience of reading "The Call of Cthulhu," it does explain why, contra Janicker, attempts to adapt the story into a visual medium somehow fail to satisfy, why artists feel compelled to create—and readers feel compelled to obtain—countless images of Cthulhu. These images, no matter how gorgeously rendered, flatten the story's many layers. Indeed, in the text, the distance that separates readers from Cthulhu is immense, for they encounter it through a series of written descriptions of artistic representations, some of which are not viewed by the narrator, but by his uncle. Even when Cthulhu finally emerges from R'lyeh, readers "view" it through Thurston's summary of Johansen's diary. In the comic books and graphic novels inspired by the story, there is no way to recreate these layers, and the haziness and doubt that shapes how readers experience the original story is replaced by clarity and certainty. In an important sense, these layers *are* the story, and Lovecraft relies on them, and the stylistic approach to description analyzed above, to frustrate readers' attempts to visualize Cthulhu and thereby create tension, a tension that illustrations dispel the moment they are seen.

Unless visual artists are content to depict next to nothing, they must provide readers with the very sight that Lovecraft has tried to hide: a clear and direct look at Cthulhu. Most illustrators, including Shephard and Baranger, have done exactly this (see figures 3 and 4), and as a result, that which, in the story, could not be represented in art or articulated in words readers can now describe, if they chose, quite easily. To preserve the mystery inherent in the text, some have employed a more impressionistic approach, offering the viewer, as Gianni does, little more than an indistinct mass of shadows (see figure 5), but the story itself, by relentlessly teasing its readers, creates a demand for realism. While reading the story, readers want—or think they want—clarity. This is the paradox facing would-be illustrators: by continually undermining any attempt at visualization, the story generates, in the minds of its readers, a desire for a clear, concrete image, for a look at that which Lovecraft has refused to show them, even though such an image, if produced, would cause the story itself to deflate. Even if artists could square this circle—and Gianni's blurry, rain-soaked illustrations of Cthulhu come closest—no image can capture the ontological impossibility Lovecraft describes. As Harman has noted, what illustrations *can* show—a gargantuan, winged anthropoid with the head of an octopus—is precisely what, according to Lovecraft, Cthulhu is *not*. Constrained by its very nature, no visual image can reproduce what Harman, who denounces the "t-shirts and fantasy paintings" that "depict Cthulhu straightforwardly as a dragon with an octopus head," calls the "allusive aspect of Lovecraft's style—the gap he produces between an ungraspable thing and the vaguely relevant descriptions that the narrator is able to attempt" (24).

Despite the unsatisfying nature of these attempts to depict Cthulhu, these images reveal something important about the story, which can be read as a commentary on art and its creation. Note that, in addition to references to Smith, Sime, and Angarola, artists and works of art appear throughout the story as characters and plot devices. Having dreamed of Cthulhu, these artists are all struggling with an impossible task. By striving to create a representation of the monster, they are trying to turn something as amorphous as a dream into something as concrete as a painting or a sculpture. In a sense, that is part of Cthulhu's call. It acts as

Fig. 3. Dave Shephard. *Dark Tales: The Call of Cthulhu: A Graphic Novel,* by H. P. Lovecraft (116). © Quarto Publishing plc

Fig. 4. *The Call of Cthulhu*, by H. P. Lovecraft, courtesy François Baranger.

Fig. 5. From *The Call of Cthulhu: A Mystery in Three Parts,* by H. P. Lovecraft, courtesy Gary Gianni.

their Satanic muse, driving artists to create, even though its very nature frustrates and ultimately dooms their attempts. In the story, the domineering, godlike monster represents, along with so many other themes, the unobtainable aspirations of the artist, the irrepressible desire to preserve and solidify what are nothing more than fleeting and amorphous notions—dreamlike images and sensations that, despite the artist's best efforts, can never really be shared. Despite his lack of self-awareness, even the stolid Thurston seems to hear the call, for his written narrative is an attempt at a similar goal. He, too, is trying to describe that which defies description—and yet demands it. Just as Wilcox needs to sculpt Cthulhu, Thurston feels compelled to write about him. Why else would he pen an account that he does not want anyone to read?

Like the characters he depicts, Lovecraft himself, of course, also heard this call, heard it loudly and clearly throughout his life. In that sense, he and Wilcox, who fills the place Lovecraft himself occupied in his original dream, are twins: they are both, in their respective mediums, struggling to stabilize or preserve a hazy and ephemeral impression. Lovecraft, as he states repeatedly in his letters, wrote fiction precisely because it offered him a means of capturing such impressions. "My reason for writing stories," he claims in "Notes to Writing Weird Fiction," "is to give myself the satisfaction of visualising more clearly and detailedly and stably the vague, elusive, fragmentary impressions of wonder, beauty, and adventurous expectancy which are conveyed to me by certain sights [. . .], ideas, occurrences, and images encountered in art and literature" (CE 2.175). And yet, this desire to transform the vague, the elusive, and the fragmentary into the clear, the detailed, and the stable would prove to be as frustrating as it was irresistible. Dissatisfied with his own art, Lovecraft felt, toward the end of his life, that he had failed to achieve his goal:

> In everything I do there is a certain concreteness, extravagance, or general crudeness which defeats the vague but insistent object I have in mind. I start out trying to find symbols expressive of a certain mood induced by a certain visual conception [. . .], but when I come to put anything on paper the chosen symbols

seem forced, awkward, childish, exaggerated, & essentially in-
expressive. I have staged a cheap, melodramatic puppet-show
without saying what I wanted to say in the first place. (*Dawnward Spire* 494)

After comparing the elusiveness of "The Call of Cthulhu" to the
countless images it has spawned, we might arrive at a different
conclusion.

Works Cited

Baranger, François, illustrator. *The Call of Cthulhu*. By H. P.
    Lovecraft. n.p.: Design Studio Press, 2019.

Gianni, Gary, illustrator. *The Call of Cthulhu: A Mystery in Three
    Parts*. By H. P. Lovecraft. Ed. Marcelo Anciano. Santa Cruz,
    CA: Flesk Publications, 2021.

The H. P. Lovecraft Archive. hplovecraft.com/about/search.aspx.
    Accessed 29 Sept. 2023.

Harman, Graham. *Weird Realism: Lovecraft and Philosophy*. Win-
    chester, UK: Zero Books, 2012.

Jamison, Richard F. Letter. *Weird Tales* 29, No. 4 (April 1937):
    506.

Janicker, Rebecca. "Visions of Monstrosity: Lovecraft, Adapta-
    tion and the Comics Arts." *Journal of the Fantastic in the Arts*
    26 (2015): 469–88.

Joshi, S. T. *A Subtler Magick: The Writings and Philosophy of H. P.
    Lovecraft*. 1996. Berkeley Heights, NJ: Wildside Press, 1999.

Lanzendörfer, Tim, and Max José Dreysse Passos de Carvalho, ed.
    *The Medial Afterlives of H. P. Lovecraft: Comic, Film, Podcast,
    TV, Games*. Cham, Switzerland: Palgrave Macmillan, 2023.

Lovecraft, H. P. *Letters to C. L. Moore and Others*. Ed. David E.
    Schultz and S. T. Joshi. New York: Hippocampus Press,
    2015.

———. *Letters to Robert Bloch and Others*. Ed. David E. Schultz
    and S. T. Joshi. New York: Hippocampus Press, 2015.

———. *Miscellaneous Letters*. Ed. David E. Schultz and S. T.
    Joshi. New York: Hippocampus Press, 2022.

———, and Clark Ashton Smith. *Dawnward Spire, Lonely Hill:
    The Letters of H. P. Lovecraft and Clark Ashton Smith*. Ed.

David E. Schultz and S. T. Joshi, New York: Hippocampus Press, 2017.

Mariconda, Steven J. "H. P. Lovecraft: Art, Artifact, and Reality." In Mariconda's *H. P. Lovecraft: Art, Artifact, and Reality.* New York: Hippocampus Press, 2013. 92–109.

Ralickas, Vivian. "Art, Cosmic Horror, and the Fetishizing Gaze in the Fiction of H. P. Lovecraft." *Journal of the Fantastic in the Arts* 19 (2008): 297–316.

Sederholm, Carl. "What Screams Are Made Of: Representing Cosmic Fear in H. P. Lovecraft's 'Pickman's Model.'" *Journal of the Fantastic in the Arts* 16 (2006): 335–49.

Shephard, Dave, illustrator. *Dark Tales: The Call of Cthulhu: A Graphic Novel* based on a story by H. P. Lovecraft. San Diego: Canterbury Classics, 2018.

Smith, Don G. *H. P. Lovecraft in Popular Culture: The Works and Their Adaptations in Film, Television, Comics, Music and Games.* Jefferson, NC): McFarland, 2006.

Wood, Andrew Paul. "A Ghoul's Progress: On Art, Ekphrasis, and Image in 'Pickman's Model.'" *Lovecraft Annual* No. 17 (2023): 36–52.

Briefly Noted

S. T. Joshi is at work on a full-length biography of Clark Ashton Smith, to be published next year by Hippocampus Press. One amusing item has emerged when Joshi examined correspondence received by Smith, now in the Clark Ashton Smith Papers at the John Hay Library of Brown University. A letter from a fan, James Sieger, dated 2 November 1960, notes the purchase of a copy of *The Abominations of Yondo* (1960) and a request for Smith to inscribe it to the actress Annette Funicello. … Hippocampus Press is also set to publish a comprehensive edition of Smith's personal library. Those who own copies of books from Smith's library are encouraged to contact the publisher, so that the volumes can be duly recorded.

The Lovecraftian Films of Lucio Fulci

Rebecca Kunkel

Lucio Fulci (1927–1996) was an Italian director whose career spanned more than three decades and various genres, although he is today best known for directing horror films and thrillers involving depictions of intense violence and gore. Alternately derided as an exploitation hack or praised as a surrealist auteur of the fantastic, Fulci's career and legacy remains controversial to this day.

While Fulci readily acknowledged the influence of H. P. Lovecraft on his work, whether any of his films really belong within the category of Lovecraftian cinema remains contested. Charles P. Mitchell's *The Complete H. P. Lovecraft Filmography* describes two of his films, *City of the Living Dead* (1980) and *The Beyond* (1981), in brief, but apparently does not regard them as sufficiently Lovecraftian to warrant more detailed treatment (16, 18). *The Lurker in the Lobby*, by Andrew Migliore and John Strysik, devotes an entry to *The Beyond* but somewhat dismissively suggests that it is only for the presumably few who have acquired a taste for "zombies with [their] calamari" (16). A 2015 article on Lovecraftian cinema in *Cinéaste* is even less charitable, stating that "Lucio Fulci's gorefests," including *The Beyond* and *House by the Cemetery* (1981) reflect his "repulsive sadism" and are "mired in superstition and Catholic guilt, which would make Lovecraft gag" (Sharrett 24).

This essay examines the significant Lovecraftian influences within Fulci's filmography. Given the generally recognized difficulty of translating Lovecraft's fiction to cinema, whether any of these constitute entirely *successful* attempts to adapt the author's aesthetic or philosophy to the screen will ultimately be in the eye of the beholder. Nonetheless, it is evident that Lovecraft's influence is present in several of Fulci's horror films, which are among the most poetic in Italy's rich tradition of Gothic horror, and is manifested in both profound and superficial ways.

Fulci in Context

Although Fulci is best known today as a director of horror films, his career in the cinema began as a screenwriter, a role in which he would continue to serve right up until his death. In addition, Fulci had already had a prolific twenty-year career as a director before producer Fabrizio de Angelis hired him to direct his first supernatural horror film, *Zombie Flesh Eaters* (1979). Up to that time, most of the films that Fulci directed were comedies, with a few forays into adventure, western, and thriller genres. This sort of genre-hopping was fairly typical for journeyman directors in Italy at the time. Fulci, like contemporaries such as Sergio Martino and even Mario Bava, who today are primarily known for their thriller and horror films, worked across a variety of different genres throughout their careers.

Although Fulci was brought in rather late in the game to direct *Zombie Flesh Eaters*, the film became an unexpected box office success (Thrower 179). This success allowed him to assume a greater degree of creative control over his next several horror films, co-writing the scripts and often reassembling members of the same crew, including screenwriters Dardano Sachetti and Elisa Brigante, cinematographer Sergio Salvati, editor Vicenzo Tomassi, makeup effects artist Gianetto de Rossi, and composer Fabio Frizzi. These collaborators were present in some combination and left their stylistic marks on three of Fulci's best-known and most highly regarded films made in this era, which are often referred to (unofficially) as the Gates of Hell Trilogy: *City of the Living* Dead (1980), *The Beyond* (1981), and *House by the Cemetery* (1981).

Although Fulci enjoyed a career renaissance as a result of his success with the horror genre, throughout the early 1980s he also continued to work on a variety of projects that ran the gamut of genre cycles, including post-apocalyptic (*Gladiators of 2072*, 1984), high fantasy (*Conquest*, 1983), and even a *giallo*-turned-*Flashdance* knockoff (*Murder Rock*, 1984). Fulci's later career unfortunately coincided with a general decline in the Italian film industry (Bruschini and Tentori 88), and a combination of the director's ill-health and inadequate funding compromised many of his later efforts.

Fulci repeatedly credited inspiration from three literary figures on his horror films: Edgar Allan Poe, Antonin Artaud, and H. P. Lovecraft. While he readily acknowledged Lovecraft's influence, he remained somewhat vague on the details and never attempted a direct adaptation of any Lovecraft story as he did with the Edgar Allan Poe tale "The Black Cat" in 1980. In an interview given near the end of his life he conceded:

> I've read all Lovecraft's work, which is pretty heavy-going and I've always enjoyed Poe, though, in my opinion, the extent and manner in which reading works of this genre influences you depends on your own imagination. As Gramsci said, "Culture doesn't mean possessing a bag full of notions, it involves filtering these notions through one's own sentisivity." (Palmieri and Mistretta 58)

Dardano Sacchetti also admitted to reading Lovecraft in his youth (Interview). Thanks to work by film historian Roberto Curti in the archives of the *Centro Sperimentale di Cinemagrafia*, many of the specific Lovecraft references in the films that Sacchetti co-wrote with Fulci can be definitely attributed to Sacchetti's contribution to the scripts. In spite of this, Sacchetti tended to downplay his own interest in Lovecraft. Referring to the volatile relationship between the two men that eventually resulted in a permanent falling out, Sacchetti indicated that "Lucio realized he was a great horror director only later, when the magic moment had passed. ... My clashes with him stemmed from the fact that I was pushing modern horror, while he wanted to anchor himself in the nineteenth century classics (like Lovecraft)."

These statements notwithstanding, Fulci's failure to be embraced as a Lovecraftian filmmaker—unlike, for example, John Carpenter, who was active in the same years—may be in part due to the fact that Fulci continues to be associated with what has alternately been termed vernacular, exploitation, or "Euro-trash" cinema. By and large, Fulci worked on films intended for a mass audience in genres shaped by the prevalence of second- (*seconde vizione*) and third-run (*terza vizione*) theatres located in suburban and rural areas of Italy. The working-class audiences that filled these theatres were there equally to socialize and to be entertained by the film (Wagstaff 253). In his study of the *giallo*—the stylish hybrid of the murder mystery and proto-slasher horror film that peaked in Italy in the 1970s—Mikel J. Koven explains that "Italian horror films, not just giallo, are notorious for their graphic and 'elaborate' set pieces," which developed out of the need to "periodically grab its audience's attention" (126). The best Italian genre films often displayed a skilled orchestration of collective attention at key inflection points (the set-pieces), while the logic-optional plots left the audience more or less free to converse during slow bits of dialogue. It is important to keep this context in mind when approaching Fulci's films, since the criticism so often leveled at Fulci and other Italian genre filmmakers—that their films do not "make sense"—should not be understood as a universal mark of poor quality. Rather, it is a culturally specific judgment shaped by the hegemonic American context of Hollywood filmmaking which anticipates that audiences will sit silent and enraptured for the duration of a given film (Koven 26).

The second- and third-run theatres also saw a high degree of turnover, and it was not unusual for cinemagoers to return to the theatre every night expecting to see a different film (Koven 13). To meet this demand, Italian genre films also tended to be low-budget affairs, made as quickly and cheaply as possible. Imitation, usually of a better-known and more successful American predecessor, proved to be an important part of marketing the films as well as meeting demand (Koven 14). Typically, this occurred in one of two ways. First, a film could be marketed in Italy as an unofficial "sequel" without the blessing or involvement of any of the original cast or crew (Baschiera 47). A second but closely related phenomenon was the *filone*, in which a successful "original" film would generate a rapid-fire cycle of imitations

(Olney 25). Fulci, either wittingly or unwittingly, participated in both versions of this sincerest form of flattery, as when *Zombie Flesh Eaters* was marketed as a sequel to *Dawn of the Dead* (1978). His subsequent films featuring zombies, including *City of the Living Dead* and *The Beyond,* may be viewed as further entries in the same zombie *filone* that the popularity of *Zombie Flesh Eaters* helped to cement.

Finally, all the films discussed here feature dubbed dialogue, typically considered a signifier of a "lowbrow" or "trash" foreign films. Dubbing of foreign-language films is stereotypically associated with bad films, with the more respectable films being given the "authentic" treatment of subtitling that left the original soundtrack intact (Olney 28). However, it was common practice for nearly every film produced in Italy during this period to be dubbed in post-production (Monaco 145). At any rate, Fulci's use of international casts with English-speaking actors in lead roles (another common industry practice) insured that even the Italian-language version of the film had to be dubbed and was thus no more authentic than the English-dubbed version.

While the foregoing description may make it appear as if Italian horror films were unintelligent and derivative, for many genre fans the artistry and creativity to be found in many of these films is all the more endearing for their economically imposed limitations. As singular a filmmaker as Fulci was, his films should be evaluated in this context, in which he was a particularly interesting but not wholly sui generis participant. While the temptation to view Fulci's work as a kind of auteurism is not completely misguided, there were many countervailing tensions determined by the economic demands of film production in Italy at the time. It is these tensions, between a kind of visionary style and the often mundane demands of producers, that created some of his most interesting work, as well as his occasional misfires.

City of the Living Dead

Production on *City of the Living Dead* began soon after the release of *Zombie Flesh Eaters* (Sacco 79). Along with *The Beyond,* this is the Fulci-directed film in which the debt to Lovecraft is most overt, being linked directly to Lovecraft's quasi-mythical New England by being set in his fictional town of Dunwich, Massachusetts. While critics have often glossed over the other Lovecraftian components of the film, in its essential parts the basic narrative also appears to be indebted to Lovecraft's novella "The Dunwich Horror."

In *City of the Living Dead*, a barrier between worlds is punctured by the suicide of a priest named Father Thomas (Fabrizio Jovine), which opens a "gate to hell" beneath the cemetery in Dunwich. The main protagonist of the film, Mary Woodhouse (Catriona MacColl), is a psychic who sees this event in a vision while participating in a séance. Following her vision, she appears to drop dead from fright and is nearly buried alive before she is saved by a reporter named Peter (Christopher George) who is investigating her death. Through Mary's friend and fellow psychic, Mary and Peter learn that the *Book of Enoch* contained a prophecy that the suicide of a priest would cause the dead to rise and create hell on earth if the gate to hell is not closed by "All Saints Day." Mary and Peter set out to find Father Thomas's grave and attempt to close the gate. In the meantime, all hell is in fact breaking loose in Dunwich, as the revenant of Father Thomas commits murders whose victims in turn rise to take still other victims. After Peter is killed in the cemetery, Mary is joined by a Dunwich resident, a psychiatrist named Gerry (Carlo de Mejo), beneath Father Thomas's tomb. In the final confrontation with Mary, Father Thomas is apparently defeated, bursting into flames alongside his undead followers. However, the final freeze frame of the film, which splinters and fades entirely to black, overlaid with Mary's scream, sows doubt about whether the apocalypse has actually been averted.

The film's reference to the Book of Enoch is a variation on a Lovecraftian device, a pseudo-citation to a book of ancient occult lore intended to underscore the reality of the supernatural events taking place within the story. Although the Book of Enoch is a real ancient Jewish text, and not one of Lovecraft's pseudo-bibliographic inventions, it seems to be one of the real-world models upon which Lovecraft's own fictional occult works are based. Lovecraft mentions the Book of Enoch in "Supernatural Horror in Literature," an essay written between 1925 and 1927 and first published in 1927, around the time the *Necronomicon* made its first appearance in his fiction. In it he states:

> Cosmic terror appears as an ingredient of the earliest folklore of all races, and is crystallised in the most archaic ballads, chronicles, and sacred writings. It was, indeed, a prominent feature of the elaborate ceremonial magic, with its rituals for the evocation of daemons and spectres, which flourished from prehistoric times, and which reached its highest development in Egypt and the Semitic nations. Fragments like the Book of Enoch and the Claviculae of Solomon well illustrate the power of the weird over the ancient Eastern mind, and upon such things were based enduring systems and traditions whose echoes extend obscurely even to the present time. (*CE* 2.85)

This Lovecraftian deep cut appears to be Sacchetti's contribution to the script, as references to the Book of Enoch, including a final twist ending that did not make it into the film, were already present in Sacchetti's original 34-page story for *City of the Living Dead* (Curti 45). Although the film mentions the Book of Enoch only once in passing, it retains its function of conveying the sense of deep time and ancient prophecy behind Mary's psychic vision.

Where the film departs substantially from Lovecraft and "The Dunwich Horror" is in its characters, which are far more typical of *giallo* films. The reporter, for example, is a stock character in many *gialli*, which typically center on the attempt by an amateur detective to solve a mystery in which he has become entangled (Koven 86). In *City of the Living Dead*, a secondary narrative emerges that appears to be based on ideas Fulci previously developed in his 1972 *giallo, Don't Torture a Duckling* (Howarth 204). In that film, a series of child murders takes place in a small town in southern Italy, which turn out to have been committed by a priest named Don Alberto (Marc Porel). The heart of *Don't Torture a Duckling* is the brutal lynching of the town "witch" Maciara (Florinda Bolkan) for the murders actually committed by Don Alberto. As a person with an apparent psychiatric disability and epilepsy, Maciara is an outsider in the town who also bears significant trauma resulting from the death of her own child. In addition to its reincorporation of a killer priest character, the death of Maciara also finds an equivalent in *City of the Living Dead*. One of the Dunwich locals, Mr. Ross (Venantino Venantini), graphically murders a man with intellectual disabilities named Bob (Giovanni Lombardo Radice), because Ross baselessly suspects him of the deaths actually caused by Father Thomas. Fulci described this scene as "a warning I wanted to give against a certain type of fascism, the girl's father killing the young guy in such an abject way just because the young guy is different, a frightened victim who, like the so-called witch in *Long Night of Exorcism* [*Don't Torture a Duckling*], does not understand all this hostility towards him" (Fulci, Interview 53). This scenario, which expresses sympathy with a disabled outsider, forms a fascinating counterpoint to the eugenic subtext of "The Dunwich Horror," in which it is the outsiders, the Whateleys, whom Lovecraft describes as possessing varying degrees of physical abnormality and madness, who are responsible for the violence unleashed in the story.

A further reversal of Lovecraft is evident if one considers Mary Woodhouse to be the film's replacement for Dr. Armitage. Armitage is a librarian and an academic, a Gothic hero in the mold of *Dracula*'s Abraham Van Helsing, who through a modern scientific cast of mind is able to confront and defeat the supernatural when the need arises because of his high degree of rationality. Although the psychic is also a Gothic character trope of a sort, the gift of second sight is a far more dubious qualification for heroism. Like the protagonist of Fulci's 1978 *giallo, Seven Notes in Black* (also known as *The Psychic*), it is unclear whether Mary's psychic abilities do anything other than enable her to struggle helplessly against fate as it unfolds. A scene that occurs in the Dunwich cemetery when Peter and Mary first arrive in the town underscores this lack of agency with its nightmarish logic. When Mary and Peter meet psychiatrist, Gerry, and his patient, Sandra (Janet Agren), for the first time, they are in the middle of urgently searching for Father Thomas's grave. Mary asks Gerry where the grave can be found, to which Gerry responds by asking why they need to find it. Rather than explaining while they continue the search, the quartet adjourn to Gerry's house to discuss the matter over a pot of tea. The scene concludes with the window slamming open and the characters being showered with 10 kg worth of maggots blown in through the open window.

"The Dunwich Horror" has been faulted for its simplistic moralism where good emerges triumphant against evil (*IAP* 717–18). In its departures from the story, *City of the Living Dead* presents in its own way a worldview more in keeping with Lovecraft's own philosophy of cosmicism. It presents a hell that threatens to engulf the world and an absent God, while the usual bulwarks that humanity erects against the void, in particular religion but also ostensibly normal communal life, are revealed as merely another source of chaos and death. This bleak outlook is conveyed not just through characters and plot but in the film's repeated and radical frustration of the audience's attempts to make sense of what is happening. This is a conceptual achievement that has its roots in the *giallo*, with its unabashed use of red herrings and paramount logic of the set piece. Fulci and his collaborators would continue to develop these ideas further in *The Beyond*.

The Beyond

In a frequently cited characterization, Fulci described *The Beyond* as an "absolute film, with all the horrors of our world. It's a plotless film: a house, people, and dead men coming from The Beyond. There's no logic to it, just a succession of images" (Interview 54). He then went on to argue:

> People who blame *The Beyond* for its lack of story have not understood that it's a film of *images*, which must be received without any reflection. They say it is very difficult to interpret such a film, but it is *very easy* to interpret a film with threads: any idiot can understand Molinaro's *La Cage aux Folles*, or even Carpenter's *Escape from New York*, while *The Beyond* or Argento's *Inferno* are *absolute* films. (54)

If Fulci was overstating the case of *The Beyond*'s lack of plot, he can perhaps be forgiven for his impatience with the complaint that his films did not make sense, even more ubiquitous at the time they were released. In fact, *The Beyond* does have a plot, but its many twists and turns, as well as its liberal quotations from a variety of texts and cinematic sources, defy easy interpretation and assimilation into generic conventions. *The Beyond* opens with a typically violent set piece, which takes place in the past in the year 1927, as a painter named Schweik (Antoine Saint-John), suspected of being a "wizard," is confronted by a lynch mob in his studio, crucified to the wall, and doused in acid before he is finally killed. This scene is intercut with a white-eyed seeress, Emily (Cinzia Monreale), reading from the ancient book *Eibon,* which prophesies the opening of one of the seven gates to hell. Following this introduction, the action jumps to the present day, in which Liza (Catriona MacColl), a transplanted New Yorker, has just inherited the Louisiana hotel in which Schweik's murder took place.

As workers are undertaking restoration of the hotel, one of them sees Emily from a second-story window and falls from a scaffolding. From there, Liza is introduced to a local doctor, John McCabe (David Warbeck), who arrives to take the worker to the hospital. Liza is eventually alerted to the building's dark past after meeting Emily and her seeing-eye dog while crossing the Lake Pontchartrain bridge. Not wanting to give up her windfall inheritance, Liza continues working on the hotel even as several more deaths occur around the restoration, until she herself is attacked by an undead corpse in the basement of the hotel. She encounters John as she flees the hotel, and they travel together to the hospital. They are pursued by undead corpses in the hospital and, as they flee, they find themselves back in the basement of the hotel. Looking for a way out, Liza and John find themselves in Schweick's painting, a dusty landscape where every direction they turn in is the same, and they appear blinded like Emily in the final moments of the film.

As with *City of the Living Dead,* the device of an ancient book of prophecy is used to convey a sense of ancient foreboding behind the events that unfold in the film. Here, the borrowed title of the book *Eibon* is lifted directly from fiction. The *Book of Eibon* was an invention of Lovecraft's friend Clark Ashton Smith, which Lovecraft also playfully incorporated into his own fictional list of occult works cited, alongside the *Necronomicon* and *Unaussprechlichen Kulten* in such stories as "The Dreams in the Witch-House" (Simpson 247). Again, despite his protestations to the contrary, this nod to Lovecraft and his circle seems to have been part of Sachetti's contribution to the script. In a 2015 interview, Sacchetti even amusingly claimed to have read the *Book of Eibon*, while stating emphatically that it was "wasn't the 'damned book' it wasn't the *Necronomicon*" (*Looking Back*).[1] However, Roberto Curti once again notes that despite significant changes to the script used in the film, Sachetti's original story involved the discovery of a "secret locked room in the attic, filled with strange old books, including the *Necronomicon* and the Book of Eibon" (Curti 67).

The opening flashback sequence was a late edition to the script by Fulci, with the mob violence against Schweik again recalling the chain whipping of Maciara in *Don't Torture a Duckling* (Curti 66). Here, Fulci may have drawn on the Lovecraft story "Pickman's Model" for the character of the painter Schweik. Originally published in 1927 (the date of the opening flashback), "Pickman's Model" is the story of a painter who is ostracized by the artistic establishment for his depictions of horrific scenes, revealed in the course of the tale to be depictions of reality drawn from the artist's contact with a monstrous subterranean species. Whereas "Pickman's Model" implies that the cause of Pickman's disappearance was his contact with these inhuman monsters, *The Beyond* posits an alternative explanation by vividly depicting the death of Schweik at the hands of an entirely human mob. As with *City of the Living Dead*, the elements borrowed from Lovecraft are accompanied by a thematic shift that focuses on the horror of the everyday world and the hypoc-

---

1. Sachetti may have been conflating the fictional *Book of Eibon* with the Book of Enoch, as he describes the book he read as "one of the first books by one of the first prophets, so really it's as if it were a sort of positive pre-Bible."

risy of the self-identified enforcers of normality.

The film returns to Schweik's depiction of hell as the characters enter his painting in the final scene. Sacchetti provided an insight into the Lovecraftian inspiration behind this depiction of hell, stating that "given it's hell, we depict it outside of Euclidean geometry" (*Looking Back*). Lovecraft invoked non-Euclidean geometry to describe weird dimensions outside of our own. In "The Call of Cthulhu," the artist Wilcox described his prophetic dreams taking place in a space that consisted of "geometry" that was "abnormal, non-Euclidean, and loathsomely redolent of spheres and dimensions apart from ours" (CF 2.51), while "The Dreams in the Witch House" attributes the nightmare journeys of mathematics student Walter Gilman to an unholy amalgam of "non-Euclidean calculus," "quantum physics," and "folklore" (CF 3.232). *The Beyond*'s representation of this non-Euclidean space appears to be more in line with the concept as it is applied in mathematics, as a geometry of curved or spherical space where "to go forward is to go back, where every beginning is simply a repeated end" (Grant 153). The set, created in a dusty film studio in Rome by cinematographer Sergio Salvati, provides the backdrop for one of the film's most haunting sequences. By repeatedly flipping the camera behind the characters as they run, it suggests that the scene is the same wherever they go, and that they are everywhere at once while going nowhere.

The scene and the film ends with Liza and John with eyeballs whitened, signifying that they have now seen too much and been blinded. The motif of eye trauma and blinding, which is present in several of Fulci's horror films, in *The Beyond* becomes a way of visually representing the Lovecraftian theme of madness resulting from acquisition of horrific or forbidden knowledge. This theme appears in the very opening sequence in which Emily reads from *Eibon* and then appears to be blinded, represented in the film with the use of contacts that turn her eyes milky white. The same effect is used to signify when a workman's daughter, Jill (Maria Pia Marsala), is blinded after seeing her mother killed in the hospital morgue, and again the final scene in which Liza and John are blinded after entering and glimpsing

the "non-Euclidean" space of hell. More violent blindings occur
in the film as well, as when Joe's eyes are gouged out by a zombie, and he later comes back to life and impales the maid, Mar-
tha (Veronica Lazar), on a spike, which gouges out her eye.

Fulci may have drawn on a more proximate cinematic source
for this symbolic representation of the trauma of cosmic
knowledge through eye violence, Roger Corman's 1963 film *X:
The Man With the X-Ray Eyes*. Fulci was an admirer of Corman's
work as a director and cited Corman's Poe cycle as an influence
on his own films (Interview 51). Corman was one of cinema's
earliest adapters of Lovecraft, and his Poe cycle contained one
of the first credited screen adaptations of a Lovecraft story, *The
Haunted Palace,* which was also released in 1963.[2] *The Man with
the X-Ray Eyes* follows the story of Doctor Xavier (Ray Milland),
who develops eye drops that at first are intended to allow him to
diagnose illness more accurately by seeing inside of his patients.
As his use of the drops continues, Xavier's ordinary ability to see
what is in front of him declines and his mental state deterio-
rates. He finds himself unable to turn off his extraordinary powers of sight, signified by his eyes appearing totally black in the
latter part of the film. The film's final scene finds him in a revival tent, raving about the things he sees including "in the center
of the universe, the eye that sees us all," a line that recalls Lovecraft's description of Azathoth in *The Dream-Quest of Unknown
Kadath* as "outside the ordered universe that blight of nether-
most confusion which blasphemes and bubbles at the center of
all infinity" (CF 2.100). The film concludes with Xavier taking
literally the revival minister's biblical admonition "if thine eye
offends thee, pluck it out" and pulling out his own eyes.

While *The Man with the X-Ray Eyes* is not a Lovecraft adaptation, it has been recognized as an early attempt to capture
something of Lovecraft's cosmic horror on screen that remains
highly effective despite the film's overall kitschy sensibility

---

2. *The Haunted Palace* is a faithful direct adaptation of *The Case of Charles Dexter
Ward.* To Corman's chagrin, the film was given a generic title lifted from an Edgar Allan Poe poem because his producers at American International Pictures
thought it would make the film more marketable (Migliore and Strysik 204).

(Migliore and Strysik 122). The theme of madness resulting from a too-accurate glimpse into mysteries that are usually hidden is pure Lovecraft, recalling the often quoted passage from "The Call of Cthulhu": "The most merciful thing in the world, I think, is the inability of the human mind to correlate all its contents. We live on a placid island of ignorance in the midst of black seas of infinity, and it was not meant that we should voyage far" (CF 2.21). *The Beyond* picks up on Corman's visual representation of this theme, while pushing still further in its attempt to visualize a hostile alternate dimension on screen and through the generally off-kilter atmosphere created by its assault on narrative convention.

House by the Cemetery

Although the Lovecraft influence seems more obvious in the first two films of the Gates of Hell trilogy, Fulci evidently felt that it was most significant to the third film, *House by the Cemetery*. In a study of his work published during his lifetime, *L'occhio del testimone*, Fulci was quoted as stating that "Along with Artaud and Poe, I have much studied Lovecraft, a dreamlike and visceral writer, so after *The Beyond* and *The Black Cat*, I wanted to make a film that could contain all the deliriums of the Providence writer" (Romagnoli 18).[3]

House by the Cemetery revolves around the family of a history professor named Norman Boyle (Paolo Malco), who moves from New York City to Massachusetts to a home formerly occupied by his colleague, Dr. Peterson. It is believed that Petersen killed his mistress before committing suicide. Norman intends to investigate and complete the research that Peterson was conducting before his untimely death. Norman's wife, Lucy (Catriona MacColl), is hesitant to relocate and their son, Bob (Giovanni Frezza), who begins to receive warnings from a mysterious playmate, Mae (Silvia Collatina), to stay away from the house. The

---

3. *"Insieme ad Artaud e Poe, ho molso studiato Lovecraft, uno scrittore viscerale e onirico, quindi dopo L'aldila [The Beyond] e Black Cat volevo realizzare un fulm che potesse contenere tutti I deliri dello scrittore di Providence."*

family meets a mysterious babysitter named Ann (Ania Pieroni) who shows up at the house, stating that she was hired by the real estate agency. Other strange occurrences begin to happen in and around the house: Lucy uncovers a gravestone in the front hall; a bat flies out of the basement and viciously attacks Norman; and Ann is discovered cleaning up a bloodstain on the kitchen floor. In the meantime, Norman begins to unravel the secret of the house that once belonged to a surgeon named Freudstein who conducted gruesome experiments in the basement. Bob witnesses Freudstein (Giovanni de Nava), now an undead revenant who continues to live by incorporating fresh body parts of his victims into himself, murdering Ann in the basement. Norman and Lucy are killed trying to protect Bob from Freudstein; Bob escapes only by being taken to the afterlife by Mae.

While there is still plenty of strangeness and excess to go around, the overall feeling of *House by the Cemetery* is much more coherent than the first two Gates of Hell films, while the gore is mostly contained in the film's climax. Given Fulci's statement about the significance of Lovecraft's influence on the film, it is ironic that this is the film of the three that also seems the least tinged with cosmic horror and most embedded in more conventional haunted house narratives. Certain elements—the nuclear family transplanted to a house that turns out to be the site of recurrent violence and the psychic warnings imparted to a child—seem to be clearly indebted to *The Shining* (Kubrick's film adaptation having been released the previous year), although this was a comparison that Fulci intensely disliked.[4] Another frequent comparison is to Henry James's *The Turn of the Screw*, a tale of a disturbed governess and her young charges. This comparison, at least, seems to have been invited by Fulci and/or Sachetti, as the film concludes with a pseudo-quotation attributed to Henry James: "No one will ever know if children

---

[4] "My film borrows from Henry James's works, and not, despite an accusation I have received, from *The Shining*. In *The Shining*, there was a complicity between a child and an adult—the cook of the Overlook Hotel. But in *The House Near the Cemetery*, adults are totally unimportant. I couldn't care less about this guy who goes mad in *The Shining*. I hate *The Shining* anyway" (Interview 55).

are monsters or monsters are children."

However, it is still possible to detect a note of Lovecraftian atmosphere injected into this intertextual mix, which is helped along considerably by the genuineness of the New England setting. While *City of the Living Dead* is also nominally set in Massachusetts, it was in fact shot in Savannah, Georgia, a setting that was made even less accurate with the surreal addition of exotic animal sounds to the soundtrack. *House by the Cemetery*, by contrast, is much more faithful to a Lovecraftian sense of place, with its outdoor scenes (again beautifully photographed by Sergio Salvati) in Concord, Massachusetts.

The Lovecraft influence is not pulled directly from any one theme or tale; like Freudstein himself, it is a patchwork, made up of elements lifted from various stories. Bruschini and Tentori suggest that the main sources are "The Unnamable" and "Cool Air" (81). "The Unnamable" is one of Lovecraft's more generic stories, so it is difficult to say for certain whether this observation is correct, but it is possible that the device of windows being haunted by long- dead residents and the image of the broken cemetery slab were taken from this story. "Cool Air," which concerns a doctor who keeps himself alive after death through artificial means, is a more provocative suggestion as one of the sources that Freudstein was based on. The image of the maggots spilling out of Freudstein when Norman Boyle pierces his torso may have been Fulci's way of reimagining the putrefying corpse of Dr. Muñoz in "Cool Air."

However, it should be noted that, following his professional and personal split with Sacchetti, Fulci complained that Sacchetti had lifted many of the script's ideas from a Spanish film, *La Residencia* (1969), which features a scientist who builds an ideal woman out of dead body parts in his basement (Romagnoli 18). Meanwhile, Norman Boyle's investigation into what his colleague was working on before his death under mysterious circumstances recalls "The Call of Cthulhu," in which the young narrator's investigation into his uncle's death draws him into an occult conspiracy that in turn threatens his own life. In the scene in *House by the Cemetery* that is most redolent of Lovecraft's style, Norman plays an audio tape in the library that documents his dead colleague's decent into madness as he reveals the truth of what his research has uncovered about Freudstein's experiments. There may also be some resonance with "The Rats in the Walls," in which the protagonist is driven mad when he uncovers the secrets harbored in an ancient basement beneath his family's ancestral home, although haunted houses with eldritch secrets hidden in basements figure in so many Gothic stories that it is difficult to pin down any particular one as the inspiration. Finally, there are also shades of "Herbert West—Reanimator" in the doctor's murderous experiments with reanimated tissue, although this source also seems to be overdetermined as the obvious portmanteau of his name, Freud + Frankenstein, makes it clear that both narratives share a common source.

Manhattan Baby

Released in 1982, Manhattan Baby was the last film that Fulci directed under the aegis of producer Fabrizio de Angelis (Howarth 263). The film opens in Egypt, where an archaeologist, Professor George Hacker (Christopher Connelly), is excavating an Egyptian tomb, while his daughter, Susie (Brigitta Boccoli), and wife, Emily (Laura Lenzi), are exploring local tourist destinations. Susie and Emily are temporarily separated, and a mysterious white-eyed woman presses an eye-shaped medallion into Susie's hand. Meanwhile, George is temporarily blinded and his guide is killed by falling into a pit full of spikes while the two are exploring the tomb. George survives this ordeal and the family returns to New York, where the couple's younger son, Tommy (Giovanni Frezza), and babysitter, Jamie Lee (Cinzia de Ponti), are waiting.

Strange things begin to happen once the family returns to New York: Emily's colleague Luke (Carlo de Mejo) disappears through the children's bedroom; the children are also at times found to be missing from their room after going on what they call "voyages." One day as the children are walking in Central Park with Jamie Lee, the babysitter takes a Polaroid photograph that turns out to show only the medallion. A woman picks up the photograph and returns it to the family with the name of an antiques dealer, Adrian Mercato (Cosimo Cinieri), written on the back. Emily seeks out Mercato after more disturbing occurrences befall the family, including the disappearance of Jamie Lee. Mercato warns them that the medallion is a symbol of the ancient and evil Egyptian cult of Abnumenor that predates the pyramids by several thousand years, and that Susie has absorbed its energy. At home, Susie is taken to the hospital after fainting. Mercato is killed when his taxidermy collection comes to life after channeling the evil energy away from the children. In a final scene, once again in Egypt, the same blind woman is shown pressing another medallion into the hand of a young girl.

Manhattan Baby again incorporates a dense array of textual references and sources, including many drawn from Fulci's own prior films. A blind seeress once again makes an appearance, this time in the form of an old woman who is apparently a devotee of the ancient cult of Abnumenor, while the supernatural threat centering around the two children and their babysitter recalls *House by the Cemetery*'s invocation of *The Turn of the Screw*. Roberto Curti suggests that the primary inspiration behind the film's Egyptian theme and setting was the now mostly forgotten 1980 film *The Awakening*, with elements of the booby-trapped temple taken from *Raiders of the Lost Ark* (1981) and the climax in the hospital setting drawn from *The Exorcist* (1973) (102–3).

The Italian-language version of the film also opens with a (probably apocryphal) quotation attributed to Lovecraft, a dubious honor previously bestowed on Henry James in *The House by the Cemetery*. It reads: "Il mistero non e attorno alle cose, ma dentro le cose stesse" (Mystery is not around things, but within things themselves) (Curti 103). The film's Lovecraftian themes were probably more evident in the original script, written by Sacchetti and Brigante, which described the children astral projecting into other dimensions while they slept (Curti 102), a device similar to one Lovecraft used in "The Dreams in the Witch House." Due to the uncharacteristic interference with the script by de Angelis, the astral projection theme was written out of the film, although images of the children passing through interdimensional portals remain. While some have posited the influence of *Poltergeist* (1982) on these scenes, this is unlikely as *Poltergeist* was released only afterward (Curti 102).

As it stands, the film's main debt to Lovecraft is its attempt to convey a sense of the antediluvian origins of the fictional cult of Abnumenor. Lovecraft also coincidentally produced his own Egyptian-themed work, "Under the Pyramids," ghostwritten for Harry Houdini. However, this seems to be less a case of direct influence than a common ancestry of inspiration in the real-life excavation of Tutankhamen's tomb in 1922, also the inspiration behind the influential 1932 Universal horror film *The Mummy* (Peirse 16). This was a film that Fulci saw in his youth and professed to admire (*Miei Mostri Adorati* 130).

Unfortunately, *Manhattan Baby*'s attempts to create a sense of cosmic sweep around the cult of Abnumenor and the passage through interdimensional portals was greatly compromised by the economic reality of the production, during which the producers decided to slash the budget by more than half (Howarth 262). Wherever the blame lies, while *Manhattan Baby* has its moments, it feels like a half-measure; it not only fails to commit to the all-out weirdness of *City of the Living Dead* and *The Beyond* but also lacks the relatively tight storytelling in evidence in *House by the Cemetery*.

The Curse

Unlike most of the films under consideration here, *The Curse* (a.k.a. *The Farm*, 1987) is easily recognized as a relatively faithful credited adaptation of "The Colour out of Space." What is less well-known is Fulci's involvement in the film. Although *The Curse* masquerades as a purely American venture, it was in fact an Italian co-production under the helm of producer Ovideo Assonitis. The cast and credited director, David Keith, were Americans, with outdoor scenes filmed on location in Tennessee. However, much of the film was the work of an Italian crew, and the interior scenes were shot in Rome. This fact was disguised (barely) by the use of Anglicized names for many of the crew members, including Lucio Fulci, who was credited as an associate producer under the name of Louis Fulci (AFI, "The Curse").

While Fulci allowed his name to be attached for marketing purposes to a number of questionable productions in the late 1980s under the title "Lucio Fulci Presents," the fact that the name was half obscured in the credits suggests that some work was actually done by Fulci on the film, although actually raising money would have been extremely out of character. What Fulci was getting up to on the set of *The Curse* becomes more apparent in the second half of the film, as the contagion from the "colour" begins to infect the farm and its inhabitants. For anyone familiar with Fulci's horror films, the goopy cabbages, maggot-filled apples, crazed chicken attacks, and zombie showdown that erupts in the third act appear as almost an artist's signature. This suspicion was confirmed by Fulci in a 1996 interview, who described his involvement as such:

> I got on extraordinarily well with Assonitis, filmed almost all the special effects, got well paid and was rewarded by the director David Keith . . . who thanked me saying that he wouldn't have been able to create certain effects without me. Assonitis' only mistake was to name me as associate producer, which, in America, is the title given to a creative colleague who uses a pseudonym. (Palmieri and Mistretta 63)

While *The Curse* engages Lovecraft in a way that is less conceptually interesting than Fulci's own films, it is worth seeking out for those interested in both Fulci and Lovecraft, as the director was integral to its visual interpretation of the unwholesome effects of the meteor on the life of the farm.

Demonia

Demonia (1990) sees Fulci retreading some familiar ground from the Gates of Hell films and *Manhattan Baby*, although with a different set of collaborators that included screenwriter Piero Regnoli, editor Otello Colangeli, and cinematographer Luigi Ciccarese. In the opening sequence, a lynch mob is pursuing a

group of nuns, whom they torture and crucify, intercut with a
modern-day séance in which a blonde archaeologist named Liza
(Meg Register) is receiving visions of the scene. Several months
later, Liza travels to Sicily to participate in an archaeological dig
with Professor Paul Evans (Brett Halsey). Although she is
warned by several locals as well as Evans to stay out of the ruins
of a nearby convent, she becomes increasingly fascinated by the
place. While researching its history in the nearby town she is
contacted by a mysterious woman named Lilla (Carla Cassola),
who tells Liza that the convent was formerly populated by nuns
who worshipped Satan and practiced human sacrifice. Meanwhile, several townspeople and members of the expedition are
found murdered in bizarre and grotesque ways.

   Demonia, which was initially conceived as a theatrical come-
back, is also something of a novelty, being Fulci's only foray into
the "nunsploitation" genre and containing an extended uncredit-
ed cameo by the director as a police inspector named Carter who
is investigating the murders. Unfortunately, the film suffers from
subpar production and the seemingly haphazard script that Fulci
co-wrote with Regnoli. In their study of Fulci's horror films, As
Chianese and Gordiano Lupi note that Fulci refused to edit the
film and came close to disowning it after producer Ettore Spag-
nuolo abandoned the project in the middle of filming (170).

   As it stands, the film has the kernel of an interesting idea
that is developed poorly. The scenario seems to have been
roughly based on "The Shadow over Innsmouth." The way the
first half of the film unfolds bears a resemblance to Lovecraft's
tale, as Liza's inexplicable fascination with the history of the
convent draws her into a dangerous investigation in which she is
threatened by suspicious locals who want to keep her away from
the convent's secrets. The theory that "The Shadow over
Innsmouth" is at least one of the story's sources is bolstered by
graffiti reading "Azathoth" and "Cthulhu" that can be seen in
the sealed room in which the nuns were crucified. However, the
possibility of a more interesting cosmic dimension to the story is
unfortunately undone by the far more conventional exposition
given by the seer, Lilla, halfway through the film. The quota-

tions from Fulci's own work are likewise less than satisfying. Un-like the complex outsider characters of Maciara, *City of the Living Dead*'s Bob, and even Schweik, whose differences cause them to fall prey to small-minded mob violence, it is hard to see anything sympathetic about the bloodthirsty convent nuns.

A Cat in the Brain

A Cat in the Brain (1990) is one of Fulci's strangest films, and also one of the most divisive. It has not been well received by critics, even those generally sympathetic with Fulci. Stephen Thrower, for example, described it as "packed with gratuitous carnage, but sadly it suffers from a near complete absence of *cervello*" (255). *A Cat in the Brain* nonetheless enjoys an enthusiastic cult following, as it serves as a touching albeit sardonic self-portrait of the director. Made near the end of his career, it stars Fulci as a director of horror films named (you guessed it) Lucio Fulci. In the film, Fulci's thinly fictionalized avatar becomes increasingly distraught by the gory set pieces he invents for his films. Lucio seeks help from a psychiatrist, Professor Egon Schwarz (David L. Thompson), but Schwarz instead becomes fascinated by Lucio's morbid imagination. The psychiatrist hypnotizes Lucio to appear at the scenes of murders Schwarz himself commits, and stages the crimes to look like events in Lucio's films in order to frame him.

   A Cat in the Brain was made on a budget of only about $100,000 (Howarth 330). The slight budget was made possible through the use of many of the scenes recycled from Fulci's own (real) films *Ghosts of Sodoma* (1988) and *Touch of Death* (1988), as well as scenes from films in the "Lucio Fulci Presents" series, which were incorporated into the wrap-around narrative involving Lucio and Schwarz (Thrower 255). The film thus sees its characters interacting across various layers of reality: ordinary life as presented in the world of the film; the internal reality of Lucio's fevered imagination; and the scenes from other "real" films directed by Fulci and others, which are also shown as being in the (fictionalized) process of creation. The film's version of reality is continuously punctured by Fulci's own presence in the cast playing a character clearly modeled on and named after himself, with details drawn from his own life such as the final scene which takes place on Fulci's sailboat, the *S.S. Perversion* (reprising its own cameo appearance in *Demonia*). That this degree of ontological confusion hangs together as any sort of narrative is, as much as anything, a testament to the brilliance of editor Vicenzo Thomassi.

The way the characters in *A Cat in the Brain* interact across "ontological levels" places it in one of the categories of the weird identified by Mark Fisher in *The Weird and the Eerie*. As described by Fisher, in this type of weird tale, "What should be at an ontologically 'inferior' level suddenly appears one level up (characters from a simulated world suddenly appear in the world generating the simulation); or what should be at an ontologically "superior" level appears one level down (authors interact with their characters)" (45). While Lovecraft's fiction was a less self-consciously mannered attempt to collapse the boundaries between the "worlds" of fiction, imagination, and reality, *A Cat in the Brain* echoes Lovecraft's impulse to peel back the layers of ordinary life to view the often horrifying reality beyond.

This convergence is illustrated nicely by a scene early on in the film, in which Lucio is in the beginning stages of being driven mad by his films. During a break in the filming of a violent cannibal film (the scenes are from Fulci's real film *A Touch of Death*), he enters a restaurant where he is warmly greeted by the host and offered the special of the day, steak tartare. Seeing the lump of raw meat on the plate immediately induces a flashback to scenes from the film, in which a "steak" is taken from a woman's leg. Unable to shake the images from the film, Lucio flees the restaurant shouting, "No! Not the steak tartare!"

This scene works on a number of different levels, and if one is not too distracted by the film's proverbial buckets of gore, the result is both humorous and affecting. On the most obvious level, Lucio's descent into "madness" seems to be a question of his own ontological confusion, leading him to mistake his fictional creations with reality. But this apparent confusion also seems reveal on a deeper level the real horror behind the commodity on offer. In Marxist terms, Lucio's incipient madness allows him to see through the "commodity fetish," the veil of illusion that cloaks every exchange of commodities in a capitalist society. This illusion is what allows us to ignore the reality of the labor that has produced and been exploited in the production of the commodity. In this way, the scene is reminiscent of the anti-capitalist metaphor of fellow Lovecraftian filmmaker John Carpenter in *They Live* (1988), in which sunglasses render visible the omnipresent reality of capitalist exploitation, as well as the ideological brainwashing required to disguise this reality.

Adding still another layer, in Lucio's inability to see food he formerly enjoyed without seeing violence and cannibalism there is a reflection of anhedonia, the loss of pleasure that is one of the most debilitating symptoms of depression. And so a third possibility presents itself: that Lucio's real mental deterioration is not the result of losing touch with reality so much as taking on board too much reality, which then results in the loss of enjoyment in ordinary things. His madness, at first seeming to be a confusion of the real and unreal, in fact may be something that more closely resembles the pseudo-madness of many Lovecraftian protagonists who appear mad but are in fact reacting to a confrontation with the inhospitable reality below the surface of things.

Conclusion

Fulci's reputation for excessive violence often overshadows the keen intelligence and poetic sensibility evident in many of his films. A number of his works inspired by Lovecraft, particularly the Gates of Hell trilogy, stand out as some of his most original and noteworthy creations. Others have noted the biographical parallels between the lives of Fulci and Lovecraft: "both were dismissed as hacks in their own lifetimes; suffered bouts of depression; and created fictional universes of unimaginable horror and bleakness" (Sacco 81). To this it should be added that both should be recognized as artists who aspired to, and at times succeeded in, creating the sublime from the unexpected elements of nihilism and revulsion.

Works Cited

American Film Institute. "The Curse." *AFI Catalog of Feature Films*. catalog.afi.com/Catalog/MovieDetails/57593 accessed 14 November 2024.

Baschiera, Stefano. "The 1980's Italian Horror Cinema of Imitation: The Good, the Ugly and the Sequel." In *Italian Horror Cinema,* ed. Stefano Baschiera and Russ Hunter. Edinburgh: Edinburgh University Press, 2016. 45–61.

Bruschini, Antonio, and Antonio Tentori. *Lucio Fulci: Poet of Cruelty*. Tr. Roberto Curti. Rome: Profundo Rosso, 2010.

Chianese, As, and Giordano Lupi. *Filmare La Morte: Il Cinema Horror e Thriller di Lucio Fulci*. Piombino: Il Foglio, 2006.

Curti, Roberto. *Italian Gothic Horror Films, 1980–1989*. Jefferson, NC: McFarland, 2019.

Fisher, Mark. *The Weird and the Eerie*. London: Repeater, 2016.

Fulci, Lucio. Interview with Robert Schlockoff. Tr. Frederic Levy. *Starburst Magazine* 48, No. 12 (1982): 51–55. Reprinted from *L'Ecran Fantastique.*

———. *Miei Mostri Adorati: Racconti e Scritti di Cinema*. Bologna: Pendragon, 1995.

Grant, Michael. "Cinema, Horror and the Abominations of Hell: Carl-Theodor Dreyer's *Vampyr* (1931) and Lucio Fulci's *The Beyond* (1981)." In *The Couch and the Silver Screen,* ed. Andrea Sabbadini. New York: Routledge, 2005. 145–55.

Howarth, Troy. *Splintered Visions: Lucio Fulci and His Films*. Baltimore: Midnight Marquee Press, 2015.

Koven, Mikel J. *La Dolce Morte: Vernacular Cinema and the Italian Giallo Film*. Lanham, MD: Scarecrow Press, 2006.

Looking Back: The Creation of The Beyond. *YouTube,* uploaded by giofre, 26 September 2021, www.youtube.com/watch?v= PRLXgJLc_6Q

Migliore, Andrew, and John Strysik. *The Lurker in the Lobby: A Guide to the Cinema of H. P. Lovecraft*. San Francisco: Night Shade, 2005.

Mitchell, Charles P. *The Complete H. P. Lovecraft Filmography*. Westport, CT: Greenwood Press, 2001.

Monaco, J. *How to Read a Film: Movies, Media, and Beyond.* 4th ed. New York: Oxford University Press, 2009.

Olney, Ian. *Euro Horror: Classic European Horror Cinema in Contemporary American Culture.* 2nd ed. Bloomington: Indiana University Press, 2013.

Palmieri, Luca, and Gaetano Mistretta. *Spaghetti Nightmares: Italian Fantasy-Horrors as Seen Through the Eyes of Their Protagonists.* Tr. Gilliam M. A. Kirkpatrick. Key West, FL: Fantasma, 1996.

Pierse, Alison. *After Dracula: The 1930's Horror Film.* London: I. B. Taurus, 2013.

Romagnoli, Michele. *L'occhio del testimone: Il cinema di Lucio Fulci.* Bologna: Granata Press, 1992.

Sacchetti, Dardano. Interview by Barbara Torretti. 14 October 2004, www.darkveins.com/en/interview-with-dardano-sacchetti

Sacco, Daniel. "'Living Hell': Fulci's Eternal City." *Studies in the Fantastic* No. 7 (Summer/Fall 2019): 76–88.

Sharrett, Christopher. "The Haunter of the Dark: H. P. Lovecraft and Modern Horror Cinema." *Cinéaste* 41, No. 1 (Winter 2015): 22–26.

Simpson, Philip L. "No One Who Sees It Lives to Describe It: *The Book of Eibon* and the Power of the Unseeable in Lucio Fulci's *The Beyond.*" In *Terrifying Texts: Essays on Books of Good and Evil in Horror Cinema,* ed. Cynthia J. Miller and A. Bowdoin van Riper. Jefferson, NC: McFarland, 2018. 245–54.

Thrower, Stephen. *Beyond Terror: The Films of Lucio Fulci.* Guilford, UK: FAB, 1999.

Wagstaff, C. "A Forkful of Westerns: Industry, Audiences and the Italian Western." In Wagstaff's *Popular European Cinema.* London: Routledge, 1992. 245–61.

Briefly Noted

In Spain, the publisher Aurora Dorada has issued the first of a multi-volume set of Lovecraft's tales, arranged thematically. This one is called *Relatos Macabros.* This is a distinctive *bilingual* edition (using S. T. Joshi's corrected texts), for which Joshi has written a new introduction and new introductions to the two sections of the book.

Lovecraft in the Disney Universe: Convergences and Divergences in the Expression of Horror

Pietro Guarriello

The encounter between the dark and unsettling imagination of Howard Phillips Lovecraft, the undisputed master of modern horror fiction, and the sunny, reassuring world of Walt Disney—populated by comics of an optimistic bent—might at first glance appear as a cultural oxymoron, a collision of seemingly irreconcilable narrative universes. On one side, we find cosmic horror, the unknowable vastness of an indifferent universe, the fragility of human reason in the face of ancestral entities, and the fear of the unknown that permeate the works of the Providence writer. On the other side, we encounter the comforting aesthetic, intrinsic optimism, humor, and adventurous spirit that define the stories of Mickey Mouse, Donald Duck, and the entire Disney cast.

And yet, despite this apparent dichotomy, over the years numerous writers and artists working within the Disney comics universe have found ingenious and surprising ways to pay hom-

MYRRH OF CHALDEE — TWO GRAMS!
OIL OF ASSYRIAN ARTICHOKES —
ONE JIGGER! SAP OF DEAD SEA
CATTAILS — TWO SQUEEZES!

age to—or parody—Lovecraft and his oeuvre, integrating elements of Lovecraftian aesthetics and mythology into the world of cartoon mice and ducks. In doing so, they have forged a curious and fascinating cultural crossroads. This seemingly improbable fusion has proven fertile ground for exploring dark themes, existential fears, and the fragility of sanity when confronted with the unknown—all filtered through the often humorous, adventurous, and necessarily accessible lens of Disney comics. The result is a phenomenon as unexpected as it is compelling, one that has evolved through more or less explicit references, demonstrating how Lovecraft's influence extends far beyond the boundaries of traditional horror literature, even infiltrating the ostensibly innocuous realm of comics intended for younger audiences.

An analysis of this convergence reveals a complex and multifaceted dialogue between two ostensibly opposing worlds—a process of adaptation and creative reinterpretation that, having surged as a trend in recent years, merits deeper exploration.

The earliest traces of this cross-pollination, however vague and (perhaps) unconscious, can be identified as far back as 1950, in a story by the masterful Carl Barks, one of the pillars of Disney comics. In *Donald Duck in Ancient Persia* (first published in 1950 in *Four Color Comics* no. 275), Barks, while primarily operating within the realms of comedic farce and exotic adventure, introduces elements that, in hindsight, evoke Lovecraftian motifs. The plot follows Donald and his nephews as they stumble upon an ancient Persian city, *Itsa Faka* ("It's a fake"—a pun that immediately undercuts any gravitas), long forgotten and buried beneath the sands of time. There they encounter a sinister, shadowy scientist, embodying the archetype of the "mad scientist," who seeks to revive a mummified princess using unspecified "essential salts" (sound familiar?).

Though Barks's primary intent is clearly to play with classic horror and adventure tropes, the presence of the lost city (a recurring setting in Lovecraft), the scientist meddling with arcane forces (resurrecting the dead), and the overarching atmosphere of mystery shrouding the ruins constitute a textbook horror setup. Even without tentacled monstrosities or cosmic deities, these elements subtly evoke the eerie, unsettling atmosphere characteristic of such Lovecraftian tales as "The Nameless City" and *The Case of Charles Dexter Ward*.

The story's resolution, however, veers decisively into sentimental comedy, with a love triangle involving Donald Duck, a Persian lookalike, and the resurrected princess (whose original name, *Needa Bara Soapa*—"I need a bar of soap"—is yet another gag). Yet those initial ingredients—the forgotten city, the scientist defying natural law—linger as echoes of what might be an involuntary premonition of the more explicit Lovecraftian forays Disney comics would later undertake. Barks, toying with ancient history and its mysteries, unwittingly sowed the seeds that would decades later bloom into more consciously Lovecraftian creations.

Indeed, it would take the dawn of the new millennium for H. P. Lovecraft's influence to resurface in Disney comics in a more direct and deliberate manner—particularly in European productions. A striking and remarkably audacious example arrived in 2004 from Denmark with the story *The Call of C'Rruso*, written by Mark and Laura Shaw and illustrated by Flemming Andersen. Originally published in the German *Lustiges Taschenbuch* and later appearing in the U.S. in *Donald Duck* no. 16 (IDW, 2016) and in Italy (*Paperino* no. 421, 2015, as *Paperino e il canto mutevole*), this story marks a turning point—a bold and surprisingly faithful (albeit parodic) plunge into the heart of Lovecraftian cosmic horror.

The plot begins in a deceptively conventional manner. Donald Duck, notorious for his less-than-melodious voice, enters a singing contest hosted by a famed musician, Mr. C'Rruso. He is approached by C'Rruso's identical twin, D'mmingo (the names being obvious spoofs of the legendary tenors Enrico Caruso and Plácido Domingo), who offers him a potion to enhance his vocal prowess. After winning the contest, Donald is invited to a private island for the finals—where the tale takes a decisively Lovecraftian turn.

It is revealed that reality itself—or at least the Disney world as presented in the story—is nothing but the dream of an ancient, monstrous cosmic entity named Pflegmwad, a gargantuan

cephalopod slumbering eternally within a white citadel in the
sunken city of Sp'too (a clear nod to Cthulhu's dormant R'lyeh).
C'Rruso and D'mmingo are psychic manifestations of the creature's conflicting impulses: C'Rruso (dressed in black) seeks to
awaken Pf'legmwad, ending the reality he despises, while
D'mmingo (in white) strives to keep it asleep to preserve existence. Every century, when Sp'too rises from the waves, the two
vie to sway the world's fate. Donald's artificially "perfected"
voice is, in C'Rruso's eyes, the key to rousing the entity.

When Donald, manipulated into singing within the island's
suddenly emergent temple, unleashes his voice, Pf'legmwad
awakens—and reality unravels into a Lovecraftian nightmare.
Donald and his nephews Huey, Dewey, and Louie undergo a
grotesque physical transformation, sprouting octopoid traits like
tentacles and multiple eyes (a textbook example of body horror).
The world itself warps into a reflection of the awakened monstrosity. Salvation comes only when the nephews realize that
Donald's *real* voice—his natural, gratingly awful one (which, to
Pf'legmwad's alien perception, is soothing)—can lull the entity
back to sleep. Brewing a makeshift antidote to restore his origi-

nal voice, Donald sings a lullaby, and Pf'legmwad drifts back into slumber, restoring reality.

Yet the ending is not entirely comforting—a touch wholly faithful to Lovecraft's ethos. Donald remains deeply traumatized by the revelation that his entire existence is precarious, a mere figment in the mind of an alien being that could reawaken at any moment. This lingering sense of cosmic horror and existential fragility, persisting beyond the plot's resolution, is extraordinary for a Disney comic and underscores the story's daring engagement with core Lovecraftian themes: reality as illusion and humanity's insignificance.

Nevertheless, *The Call of C'Rruso* retains the necessary levity for its audience through parody (the punning names, Donald's off-key voice as salvation) while carrying an authentic undercurrent of disquiet rarely seen in Disney comics. It sets a significant precedent, proving that even in the sunniest of universes, the shadows of the cosmos can creep in—and leave a lasting chill.

A few years later, in 2010, the Italian graphic artist and illustrator Vacon Sartirani proposed a markedly different experiment, which he defined as "post-comic," with his conceptual work *Topolino contro i vermi* ("Mickey Mouse Against the Worms"). Cited by Comic Book Resources as "a mash-up with Lovecraft's *At the Mountains of Madness*," the piece is in fact something far more complex and disquieting. Rather than crafting an original narrative, Sartirani appropriates the panels of an old Disney comic—specifically, several pages from *Le gemme del sultano* ("The Sultan's Gems") by Gian Giacomo Dalmasso and Luciano Gatto (published in *Topolino* no. 1220)—and reworks them artistically. Into these panels he inserts monstrous, wormlike, gelatinous creatures reminiscent of the viscous, organic imagery found in certain Lovecraftian descriptions (notably the shoggoths), as well as in the works of Jim Woodring or Stephen King (particularly *The Mist*).

Yet the intervention is not merely visual. Sartirani also alters the original dialogue, radically transforming the meaning of the narrative. In this manipulated version, Mickey and Minnie become disturbing figures, portrayed as "two racist lunatics," and the story takes on the contours of a racial allegory. The slimy creatures (dubbed "eidozoon") attempt to coexist with the "native mice," but face tension and discrimination. Though the work may appear controversial due to its subversive use of iconic characters and the themes it explores—racism and intolerance—it powerfully demonstrates how Lovecraftian aesthetics and atmospheric touches, steeped in alienation, paranoia, and contamination, can be employed to confront complex and unsettling social issues, even within a seemingly light-hearted and innocuous setting like that of *Topolino*.

Soggetto e sceneggiatura di **Pietro B. Zemelo**
Disegni di **Davide Cesarello**

Nevertheless, *Topolino contro i vermi* is not so much a Disney story inspired by Lovecraft as it is an artistic act of détournement that uses both Lovecraft and Disney to construct a critical commentary, thrusting Mickey Mouse into uncharted territories and revealing the thematic pliability of Lovecraft's legacy. The horror here is not cosmic in the sense of alien entities, but social and psychological—a sense of paranoia and distortion of the familiar that nonetheless echoes the work of the Dreamer from Providence.

Lovecraftian influence continued to manifest in various forms in the years that followed. In 2021, to mark Halloween, issue no. 3440 of *Topolino* featured the story *Qualcosa nella nebbia* ("Something in the Fog"), written by Pietro Zemelo and illustrated by Davide Cesarello. The tale sees Mickey and Minnie lose their way in a dense fog while driving, ending up in the village of Boscozucca, a town with an obsessive fixation on pumpkins—especially those of Halloween. The story opens with a meteor shower striking a pumpkin field, an event that causes devastation and is soon followed by the mysterious disappearance of a boy, dragged away by something invisible lurking in the bushes. Trapped in the village until the fog lifts, Mickey and Minnie become entangled in a chilling mystery.

The core element of the story, which directly ties it to Lovecraftian imagery, is its inspiration from "The Colour out of Space." Just as in Lovecraft's tale, an alien element—here connected to the meteorites and the pumpkins—contaminates the environment and alters reality, generating an atmosphere of terror and paranoia. The horror does not arise from traditional bloodthirsty monsters but from the incomprehensibility of what is unfolding: the giant pumpkins (superbly illustrated by Cesarello) come to life and attack the protagonists. Though more grotesque than terrifying in a strict sense, this representation effectively channels the Lovecraftian theme of an unknowable alien influence that corrupts normalcy and threatens sanity. The story thus succeeds in crafting a mysterious and perilous atmosphere, using the evocative setting of a fog-shrouded village and the motif of animate pumpkins as a Disneyfied surrogate for cosmic horror.

Yet even before this story's publication, in 2020, there had already been another significant Disney foray into Lovecraftian territory, again touching upon themes from "The Colour out of Space," with *L'oro venuto dallo spazio* ("The Gold from Space"), published in *Topolino* no. 3373, written by Danish author Peter Snejbjerg and drawn by Giorgio Cavazzano. What begins as a classic Scandinavian treasure-hunting adventure quickly takes a darker turn. Scrooge McDuck organizes a geological expedition to the North Pole, where he discovers a colossal meteorite composed entirely of gold, buried deep within the ice. Despite warnings about its dangers, greed compels Scrooge and his crew to reach the alien object. As they approach the meteorite, the crew members begin to show signs of encroaching madness: they lose their grip on reality, believe themselves to be fairy-tale characters or animals, and grow increasingly paranoid and aggressive.

The plot draws overtly from two of Lovecraft's masterpieces: *At the Mountains of Madness*—for its polar setting, the expedition that uncovers something ancient and alien, and the madness that ensues—and once again "The Colour out of Space," for the idea of an extraterrestrial object emanating a malign influence that destabilizes the human mind. Although the story features no physical monsters or scenes of explicit violence—in keeping with Disney's conventions—it nonetheless effectively conveys the psychological dread and mental disintegration faced in the presence of the unknown and the alien, themes central to Lovecraft's oeuvre. The moral lesson on greed is present but entwined with a narrative that balances tension and playfulness with a genuine sense of unease stemming from cosmic influence.

The year 2021 proved to be particularly fertile for Lovecraftian contaminations within the Disney universe. In *Topolino* no.

3238 appeared *Topolino e le luci di Innsmouse* ("Mickey Mouse and the Lights of Innsmouse"), written by Gabriele Panini and illustrated by Alessia Martusciello. The title is a clear play on words, paying homage to "The Shadow over Innsmouth," one of Lovecraft's most celebrated and disturbing tales. Set in the winter of 1928, the story follows Mickey as he arrives in an isolated town steeped in a hostile atmosphere. There, he is hired as a secretary by an eccentric writer of fantastic tales named Pippcraft—clearly a Disneyfied version of H. P. Lovecraft, portrayed by Goofy.

The townsfolk prove to be unfriendly, elusive, and eerily unsettling in their behavior. The narrative unfolds amidst sinister mists, mysterious lights, and a hidden secret that Mickey seeks to uncover. Although it refrains from replicating the more graphically horrific elements of the original story—such as the fish-human hybrids—it successfully captures the rarefied atmosphere, the sense of mystery, isolation, and mistrust that define Lovecraft's fictional town of Innsmouth. The references go beyond the town's name: the inhabitants' suspicion, the eerie interplay of lights hinting at unnamable presences, and the pervasive sense of estrangement all contribute to a faithful evocation. This homage manages to preserve the unsettling tone of the original tale, adapted to fit the lighter, more adventurous style typical of *Topolino* stories, proving that Lovecraftian fear can be effectively conjured without overt depictions of horror.

That same year, *Topolino* no. 3458 published one of the most emblematic stories of this Lovecraftian strand, one that openly integrates Lovecraft into the Disney world: *Zio Paperone e la maledizione delle maledizioni* ("Scrooge McDuck and the Curse of Curses"), written by Marco Nucci (with a story co-conceived with Giulio Antonio Gualtieri) and illustrated by Giorgio Cavazzano. This story introduces two key parodic elements that would become recurring features in the Mickey Mouse comics: the character of Lord Mortimer Hatequack and the cursed grimoire known as the *Tetronomiduck*.

The plot begins with Scrooge purchasing an ancient, infamous tome—the *Tetronomiduck*—at a Billionaires' Club auction, drawn to it by the diamonds encrusting its cover. The seller, Professor Howard Kingsport (a nod to the fictional Massachusetts town featured in many of Lovecraft's tales), informs Scrooge of the book's dark history and its author. Lord Mortimer Hatequack, an eccentric nobleman and scholar of the occult, was the last of his lineage, known for bizarre habits such as walking upside down and speaking in reverse. He withdrew to his mansion at 66 Black Cats Street in Duckburg, where he devoted himself to alchemy and black magic, distilling his arcane research into the *Tetronomiduck*. Realizing that the spells it contained were too powerful and uncontrollable, he entrusted the book to Kingsport before vanishing under mysterious circumstances. (It is later revealed that he had been trapped for decades within his own portrait by a spell.)

Hatequack is an unmistakable and brilliant parody of Lovecraft himself: the name "Hatequack" humorously inverts "Lovecraft" by turning "love" into "hate" and adding the suffix "quack," evocative of Disney's ducks. The *Tetronomiduck* is, of course, the Disney equivalent of the *Necronomicon*, the most infamous forbidden tome in Lovecraftian literature, a source of arcane knowledge and madness. In Nucci and Cavazzano's story, the *Tetronomiduck* indeed contains powerful curses and spells. Scrooge, skeptical as ever yet intrigued, reads aloud several passages, including the dreadful "Curse of Curses," written in runes, said to "activate all dormant curses in the world."

This unleashes chaos in Scrooge's Money Bin: his most disturbing relics—the ghost of the pirate Barbafiera, harpies, Count Papula, a mummy, the seaweed of Ciutullù (clearly a deformation of "Cthulhu"), Count Ironbelly, even the evil double of King Janus—come to life and attack him. Scrooge, aided by his loyal butler Battista and the ever-erudite Gyro Gearloose (who proves unhelpful on this occasion), must search for a counterspell in Hatequack's library. The solution is found in recalling Hatequack's habit of speaking in reverse: by reciting the formula backwards, the curses are nullified. In the end, Lord Hatequack himself emerges from his portrait, aged but ready to begin a new life—as a writer of horror tales, just like Lovecraft.

This story is a masterpiece of balance, fusing the adventure and comedy typical of Scrooge McDuck with a genuine sense of suspense and numerous clever references to Lovecraftian mythology (Hatequack, the *Tetronomiduck*, Kingsport, Ciutullù/Cthulhu among the relics). The narrative builds in tension, yet the horror is softened by humor (such as ghost-fighting and Battista's dusting antics) and character-driven charm. The *Tetronomiduck*, though powerful, does not lead to madness or annihilation, but stands as a perfect example of effective "sweetening" of horror.

The story's success led to the creation of a spin-off series titled *Lord Hatequack Presents . . .*, in which the character assumes the role of narrator of terrifying tales—much as Lovecraft would insert versions of himself into his fiction, or as the Crypt-Keeper (Uncle Tibia in the Italian tradition) did in EC Comics, another clear influence acknowledged by the writer.

The following year, in 2022, the series continued with "Lord Hatequack presenta . . . L'ora del terrore: Topolino e il mistero del museo degli orrori" ("Lord Hatequack Presents . . . The Hour of Terror: Mickey Mouse and the Mystery of the Museum of Horrors"), published in *Topolino* no. 3461, created by Giulio Gualtieri and Marco Nucci. In this adventure, Mickey finds himself entangled in the mystery of a wax museum, where the statues bear disturbingly lifelike resemblance to his most notorious enemies. The declared—or at least evident—inspiration is "The Horror in the Museum," a tale bearing the byline of Hazel

Heald but essentially written by Lovecraft. As in the original, the story plays on the ambiguity between art and reality, and the unsettling possibility that the wax figures are something far more sinister than inert replicas.

The wax museum setting provides a Gothic and eerie backdrop, and the presence of unmoving yet menacing statues instills a growing sense of unease and paranoia. Though the explicit references to Lovecraft are limited to the general atmosphere and Hatequack's role as introductory narrator, the story successfully evokes the spirit of the original tale, suggesting yet another Lovecraftian infusion into the world of Mickey Mouse—this time leaning more toward the *weird tale* and psychological horror than the mythos of Cthulhu itself.

The "Lord Hatequack Presents . . ." series has continued to explore the horror and *weird* genres within the Disney universe, often intertwining Lovecraftian references with other literary homages. One notable example is "Una gara da paura" ("A Frightful Contest"), in *Topolino* no. 3609, written by Giulio Gualtieri with visual assistance from Roberto Vian. In this story, Hatequack, Grandma Duck, Scrooge McDuck, and Ludwig Von Drake engage in a storytelling competition, each narrating a tale of terror—a clear tribute to the famous gathering at the Villa Diodati in 1816, where Lord Byron, Percy Bysshe Shelley, Mary Shelley, and John Polidori gave birth to *The Vampyre* and *Frankenstein*. Among trams that lead to horror, monstrous scarecrows, and haunted libraries, the chills are plentiful.

Within the tale, specific Lovecraftian allusions are also embedded. Gualtieri resurrects a fictional fragment that, according to him, Lovecraft never completed, and most notably, the cursed book featured in one of the characters' stories bears a large letter N on its cover—an unmistakable reference to the *Necronomicon*. This illustrates how the figure of Hatequack and his series become a narrative framework for exploring various facets of horror, while preserving a privileged link to the character's original Lovecraftian inspiration.

Another significant story tied to the *Hatequack* series, published more recently (January 2024 in *Topolino* no. 3556 and

following issues), is "Topolino e le nebbie di Meyrink" ("Mickey Mouse and the Mists of Meyrink"), written by Marco Nucci and illustrated by Fabio Celoni. Hatequack introduces the narrative by displaying a map of the Mousekatonich Valley (an evident parody of Lovecraft's Miskatonic River and its surrounding region) and its capital, Meyrink—an ancient, fog-shrouded city steeped in mystery. Despite being the name of a fictional location, "Meyrink" is a clear homage to the Austrian writer and occultist Gustav Meyrink, author of the celebrated novel *The Golem*.

Mickey, Goofy, and Minnie visit Meyrink as tourists, guided by an eerie local whose appearance strongly resembles a famous photo of an elderly Gustav Meyrink. Thanks to Celoni's masterful art (he himself resides in Prague, the city forever linked to both Meyrink and the Golem), the setting brims with architectural elements that evoke the Czech capital: spired towers, the Tarlo Bridge (a play on Charles Bridge), gargoyles, and narrow alleys. The result is an atmosphere thick with magic, alchemy, and dread. The plot intensifies when Mickey, after making a wish in the shop of Doctor Feather (a recurring Disney character often cast in mysterious roles, here possibly symbolizing the "sinister tradesman" from the Golem mythos), is transported back to the year 1924. There he encounters the terrifying Shadow Thief—a spectral figure who steals others' shadows. The story thus becomes a race against time and against this spectral antagonist, set in an even darker and more perilous version of Meyrink.

Beyond the references to Meyrink and the Golem legend, the story features further allusions: the wizard Doctor Feather's residence is called *The House at the Edge of the World*, which echoes the title of the classic weird novel *The House on the Borderland* by William Hope Hodgson—a work highly admired by Lovecraft. This narrative thus demonstrates how the *Hatequack* series evolves by weaving Lovecraftian influences together with other fantastic traditions (Meyrink, Hodgson, Blackwood[1]), utilizing setting and atmosphere as primary vehicles of unease, supported by a robust visual design that enhances its symbolic and aesthetic resonance.

An analysis of these examples reveals that H. P. Lovecraft's influence in the Disney universe manifests itself through multiple narrative and iconographic strategies. Rarely is there a direct transposition of his original stories—such an approach would be incompatible with Disney's tone and target audience—but rather a complex process of adaptation and parody, homage and reinterpretation. Disney writers draw on archetypal Lovecraftian elements: forbidden tomes (the *Tetronomiduck* as a parody of the *Necronomicon*), lost or forgotten cities (Barks's Persia, Sp'too/R'lyeh, the very city of Meyrink), ancient and mysterious

---

1. For the tribute to the figure of Algernon Blackwood, see "La lunga note dello sghignazzatore" ("The Long Night of the Sniggerer"), in *Mickey Mouse* no. 3611 (5 February 2025), where it is Goofy's great-great-grandfather, Algernon de Pippis, who embodies the British weird writer.

civilizations, malignant alien influences (such as the meteorites in "The Colour out of Space" and the comic *The Gold from Space*), contact with the unknown, and the fragility of mental sanity in the face of cosmic horror (as seen in the madness of Scrooge's crew or Donald's trauma in *The Call of C'Rruso*). Yet these elements are almost always *softened* or toned down. Explicit violence, the darkest and most unsettling ambiances, and Lovecraft's radical existential pessimism are—naturally, given the youthful readership—attenuated or transformed.

Scenes of horror are often avoided or depicted in a less explicit manner, frequently through humor, caricature (giant pumpkins, Hatequack's comic ghosts), or more moderated language. To Lovecraft's bleak atmospheric touches, the stories counterpose quintessentially Disney themes: friendship, courage, optimism, hope, and the protagonists' ingenuity. Even when confronting disturbing themes, the plots typically reach a positive resolution, with the protagonists overcoming adversity and defeating evil—though, as in *C'Rruso*, a lingering trace of unease may remain.

Lovecraftian characters, often isolated, tormented, and doomed to madness or death, are transformed: Hatequack, though a parody of Lovecraft, ultimately redeems himself and becomes a successful horror writer; Pippcraft is eccentric but fundamentally harmless. Disney protagonists like Mickey and Scrooge retain their resourcefulness and problem-solving abilities, even when faced with supernatural threats.

This adaptive operation, while it may at times result in discrepancies with the source material—for instance, the trivialization of cosmic horror through its "sugarcoating," stripping it of its original philosophical weight and reducing it to a mere narrative device or an excuse for adventure—nonetheless raises the more pressing issue of *cultural appropriation*. Indeed, the use of Lovecraftian themes and atmospheric elements in Disney comics occasionally occurs without an adequate understanding or respect for their deeper meaning, thus transforming such motifs into mere marketing tools or superficial attempts to "modernize" classic characters.

The analysis of stories like *Mickey Against the Worms*, which employs iconic characters to convey parodic "woke" messages, further highlights the need for a critical and conscientious approach to the representation of sensitive themes, lest such portrayals inadvertently perpetuate stereotypes rather than challenge them.

Despite the critiques and inherent risks of such an operation, Lovecraft's influence on Disney comics nonetheless represents a valuable opportunity. For younger readers, these stories may serve as an accessible gateway to complex themes such as the fear of the unknown, the fragility of knowledge, and humanity's true place within the universe—stimulating reflection within a framework that is both engaging and approachable. These comics can broaden the imaginative horizons of their audience, introducing them to unfamiliar, uncharted worlds inhabited by fantastic creatures and layered mysteries. Importantly, they may also inspire curiosity and a deeper interest in Lovecraft's original literature or in the broader horror and weird genres. Furthermore, by engaging with themes such as alterity and the unknown—albeit in a softened manner—these narratives might even contribute to fostering tolerance and open-mindedness.

The fusion of Lovecraftian cosmic horror with the reassuring world of Disney comics demonstrates, if any proof were still needed, the medium's inherent ability to explore a vast emotional range and to engage with complex topics in ways that can be tailored to diverse audiences.

Iconography, too, plays a crucial role. Certain Disney artists—such as Cavazzano and Celoni—have incorporated visual elements that closely echo Lovecraft: tentacled creatures (like Pf'legmwad or the ducks transformed in *C'Rruso*), implied non-Euclidean geometries (in the architecture of R'lyeh or Meyrink), cyclopean structures, and Gothic or fog-drenched atmosphere saturated with mystery. These visual cues help to evoke the terror of the unknown, even though they are frequently tempered by irony, caricature, or the characteristically comforting Disney style.

From a sociological perspective, this intermingling of Lovecraft and Disney can be seen as a reflection of the growing com-

plexity of the contemporary world. In an age where the certainties of the past are increasingly in question and the individual is
confronted with radical uncertainty, Lovecraftian cosmic horror—with its emphasis on the insignificance of humankind and
the intrusion of irrational forces—resonates with the anxieties of
a globalized, technologically advanced, yet fragile and disoriented society. The very fact that such themes have permeated narratives aimed at younger audiences signals a profound cultural
shift—a need to symbolically and imaginatively confront the
limits of human knowledge and the forces that lie beyond our
control.

And thus, even the Disney universe—traditionally founded
upon order, reason, and happy endings—tentatively opens itself
to the exploration of chaos and the irrational, the very core of
Lovecraft's oeuvre. This does not necessarily indicate a descent
into nihilism, but rather a form of enrichment: an attempt to in-
tegrate the shadows of the unknown into the ostensibly sunlit
tableau of the Disney world.

In conclusion, the influence of Howard Phillips Lovecraft on
Disney comics—particularly within long-standing titles such as
Topolino and *Donald Duck*—is a more pervasive, complex, and
multifaceted cultural phenomenon than one might initially assume. Far from being a mere marketing ploy or the subject of
occasional parody, it constitutes a dialogue—albeit often filtered
and adapted—between two influential, if seemingly antithetical,
imaginaries. Through direct quotations, homages to specific tales, the creation of parodic characters such as Lord Hatequack
and Pippcraft, the use of narrative archetypes such as the forbidden book and the lost city, and the construction of an atmosphere rich in mystery and unease, Disney writers have
demonstrated the possibility of exploring Lovecraftian themes—
cosmic horror, madness, the unknown, and existential fragility—
within a narrative framework designed for a broad readership.

This process of "softening" and adaptation may at times risk
trivializing the philosophical depth of Lovecraft's work, yet it also renders complex concepts more accessible, encourages critical
reflection, and attests to the remarkable capacity of the comic

medium to function as a vehicle for the exploration of a wide range of emotions and ideas. This is why the meeting of Cosmic Horror and Disney Magic—however improbable—will, I believe, continue to generate original and thought-provoking stories, bearing witness to the enduring influence of the Genius of Providence and the astonishing versatility of the Disney narrative universe, capable even of embracing and reworking the darkest shadows of literary imagination. What remains to be seen is how this trend will evolve in the future, and what new, unexpected convergences may yet emerge from the encounter between these two titans of the collective imagination.

Briefly Noted

Cadabra Records has issued a massive eight-LP recording of *The Case of Charles Dexter Ward*. The novel is read by Andrew Leman, and there is artwork by a number of artists, including Santiago Caruso and Jason Eckhardt. S. T. Joshi has contributed two essays, one on the novel itself and another, more extensive piece on "Lovecraft and Weird Fiction on Audio."

The Call of the Eco-Weird in Fiction, Films, and Games, edited by Brian Hisao Onishi and Nathan M. Bell, has been published by Palgrave Macmillan. This book features splendid essays on Algernon Blackwood, H. P. Lovecraft, and other weird writers. Another scholarly work is of note. Steven J. Mariconda, who for decades has been one of the leading scholars on Lovecraft, has contributed an article—"To Thrill and Agitate: Complex Figuration in Lovecraft and Emerson"—for an academic volume on Ralph Waldo Emerson, *Father of the American Mind,* edited by Emile Alexandrov and Steve Stakland. The book will be published next year by Routledge.

"Iä, Iä!": Its Origin and Significance

Stephen Walker

Not an arbitrary assemblage, Lovecraft's invented, unruly "Iä" is fashioned through its likely footing in Greek and Latin.[1] These two languages show up with something like a flourish in his fiction and come out here and there in his correspondence, their allure going back to his youth.[2]

Greek, unlike Latin, possesses the punctuation marks of the apostrophe[3] and diaeresis. In the gaudy Cthulhuese *"Ph'nglui mglw'nafh Cthulhu R'lyeh wgah'nagl fhtagn"* the former mark credibly signifies a lacuna for a clitic or incommunicable sound and

---

1. To locate the presence of "Iä" I have word-searched online *The Complete Works of H. P. Lovecraft* and *The H. P. Lovecraft Archive*. Faults in its text can mean faults in this research; even without faults there, faults may be here. For "Iä" in different languages—none in Greek or Latin—see en.wiktionary.org/wiki/ia. It is possible, if unlikely, that "Iä" is not a foreignism but from an English work that HPL had encountered and adapted.

2. He wrote to Robert E. Howard that in high school, "Latin and Greek were my delight" (*Means to Freedom* 583).

3. "Elision also occurred in Ancient Greek, but in that language, it is shown in writing by the vowel in question being replaced by an apostrophe, whereas in Latin elision is not indicated at all in the orthography" ("Latin Phonology and Orthography," *Wikipedia*). Since the apostrophe was a common and even affected feature of Lovecraft's eighteenth-century inspired poetry and signified omission (typically replacing the "e" in a verb's past tense that ends with "d"), its appearance in his created language may be an acknowledgment of this; for leave it to him to synthesize seemingly unrelated material. In his poetry the diaeresis is infrequent and almost always with an "i" in a proper name (e.g., within the poem "Nathicana"). Apparently, a diaeresis atop an "a" makes its single if resolute appearance in "Iä." (For the languages that possess an "ä," see "Ä" in *Wikipedia*. Of them, Lovecraft would have most likely borrowed "ä" from German.)

may have been borrowed from Greek, where it is present, and represents an imaginary vowel[4] tying the consonants, contrasted with the vowels "iä." The other mark tops the Hellenic "ï" and "ü," but the Greek lacks the "ä." (A secondary function of both marks in Lovecraft is to imply the alien contamination of language.) Beyond punctuation, Greek's foundational influence on Lovecraft's invented language is in its heterodox and occasional combination of consonants, as with "chthonic," which is like a semi-jelled version of "Cthulhu." That Greek is written in a non-Roman alphabet furthers its exoticism and remoteness.[5] Nor should we overlook that it was from the coalescence of Greek fragments that the etymological creation of the *Necronomicon* emerged.

A search in the Greek to English *Eulexis LSJ* yields several definitions for "ia," the first being "ἰά [1] Ion. ἰή, ἡ, = ἰωή, voice, cry, Orac. ap. Hdt. 1.85, A. Pers. 937 (lyr.); σύριγγος ἰά E. Rh. 553 (lyr.)," whose meaning, as affiliated with sound, is contextually appropriate; Liddell and Scott's *A Greek-English Lexicon* (1843) supports similar results. Perhaps related to this through its first two letters is the name Iacchus, which (states *Wikipedia*) "seems to have originated as the personification of the cultic exclamation, Iacche, cried out by participants during the Eleusinian procession, with the exclamation itself, having apparently derived from ιαχή ('cry'), ιάχω ('to cry')."[6] It has been suggested that the cry 'iacche' over time came to be interpreted as the vocative form of a name 'Iacchus.'"[7] Mine may be a forced interpretation of a coincidence; still, Lovecraft could be playing on the similarity of "ἰά" to the first letters of Iacchus, knowing of its

---

4. While it seems that no language lacks vowels, in English vowels have a fluid standing. "The distinction between consonant and vowel is fundamental, but some sounds sit uneasily between the two" (Crystal 242).

5. Mr. Blackwood in Edgar Allan Poe's satiric "How to Write a Blackwood Article" touts: "In a Blackwood article nothing makes so fine a show as your Greek. The very letters have an air of profundity about them . . . there is nothing like Greek for a genuine sensation-paper.'"

6. Greek also has interjections prompted by horror. See Nordgren, notably the chapter on "Semantics." One transliteration for a reaction to horror is "Da!"

7. Robert Graves, the poet and author of *The Greek Myths* (1955), translates "Iacchus" as "boisterous shout".

context as a "cultic exclamation".[8] Since Lovecraft had access to the *Encyclopædia Britannica*, its entry for Dionysus (Greek god of wine and fertility) has relevance as a source.[9] It supplies two Thracian names that "like Iacchus [and others] . . . have been connected with the loud 'shout' . . . of his worshippers" (8.287).[10] More directly, an epithet for Dionysus, Bromius, applies to "roaring" and related loud rowdiness.

Another possible influence, through spelling and meaning, is the mortal lover of Zeus, Io. Her etymology is from either "moon" or, attractively, the vocable characterizing a hawk's shriek. In the *Hymn to Apollo* by the Greek poet Callimachus, the goddess receives several addresses ("Sound Io! Io!" and the like)[11] that have the makings of redundancy, through "sound" (shout) and the similarity between "Io" and "iä". Nor overlook the exclamation mark that boosts the name and most addictively clings to "Iä."

Not as a name, but as a sound, Latin finds vocalization in "io," for all its five meanings are cries; the most relevant translation exists as "Hurrah! (ritual exclamation of strong emotion/joy)."[12] A

---

8. Ironically, a reverse of the vowels "ia" imitates the utterance of lament in a poem, purportedly by the Greek Moschus, the line reading "Hyacinth, babble thy letters and print 'ai ai' on thy petals" (Hadas 357). The poem, incidentally, seems a forerunner of Milton's "Lycidas."

9. While allusions to the Latin Bacchus appear in Lovecraft's fiction, its Greek counterpart Dionysus is never named; except, as one of the commonest late Greek names, "Dionysus" in the West became "Denys," which is the first name of the character in "The Moon-Bog." HPL's letters do make direct mention of the Dionysian, etc., as in referencing "the mystery of the Orphic, Dionysiac, Apollonian, & Pythagorean cults" (*Letters to James F. Morton* 240).

10. Dionysus was also "associated with the Phrygian goddess Cybele," the Magna Mater of "The Rats in the Walls," my allusions to which story will appear repeatedly in this commentary. Since I have dragged in one Lovecraft story, I will mention another, "The Tree," in relation with the god: "It is suggested that the cult of Dionysus absorbed that of an old tree-spirit" (*Encyclopædia Britannica* 8.288).

11. Hadas 296.

12. *Latdict*, www.latin-dictionary.net/search/latin/Io. The source is the 1982 *Oxford Latin Dictionary*.

proper name in Greek, the Latin "Io" as an interjection can mean "Hurrah! (ritual exclamation of strong emotion/joy)" or "Ho!" or "Look!," all suitable translations for the fictional "Iä."[13] More synonyms in this category are "Hail!" and "Praise!" and "Viva!" In Roman mythology, there are instances of names preceded by acclamation. Catallus' "Epithalamium" has several stanzas that end "Hail, Hymen, Hymenaeus."[14] My search for examples in the texts of Latin writers was middlingly successful (something from Horace), but for Virgil and Caesar, the Latin translations of Homer, etc. the fates have not smiled. If "io" was a rarity in Latin literature, it may be less so in Roman history, with which Lovecraft was well acquainted. During Roman triumphs the cheer from the crowd was "*io triumphe*" (see Versnel 1).

English strengthens the Latin possibility. The Elizabethan poet Edmund Spenser, in his "Epithalamion," delivers the line "'Hymen, io Hymen, Hymen!' they do shout"; and more pointedly another Elizabethan, Thomas Dekker, plays the line "Io to Hymen." As the Greek god of marriage, Hymen is the respectable facet of Lovecraft's Shub-Niggurath; and "shout" harkens to the aforementioned Iacchus, with "Io" self-explanatory in its resemblance and function.

A Latin presence has another attractiveness as a source for "Iä." Lovecraft had superior affection for it over Greek. "In

---

13. *Latdict.* latin-dictionary.net/definition/24685/Io Whether the game of *Scrabble* got "io" from Latin, it recognizes the word as expressing "joy or triumph" (Dunn and Aragonés, *ZOUNDS! A Browser's Dictionary of Interjections*, 3). Aside from his synthetic iä, HPL now and then drew on authentic Latin interjections in his letters: "ædepol!" (for surprise) and "eheu!" which, coincidentally or not, has for its meaning, "alas!," "oh, no!," etc., and is a repudiation of the celebratory. That persists in his favorite exclamatory phrase, "God Save the King!" A study in his fiction and letters of the exclamation mark, italics, all caps, bolding, and any other shapes of emotional emphasis would be instructive, if nothing else dissecting his stratagems for manipulating atmosphere or proving what strongly affected HPL. He seems to force, to reify his written feelings into a sensuous presence.

14. Hadas 28. Hymen "is a god of marriage ceremonies who inspires feasts and song," which seems a removed, honest cousin of that representative of fertility, Shub-Niggurath.

school I took to Latin as a duck to water . . . Greek I liked & respected—but I found it difficult, & tended to translate it mentally into Latin."[15]

Io in poetry survived to Lovecraft's day. Those occultists who insist on a link between him and Aleister Crowley can find sustenance in io's connection to Pan—who earns more commentary a bit further—in the latter's "Hymn to Pan," with its refrain "Io Pan! Io Pan Pan!" The poem appeared in 1919.

Culturally, if not absolutely linguistically, Greek has an edge over Latin as an incubator of "Iä." In *The New Annotated H. P. Lovecraft* Klinger writes of Shub-Niggurath, "That the Hellenes were her early worshippers is indicated by the cry 'Iä!,' identified with the Bacchantes, according to Robert M. Price, in 'Lovecraft's "Artificial Mythology"'" (359).

The crypto-voluptuary Shub-Niggurath is the most frequent consort of "Iä," and the interjection allusively reflects her Dionysian sexuality and eroticism stained with horror.[16] In the matter of the Greek god, the idea of fertility had reinforcement because the majority of his hobnobbing followers were women. Mediators of fertility and the demonic, the Priapean Dionysus and goatish, prolific S-N have behind them mythologies, including the biblical, and their accompanying commentaries, though to be fair, Dionysus has been able to evoke commentary for thousands of years, S-N only since the 1920s. At base the figures are cultural archetypes, which accounts for their persistence and their nutrition for gaggles of scholars.

Shub-Niggurath is famously described as "the goat with a thousand young," her epithet defining fecundity, with "thousand" intended in the biblical sense of "many" or "numerous."[17]

---

15. *Dawnward Spire* 499. HPL learned Latin before Greek, as early as 1898. In the 1904–05 school year Latin was one of his courses—for which he got the grade of "87," when I might have expected something higher, like about 100—and in 1906–07 his courses included "Greek Texts," "Latin Grammar," and "Latin Texts," each accorded "85" (see *IAP* 61, 100–101).

16. The subject of Shub-Niggurath has proved such a delectable quicksand for exposition that she threatens to outshine "Iä," the boding star of the title.

17. The Bible need not be the inspiration. Shakespeare, Milton, Keats, Poe,

The 1910 *Encyclopædia Britannica* proclaimed Dionysus "a nature god of fruitfulness and vegetation" (286) and, according to Frazier's *Golden Bough*, an "animal whose form Dionysus assumed was the goat." According to a few sources, the goat figures early in the development of Dionysus, once known as Zagreus, "the horned child," whom Zeus changed into a goat and then a bull in order to disguise him. Nature hybrids, such as centaurs and sileni, participated in the cult of Dionysus, as did fauns and satyrs, "the goat-like fertility spirits of mountains and forests who formed part of Dionysus' train," which points to the figure of Pan (*Funk & Wagnalls* 2.975).[18]

To fortify the skein from the goatish satellites of Dionysus— satyrs and fauns—and, a hopscotch away, Pan, with the Judeo-Christian devil development, the Book of Leviticus features Azazel, perhaps a demon or evil spirit that received a goat (scapegoat) as a sacrifice. Muddying matters, "the Hebrew word that is translated as 'scapegoat' in the King James Version is actually Azazel" (Asimov 159).[19] In later legends Azazel assumed the role of a

---

and others made "thousand" stand for the idea of "many." Likewise, HPL had the word function poetically in his fiction, as with "Thalarion, that dæmon-city of a thousand wonders" (CF 1.107), "the thousand glimpses, doubts, and suppositions which had come to torment the friends and parents of Charles Ward" (CF 2.345), and so on. As for "young," in the *Oxford English Dictionary* one definition is "A young animal, esp. before or soon after birth or hatching." Over half of the usage examples prefix "young" with "one" or "single," a proven numeric path that could have provoked Lovecraft to up the ante to "thousand young" ("Young, N. (1), Sense 2.a.").

18. Unlike the über-male Pan, Dionysus is gender challenged. While Shub-Niggurath is never fictionally pigeonholed as female, the inference is there. Cthulhu, Nyarlathotep, etc. seem guy gods rather than epicene, with each a "he," though sometimes an "it."

19. Borrowing from Graves—who, in *The White Goddess*, gave Pan the alternate name of "goat-Dionysus"—Stock finds "Azazel was possibly tangled up with worship of Dionysus" (60). He throws in the descriptive phrase "goat-demons" for a satyr or devil. HPL had read about the connection of the goat with evil. Charles Lamb wrote "the wicked are expressly symbolized by a goat" in his essay "Witches and Other Night-Fears," used as an epigraph to "The Dunwich Horror," the same epigraph that Stock sticks atop one of his book's chapters. Perhaps he got this from HPL, for he reveals that he "first came to

fallen angel who, in a Great God Pan instance, begot children from mortal women. Could the satanic Azazel have had a part in Lovecraft's choice of describing Shub-Niggurath as a "Goat"?

Azazel is a conceptual bridge between Pan, that horned half-goat, and Satan. Spence found "the devil is frequently represented under the shape of a goat" (185; the original edition of 1920 was in Lovecraft's library); and according to Russell, "The Christians associated all the pagan deities with demons, but Pan more than others" (17).

As a Dionysian being, Pan in mythology has been opposed to Apollo—the Apollonian—which began with a music contest betwixt the two that Apollo won. This opposition continued in the Renaissance, with the Earl of Oxford writing complainingly of women, "How oft from Phoebus do they fly to Pan," Phoebus being another name for Apollo; one interpretation of the line is that women prefer pleasure over seriousness, or girls just want to have fun. However, in his poetry Lovecraft benignly accepts Pan as a typical pastoral personification. Another poetic tradition identifies Pan with Jesus Christ (who also has parallels with Dionysus), but in this context that is irrelevant, if ironic.

Pan gained part of his diabolism from Dionysus, "one of the most complicated of the ancient Greek gods" (Feder 119) and, adds *Wikipedia*, possessed a godship that among other things included "fertility, festivity, insanity, ritual madness." Stock considers that god a demon. Taking a cue from Margaret Murray's *Witch-Cult in Western Europe*, he states that "Dionysianism evidently survives in the demonolatry of the Christian era. The god himself has long been viewed by Christians as the most demonic of pagan deities" (11). "Iä" becomes part of a gumbo of connections, the goat and the god as evil spirits supplementing Shub-Niggurath. To put it in a formula, Dionysus and Shub-Niggurath have a connection with the implicitly Satanic goat and share the attributes of fecundity, carousal, and a sense of runaway worship. Appropriately, the classically pedigreed "Iä" follows the

---

love reading through" Lovecraft and others (xv). Providentially, "Dunwich" was written in the same year that introduced "the Goat of a Thousand Young."

protocol of welcoming or hailing Shub-Niggurath (most commonly) or other cosmological exotics, which points diversely to the rowdy-dowdy celebratory (especially the birth of new life in the matter of S-N), to the incantatory, and to the invocative that strains for the sublimity in horror; and there may also be a shadow of the elliptically inarticulate.

In the cult of Dionysus, the satyr and maenad, carnivaling with frenzied abandon, are reminiscent of the "hybrid spawn" composing the cult members in "The Call of Cthulhu" who eschatologically believe "mankind would have become as the Great Old Ones; free and wild and beyond good and evil, with laws and morals thrown aside and all men shouting and killing and revelling in joy. Then the liberated Old Ones would teach them new ways to shout and kill and revel and enjoy themselves, and all the earth would flame with a holocaust of ecstasy and freedom" (*CF* 2.39–40).[20] Lovecraft's politically tinctured and stealthy editorial exaggerates the present's modern and Dionysian trend as the shambles of civilization. The connection with Dionysus—one of whose roles was as inspirer of "ritual madness"—had earlier been prepared for in the tale, with Cthulhu worshippers moving "in endless Bacchanal" (Bacchus was the Roman version of the Greek god).

Lovecraft's knowing inclusion of the phrase "beyond good and evil"—which he liked, having earlier wielded it in a 1924 letter to Edwin Baird—is the title of a book by philosopher Friedrich Nietzsche, whose earlier *The Birth of Tragedy*[21] promoted

---

20. Cf. "The worship of Dionysus was centered in . . . freedom and ecstatic joy and . . . savage brutality" (Hamilton 57). The "Cthulhu" passage not only points to the celebratory but smacks of the apocalyptic—a biblical shadow runs through various stories—and "Iä" scoops up this aspect as well in its intent. Waggishly HPL could take the opposite, super-rational extremity, as when he asked, "What is a beauteous nymph? Carbon, hydrogen, oxygen, nitrogen, a dash or two of phosphorus & other elements—all to decay soon" (*Letters to Rheinhart Kleiner* 153). Cf. the Poe narrator in "Berenice": "feelings, with me, had never been of the heart, and my passions always were of the mind."

21. There is more of the philosopher's outlook in the passage than "beyond good and evil." De Camp wrote that Lovecraft "admired Nietzsche's reduction of human morals to an anthropological, materialistic basis" (236).

the contrasting concepts of the Apollonian—the ordered and harmonious—with the Dionysian,[22] whose effect the passage hints at. Nietzsche held a place in Lovecraft's outlook (one of his essays is "Nietzscheism and Realism"), and there is much commentary by critics on the influence of the philosopher on Lovecraft.

As for "Iä!," it has a prolepsis or nascency in the allusions to "shouting" and "shout," vocal extensions of ecstasy and freedom and, since so often connected with the fertile Goat, as a code for sexual license. Earlier in the tale there is "a subterrene voice or intelligence shouting monotonously in enigmatical sense-impacts uninscribable save as gibberish [i.e., Cthulhuese]" (*CF* 2.26). Shouting, not yet specified as "Iä!," is an attribute of an infernal intelligence synesthetically reciting a ritual. Another Lovecraft work where the shout is invocatory is in *The Case of Charles Dexter Ward*.

With its fixture in the Dionysian, the concept of ecstasy deserves some attention.[23] The word in the phrase "a holocaust of ecstasy" is its second appearance in the story; earlier the orgiastic coterie were depicted by "howls and squawking ecstasies" (*CF* 2.35). The word is more than just another Dionysian link, with "Iä" as an emblem, an affect of the literal ecstatic, whose etymology, as *ekstasis,* is from ancient Greek and means "to be or stand outside oneself." Through *ekstasis* worshippers enjoyed "a

---

22. "Apollo promised security" while "Dionysus offered freedom" (Dodds 76). Dodds refers to "the two great Dionysian techniques—the use of wine and the use of the religious dance" (69), both of which were antithetical to HPL, a supporter of Prohibition and who, concerning dance, quoted Cicero, "Almost nobody dances sober unless they happen to be insane." I was unable to discover if "Iä" was even extenuatingly connected to Dionysus through dithyrambs, those hymns sung and danced to celebrate him, but I found no model, no interjection preceding the name of a god. Dodds calls Dionysus "a god of the people" (76), another reason the aristocratic-loving Lovecraft would have sided against him. (As a bibliographic courtesy I acknowledge that I found the Dodds book through Salonia, "Cosmic Maenads and the Music of Madness: Lovecraft's Borrowings from the Greeks.")

23. Rather than "Dionysian *ecstasy,*" R. D. Stock prefers "*rapture,* which connotes being caught up or gripped" (15).

going out of their souls to meet and be one with Dionysus" (Durant 187). This is thematically Lovecraftian. It is several times evoked in Lovecraft's second favorite horror tale, Arthur Machen's "The White People," where horror is "ecstasy of the soul; a transcendent effort to surpass the ordinary bounds," an echo-to-be of painter Pickman's "'I tell you, people knew how to live, and how to enlarge the bounds of life, in the old times!'" (CF 2.61). According to Stock, Lovecraft like Machen "could work ecstasy out of horror" (370).

While "Iä!" could have originally emerged in a conversation or his letters,[24] its fictional inauguration was in "The Last Test" under the Adolphe de Castro byline. In this story the speaker, with fear and frenzy, talks of an old man who "had worshipped at the underground shrines of Nug and Yeb—Iä! Shub-Niggurath!" (CF 4.142). This interjection ends the passage, for the speaker is told to "Shut up." The demonstrative outburst has overwhelmed reportage; the pleasure-loving and even morally anarchic Dionysian beats the Apollonian, intellectual values that Lovecraft favored, for it undergirded the continuity of civilization. Stock argues that despite Lovecraft's Apollonian temperament his "demons are decidedly Dionysian" (370). With a contrary insight he calls them "oppressive, not liberating." Of "The Dunwich Horror" he writes that the invisible monster was "exorcised by some very Apollonian professors" (372). The temptation is to identify Lovecraft exclusively with the Apollonian and demonizing, literally, carnal pleasure.

The speaker's Dionysian outburst must be curbed, shut up, perhaps because he will reveal too much or has become hysterical. If the latter, the phrase gives a glimpse of the speaker's mental collapse, but it is also gratuitous in that it does not further the narrative. This is true for other stories, such as "The Dunwich Horror."

In that tale, a combustion of exuberance irrupts in the Dunsanian-cadenced *Necronomicon* quotation where "Great Cthulhu is Their cousin, yet can he spy Them only dimly. *Iä! Shub-*

---

24. How HPL used "Iä!" in his letters could add to its meaning, but I have not the resources to locate the word.

Niggurath! As a foulness shall ye know Them" (CF 2.434).[25]
Through the floridity of italics during the cryptic fluidity of circumstance, Lovecraft established the prominence of this seemingly spontaneous flotsam from his creative unconscious. As
with "The Last Test," if omitted the narrative would not miss it.
Perhaps the breaking in of *"Iä! Shub-Niggurath!"* is the equivalent of today's jump scare—an intent to startle—or may be plot-
ted as a disrupter to show the already agitated Arab author has
been temporarily and calamitously awed, with the suggestion
that more is going on beneath the surface. In the way that Bee-
thoven's opening of his *Eroica* symphony smites the audience
with its iconoclastic audacity, preparing it for another realm, the
shout of "Iä!" typically precedes Lovecraft's alien language and
the horrific consequences that implies. Its disruption additional-
ly functions as a sort of a paragraph break.

Burleson compares the fate of the surviving Dunwich twin
with that of Jesus Christ dying through the former's faltering
words "'HELP! HELP! . . . *ff—ff—ff*—FATHER! FATHER!
YOG-SOTHOTH!'" (CF 2.464). Similarly, the exclamation
"Iä!" followed by the name of a deity is a parody of a prayer address in this and other tales. Lovecraft is stripping prayer of its
Christianity and reverting it to its forerunning roots of paganism
and magic.[26] I wonder if the sermons of evangelist Billy Sunday—a contemporary and like Lovecraft a temperance advocate—could have been a parodic, emotional example, what with
their plethora of exclamations.[27] If one sees a speaker as having

---

25. I wish that HPL had attached the epithet "the goat with a thousand
young," because of the tale's allusion to "Arthur Machen's Great God Pan"
(CF 2.436), that character complement to Dionysus.

26. "During the 19th century, when various evolutionary theories were in
vogue, prayer was viewed as a stage in the development of religion from a magical to a 'higher' stage. Such theories . . . saw in prayer no more than a development of magic or incantation" (www.britannica.com/topic/prayer). As
Christianity replaced or suppressed the pagan gods, the Lovecraft Mythos is
doing through fiction the same to Christianity, albeit not without the tools of
parody or satire.

27. HPL ends his 1915 satiric poem "The Isaacsonio-Mortoniad" with his
friend-to-be, James F. Morton, "goring Billy Sunday" (AT 220), and in a 1916

worked himself into a trance-like state, what comes out is glossolalia—an Iä! Shub-Niggurath! moment—which goes back as far as ancient Greek mystery religions and is as new as today's Pentecostalism.[28]

Written around the same time as "The Dunwich Horror," "The Electric Executioner" saw print earlier.[29] Smitten with "Iä!," Lovecraft stuffed in six instances of it, solo or immediately repeated, enhancing its rudimental theatricality. It surfaces as part of a chant where it precedes the names of the Aztec gods with the variant spellings of "Huitzilopotchli," "Tloquenahuaque," and "Tonatiuh-Metztli."[30] The word has been semi-detached from the Mythos and linked to Nahuan-Aztec mythology, as in "'Iä! Tonatiuh-Metztli! Cthulhutl!'" The tailored spelling of Cthulhu is a creolization of Nahuan-Aztec fertilized by Lovecraft's fabricated speech. The function of "Iä!" is pretty clearly celebratory and, due to its unfamiliarity, estranging.

Yet there is a diffusion of alternate readings for "Iä!" in its passel of contexts, perhaps less obvious. Seen as antagonistic and defiant, it explodes, the protocol warning that unfathomable Shub-Niggurath or Cthulhu is coming to reckon, that a new sheriff is in town. One kinship behind the interjection is "lo!", as in look! or behold![31] It forces the attention, especially when before a named being.

"The Whisperer in Darkness" reduces the bravado of "Iä!" to its most conventional, ceremonial, and panegyric. Again, it is hitched

---

"Department of Public Criticism" column tars Sunday as a "slang-mouthing 'evangelist'" (CE 1.128).

28. A former member of the Lovecraft circle, Ira A. Cole, became a Pentecostal preacher who, relates HPL, "reached the hallucination stage—he fancied strange voices spoke gospel messages through his tongue—in languages he did not understand" (A Sense of Proportion 54).

29. In this and his other revisions I am supposing that "Iä!" etc., as with the preponderance of the texts, is exclusively Lovecraft's work and becomes a kind of personal signature while substantiating the reality and ubiquity of the Mythos.

30. Respectively, the sun as well as the butcherly war god; creator god; and the gods of the sun (Tonatiuh) and the moon (Metztli).

31. "Lo!" is a copious presence in Alexander Pope's translation of Homer's two epics, whose style HPL emulated in his 18th-century poetry phase.

to Shub-Niggurath and the illuminating epithet "the goat with a thousand young."[32] Comparable to "The Dunwich Horror," italics have been added to the recipe, but always with a reverent exclamation. While it *emphasizes* and draws the eye, it also reminds the reader of the convention of italicizing foreignisms. Its function in "Whisperer" is orthodox, like a Latin chant, settling comfortably as part of a ritualistic litany.[33] Lovecraft is exploring potentials of the phrase. Earlier in "Whisperer" there is also an allusion latent with the Dionysian milieu. The Mi-Go aliens are compared with the "natural personification which filled the ancient world with fauns and dryads and satyrs" (CF 2.473).

During the throes of writing "The Whisperer in Darkness" he worked up "Medusa's Coil," where "Iä!" and Shub-Niggurath remain indivisibly pinioned, like the two Kuiper Belt asteroids married into one, the Lovecraft-sounding Arrokoth (formerly Ultima Thule, itself inescapably swaddled in a furtive aura of Poe plus Lovecraft). An "ancient Zulu witch-woman"[34] howls the phrase, which accompanies *"N'gagi n'bulu bwana n'lolo!"* (CF 4.329). The narration grafts on the sinister implication: "Some of the words she used betrayed her closeness to daemonic and palaeogean traditions" (CF 4.329). The familiar Africanism of

---

32. This is the single story that associates the name with "black"—"Black Goat of the Woods"—though from some of what has been written about the deity (including the *Wikipedia* entry) readers would be convinced that the descriptor is invariable and prominent in all stories featuring S-N. Those with a predisposition to find racial clues are especially incriminated. In fairness, the subliminal ethnophaulism implied within the second part of the name is reminiscent of "black."

33. A remark by Dodds is applicable enough: "the road to salvation is found not in reason but in ritual" (287). He was targeting the assumption of a classical treatise on magic—which could be a précis of the *Necronomicon*—that he labeled "a manifesto of irrationalism."

34. She and the more notorious witch, Keziah Mason of Lovecraft's "The Dreams in the Witch House," incorporate the Dionysian. I am basing this on the belief of Stock, who finds such an affinity in Medea et al. By extension, it seems reasonable to see in Shub-Niggurath the assimilation of the spirit of a witch, who has a close association with a goat, as in Albrecht Dürer, *Witch Riding Backward on a Goat* (ca. 1500). Centuries later, a "goat-devil" is silhouetted by Goya in *The Witches' Sabbath*.

"bwana" authenticates the other words that attempt to present Swahili or other African language.[35] This phrase is followed by "Ya, yo," then later in the paragraph, "Ya, yo!" precedes the repetition of the Africanisms. The letter "y" as a sometimes vowel that replaces "i" here stealthily transforms "Ya" into a pseudo-"Iä," a bit of echoic deception.

In "The Shadow over Innsmouth," the epizeuxis "'Iä! Iä!'"[36] crops up in the elucidative mouth of Zadok Allen, who is a carousing modern-day follower of Dionysus—assuming the god's approval of bootleg—and perhaps forces himself into intoxication as an escape from what he knows. The outburst might mean that his awareness is wandering, or being directed, and *in vino veritas* spouts the forbidden—in the manner of "The Electric Executioner"—or part of him is undergoing a conversion (a word, here, also to suggest a religious metamorphosis into the Esoteric Order of Dagon cult of the story). However, for the narrator, the truth is that "Old Zadok was fast lapsing into stark raving, and I held my breath. Poor old soul—to what pitiful depths of hallucination had his liquor, plus his hatred of the decay, alienage, and disease around him, brought that fertile, imaginative brain!" (*CF* 3.197). No burping of "Shub-Niggurath" this time, but as with "Dunwich" the fascination relates to Cthulhu. In the climax, the words from the narrator echo as *"Iä-R'lyeh! Cthulhu fhtagn! Iä! Iä!"* (*CF* 3.230), tying him to the backsliding Allen. This is the single instance that dumps in

---

35. Wood identifies the babble as a "cod Swahili variant" (145). I briefly put some of the words into a Swahili online dictionary, but the results were discouraging. However, an online search by word revealed "N'gagi" to be the name of a male gorilla who died in the San Diego Zoo in 1944 at the age of 18; the 1960 title *Biggles and the Leopards of Zinn* has a witch-doctor called "N'Bulu"; and according to Artificial Intelligence, "Lolo" is an African word that can refer to a chief's wife, a Nigerian actress, or a musical instrument.

36. Not only does the doublet "Iä! Iä!" also appear in "The Horror in the Museum" (*CF* 4.438), but replays of words with exclamations show elsewhere in Lovecraft's work. "The Statement of Randolph Carter" bears the desperate line "'Beat it! Beat it! Beat it!'" (*CF* 1.138) and "The Curse of Yig" has a somewhat similar, "'Go away! Go away! Go away'" (*CF* 4.177). As with italics, the purpose is emphasis.

R'lyeh, complete with a hyphen variant. If the hyphen is a typo, how to decipher it? It could be following grammatical rules within a totally alien tongue. (That has to be a copy editor's downfall.) Lovecraft is otherwise playing with the consistency of "Iä." In its brief career, this is the only story where it comes at the end as well as the beginning of a phrase. The replication declares Zadok and the narrator are really *enthusiastic,* both in that word's distinct and its etymological sense.

While Zadok Allen is the character most embodying the Dionysian, Walter Gilman of "The Dreams in the Witch House" comes closest to the Apollonian. The reader is informed that he "ought not to have studied so hard" (CF 3.232) in those entangled touchstones of rationality, mathematics and physics. The outcome of excessive immersion is Dionysian subjugation. Near the end of the tale we enter into Gilman's hypnagogic head, and see the progression "—the prayers against the Crawling Chaos now turning to an inexplicably triumphant shriek—worlds of sardonic actuality impinging on vortices of febrile dream—Iä! Shub-Niggurath! The Goat with a Thousand Young . . ." (CF 3.269). These last words—prefaced by "dream" and trailing off into ellipses—paints the jungle of a nightmare at its worst—facing the *mysterium tremendum*—and the traumatized Gilman then subsides into unconsciousness. The paean of "Iä!" etc. signals the scourge of a climax and deafening end.

Lovecraft's evoking of an anti-anthropomorphic god as a symbol of an inhuman enlightenment[37] has a prototype in the flight of the narrator of "The Rats in the Walls," afraid he will eventually meet "Nyarlathotep, the mad faceless god, [who] howls blindly to the piping of two amorphous idiot flute-players" (CF 1.395); the next paragraph ("My searchlight expired . . .") returns to the relative sobriety of observational reportage. The word "Nyarlathotep," like "Iä! Shub-Niggurath!," is, to strip a term out of T. S. Eliot, an objective correlative.[38] Whether

---

37. The perversion of enlightenment, that guerdon of several religions, is "things that man was not meant to know."

38. Nyarlathotep and Cthulhu have onstage roles in stories, while Shub-Niggurath et al. intimidate through the power of their names, supported by the

Nyarlathotep or "Iä," the rude and impetuous presentations of uncertain meanings deepen an estranging and subliminal quality of uncontrolled fear through the addition of atmospheric miasma.

Gilman may be chanting "Iä!" etc. because his mind has been abstracted and is one with the horror,[39] a result of killing the enterprising witch (illustrating Nietzsche's oft-repeated "He who fights with monsters should be careful lest he thereby become a monster"). Being absorbed into the thing dreaded is not unique to this story, for Lovecraft has many protagonists struggle against this predicament, from the 1917 "The Tomb" (in protoform) to the 1935 "The Haunter of the Dark." If the chant is not hiding within the turmoil of Gilman's thoughts, then he is hearing it with the outer ear, which means the essence from the Mythos has broken through.

This is the first story where the word issues from a noninitiate. Before, the exclamation came from the mouths of people already schooled in the world it represented. They are familiar with the jargon, with the language of the Other. Gilman could only learn of "Iä" from the witch or his experience in hyperspace, and attests to his conversion, to his occult damnation.

In "The Man of Stone" the villain finds a magic formula for vengeance and writes gratefully in his diary from his spirit's depths, "Iä! Shub-Niggurath! The Goat with a Thousand Young!" (CF 4.382). Later he gloatingly exults: "*Iä R'lyeh!* Praise the Lord Tsathoggua!" (CF 4.384), a perverted and parodic emendation to the simple directive "Praise the Lord," a common phrase in the Bible.[40] Examined in terms of Christian religious equivalents, "Iä!" is "Hallelujah!," which literally means "Praise the Lord." "Iä" could be a severe back-formation of Hallelujah,

---

appropriate context. In the matter of S-N, "Iä"'s paradigmatic function as celebratory rationalizes the insertion of its name.

39. Crawshay-Williams wrote, "the word 'mind', though originally a label for a complex of mental events, often becomes hypostatized into an entity" (106). Especially in HPL's later work, the mind seems independent of the body.

40. The Bible, deflected into parody, offers material for several HPL stories. The aim is not parody alone, but credibility, for when a model is excavated for humor, some of its authority gets pulled along.

concentrating on the last syllable. Since the letter j was in the
Middle Ages begot from i, the spelling reverts to Halleluiah.
Even more relevant, the Latin mother of the word was spelled
"Alleluia" (*OED*). The pronunciation of the final syllable passes
muster for one variant of "Iä."

"Iä" reaches its oratorical glut in "The Horror in the Museum" through the chattering, histrionic Rogers, a villainous, pulp
P. T. Barnum and wayward acolyte for the god Rhan-Tegoth,
whose name is never graced with a festoon of "Iä"s, but in one
instance has before it another tumultuous interjection, "'Ei! Ei!
Ei! Ei!'" (*CF* 4.442), showing how Lovecraft loved his vowels (I
am assuming that this was his concoction rather than that of his
client, Hazel Heald). Befuddled with jubilance, impresario Rogers seals his commitment to his god, thanks to his cathartic and
elocutionary profligacy of single and doubled "Iä"s ("Iä! Iä!"),
confirming ritual and conferring factuality. They also carry practical rhythm and they transition into Rogers's flamboyant decla-
rations. Through its proximity to naming S-G etc., "Iä" absorbs
an awesome and unimpaired aspect or attribute of the deity, so
presumably the ululations (cthululations?) likewise promote terror and awe.[41] At the same time, there is what linguist Charles
Kay Ogden calls "a relic of primitive word magic," that "Iä" is an
incantation, a word symbol that causes something to happen.
Below the celebratory and supplicatory is the operational, the
theurgic, seeking the manifestation of a god, named or unnamed. As such the word has an opposition jeer against the apo-
tropaic, such as the cross (vampires) or August Derleth's star-
stones. In Lovecraft stories, things are summoned with spoken
spells, of which "Iä" could be a recipe's numinous ingredient. Af-
flictive monsters are also expelled with a similar process, as in
"The Dunwich Horror" or *The Case of Charles Dexter Ward*.

In "The Thing on the Doorstep" the expression first shoves
into the text as the narrator relates a panicked visit by his

---

41. One of the deities mustered, Chaugnar Faugn—a Frank Belknap Long invention—I will force into my advocacy for Dionysus-Pan-goat by arguing the
pronunciation of "Faugn" is by no coincidence "faun." An unrelated interpretation is that "Faugn" distorts into the revolted reaction "faugh!"

friend, the wife-victimized Edward Derby, who confesses: "'I never would let her take me, and then I found myself there. . . . Iä! Shub-Niggurath! . . . The shape rose up from the altar, and there were 500 that howled'" (CF 3.337–38). As with "Dunwich," the removal of "Iä" would not interrupt the flow. What it does accomplish is to accentuate the servile fearfulness of Derby. Like Zadok Allen, he is calling on the deity for succor, unless he is harkening to the tale's theme of possession, with a remnant of wife Asenath ventriloquizing him. Particularly in this tale, there is the suggestion of "trance utterance and glossolalia"[42] common to a species of mediumship, though the source speaker is not a deceased spirit. Lovecraft's robust scorn of the occult did not prohibit him from exploiting its tools.

Later Derby has a similar experience that leads to the same runaway vehemence, the words racing: "'that she-devil—even now—Ephraim—Kamog! Kamog!—The pit of the shoggoths—Iä! Shub-Niggurath! The Goat with a Thousand Young!'" (CF 3.349). I call attention, important or minor, to the dissimilar punctuation. The ellipsis separating the first outbursts suggests an interval between the phrases due to a disordered identity battling invasive assimilation and trying to pull itself together verbally. The second instance provokes an opposite reaction, the dashes implying hysteria and trying to gasp out too many impetuous words.[43]

The physical outburst of "Iä!" corroborates the absolute displacement of Derby's identity, a psychic digestion by the voracious, dallying Asenath. Derby's "soul"—a word that appears variously in Lovecraft—leaves his body for another that is en-

---

42. "Medium," *Encyclopædia Britannica* 18.69. For Spence, one early habiliment of mediumship was "demonic possession," which suits this tale.

43. Ellipses typically accompany textual fragmentation, signifying a mind's sundering or reversion to a state of dissociation (think of "The Rats in the Walls" or "Nyarlathotep"); it is the Lovecraftian version of "stream-of-consciousness." It is possible that Lovecraft could have been arbitrary with his ellipses, replacing them with dashes, but I am putting faith in the integrity of the text, taken from Lovecraft's autograph manuscript. Of the story's typed manuscript ("by an unknown hand") there "are extensive alterations of HPL's punctuation (especially as regards ellipses)" (Joshi in *CF* 3.324).

dowed with supernatural powers.[44]

"Iä" and ecstasy are entwined in "The Diary of Alonzo Typer." Villagers of the place named Chorazin[45] "emit sounds in a kind of diabolic ecstasy" (that the italics embellish) "'*Iä! Shub-Niggurath! The Goat with a Thousand Young!*'" (CF 4.595),[46] another instance of a ritual chant, as in "Whisperer." Discomposure comes not singly from the thing addressed but from the fanaticism of the group; as everywhere, those who lose themselves in the corybantic and in excess—from whirling dervishes to certain contemporary sects—invite curiosity or wonder or laughter or fear about the lengths to which their convictions take them. And while "Iä" lives in both Lovecraft's own and in his revisions, in the latter he perfunctorily tells rather than implies to get on with the story, for the revisionist owns a separate suite of writerly values. He asserted that "not much of my own

---

44. While associated with Platonic thought, Dodds has a dandy phrase I will apply to the skill of Derby's camouflaged nemesis, Ephraim Waite: a "detachable 'occult' self," which Empedocles has aptly called "the daemon." Dodds's comment on Greeks and "psychic intervention" can be repurposed for the theme in Lovecraft where identity is dispossessed: "If character is knowledge, what is not knowledge is not part of the character, but comes to a man from outside. When he acts in a manner contrary to the system of conscious dispositions which he is said to 'know,' his action is not properly his own, but has been dictated to him. In other words, unsystematised, nonrational impulses, and the acts resulting from them, tend to be excluded from the self and ascribed to an alien origin" (17). The "outside" is not simply Ephraim Waite and his "psychic intervention," but the "unsystematised, nonrational impulses" for which the Mythos gods are codifications and corporifications.

45. A town that was cursed in the Bible, this is an atypically blatant hint by HPL; call it his covering of tracks as a ghostwriter. If he didn't provide the allusion, perhaps this is the residue of William Lumley's contribution.

46. Cf. "Exclamatives are all prosodically marked by exaggerated acoustic intensity (wide-ranging peaks and troughs) that is indicated orthographically by an exclamation mark, !"—Keith Allan, "Mood, Clause Types and Illocutionary Force," quoted in Nordgren 83. There is no "Iä" in the book, though there are tantalizing variations, like the metathetic "ai." "There is a limit to the number of possible short combinations of sounds, especially vowel sounds, which in turn may explain the fact that most languages seem to share the interjections [au] and [ai]" (Nordgren 13).

style gets into my revisions" (*Letters to Woodburn Harris and Others* 338).

The next-to-last paragraph with the purgatorial scribbling of Robert Blake in "'The Haunter of the Dark" ends (again with ellipses): "boarding at that tower window cracking and giving way. . . . Iä . . . ngai . . . ygg . . .'" (*CF* 3.477). This "Iä" may very well signify Blake's beset and disintegrating mind wavering into propitiation or rapturous worship of the Haunter, with all its terrible potency. Like Derby, Gilman, and Allen, the vocalization designates victims who, unprepared, have glimpsed the esoteric, in contrast to the caterwauling believers drenched with zealotry. "Iä" is a prelude to the seeming gibberish of "ngai" and "ygg." Perhaps its position is an intermediary between this plane and meaningless sounds. Or perhaps, dislocated, after "Iä" he is trying to form words, one of which has a removed resemblance to "ungl" in "The Rats in the Walls," showing Lovecraft was consistent even in ostensibly random sounds.[47]

"Iä" is a signifier of worship and an anointer that the Haunter commands, the obeisance and emoluments to a god who expects offerings. Acculturated by his Baptist upbringing and through the coinings of his imagination, Lovecraft would have adjusted the credibilities about the destiny, after death, of the soul and its return ("Gone Home") away from a benevolent, immortal god. There is dualism between body and mind; and with the latter, jammed into a stand-in for the soul, the essence of Blake has become part of an alternate god. Typically, Lovecraft has brandished and subverted religion for irreligious, if artistic, ends.

Quantitatively, "Iä" is found once in "The Last Test," "The

---

47. As I have argued, so-called gibberish or vocables in HPL are neither random nor unpremeditated. For example, through embedded text, "ungl"—what HPL designates an "ape-cry" in "Rats"—looks as if he had excerpted the middle letters of "jungle," which is sublimation at work; devolving, de la Poer is returning to that primitive place. And—to be gratuitous in my decoding— "rrrlh" in "Rats" looks like a squashed "R'lyeh," the vowels being excised; restored, the utterance is "rrrlyeh" (this interpretation has been independently confirmed, if that means anything, by AI results). For HPL's seriocomic attitude toward the letter r, see the Notes section concerning "Epitaph on ye Letterr Rrr. . . . . . ." in *AT* 494.

Dunwich Horror," "The Dreams in the Witch House," "The Haunter of the Dark" (where it is bereft of a "!" and surrounded by ellipses), and "The Diary of Alonzo Typer"; twice in "The Man of Stone" and "The Thing on the Doorstep"; thrice in "Medusa's Coil"; and four times in "The Whisperer in Darkness" and "The Shadow over Innsmouth." "The Horror in the Museum" holds the record with twelve.[48] Shub-Niggurath appears in seven of the eleven stories, always preceded by "Iä" and seldom amputated from its "goat" appellation.

This closes the inventory of implicated fiction titles. While "Iä" is quoted in his letters, in them its apt counterpart is Lovecraft's interjections in authentic Latin: "ædepol" (for surprise) and "eheu!" (more frequently the phrase "eheu fugaces")[49] that has for its meaning, "alas!," "oh, no!," etc. and, coincidentally or not, is a repudiation of the celebratory, which persists in his favorite exclamatory phrase, "God Save the King!"

"Iiiiichaaaaaaach!" has a squinting resemblance to "Iä!," but in this case it is onomatopoeia for a yawn that appears in James Joyce's *Ulysses*.[50] The work undermines language no less than Lovecraft. In the Circe episode, adrift in magic, "language tends to become mere noise or—the visual equivalent of noise—a mess of letters," a breakdown that catches "Joyce's pleasure in the fracting of language and the notation of noise" (Burgess 23, 24).[51] However intriguing the insights about Lovecraft that would come from exploring the language of *Ulysses* and its dream counterpart, *Finnegans Wake*, to enter is to be lost in the walls of Eryx.[52]

---

48. I have been anticipated in assessing interjections by Harkey ("A Note on Fortunato's Coughing"). He counts and categorizes "ugh!," "ha!" etc. in Poe's fiction.

49. I have found these Latin examples principally in the letters to Morton, where Lovecraft would also spark out Greek charactery. Morton brought out the classicist in him. "Eheu fugaces" is a quotation from Horace (*Odes* 2.14.1).

50. Although never read by him, HPL called it one of the "significant contributions to contemporary art" (*CE* 2.77).

51. Without a twinkle Crystal charmingly defines interjections as "emotional or functional noises" (216).

52. *Finnegans Wake* has "The datter, io, io, sleeps in peace," though I suspect

"Iä!" is the opposite of a yawn. Though printed, it is visceral, a bellowed interjection like the "barbaric yawp" of Walt Whitman (whom Lovecraft despised). Lovecraft is fixing in orthography an utterance, sheer sound vanquishing its representative letters, which in the instance of "a" is refined through the diaeresis, a mark associated with poetry rather than prose that enhances the attributes of cadence and vocal value. This ploy in his fiction seeks to attack the ear with what he called "rhetorical effect," as for example in the verbalization of "ungl," "rrrlh," and "chchch" from "Rats."

How is the gleeful disyllable "Iä!" pronounced—roared, rather, given that it is a scion of galactic origin? Backing up Lovecraft's view that human ingenuity and vocal organs founder in the unutterableness of alien language pronunciation, Nordgren states: "Sound patterns of interjections can be said to be partly arbitrary, partly motivated by the human physique" (13).[53] Nonetheless, a certain standard can be guessed at, especially through the diacritic ukase in its audacious incursion above an unadorned "a." *Wikipedia* designates ä an "open central unrounded vowel," which I hear as a bellowed "ah."

The sound of its partner letter is up for grabs. It could be separately produced as "eye," but a deep "e" feels appropriate, as it might have been before the Great Vowel Shift.[54] I have heard the interjection in movies (if that is an authoritative guide) and seen it through online sources as "ee-ah," which is how my auditory imagination materializes it. This is very much like the cowboy's "yee-hah," a coincidental vocable, and from the prospect of meaning "hurrah" is an attractive candidate, expressing "sudden euphoria" (Dunn), a disruption to the mundane and secure order.

"io" leans toward the name of the goddess. But any number of interpretations can be licensed.

53. I have argued against the first part of his dictum, by implication, that "Iä" and other vocables are "arbitrary." I maintain they are consciously, or even instinctively, fashioned.

54. "Long i in mite was pronounced as /iː/, so Middle English mite sounded similar to Modern English meet."—"Great Vowel Shift" in *Wikipedia*. Or could a Greek pronunciation be an alternate culprit?

And in its pronunciation where does the stress lie—first or second syllable? Were I a voting savant, I would choose the second, but a similarly convincing case can favor the first.

Vowels are the sinews of sounds. Lovecraft's choice of marrying the letters i and ä feeds into the tricky merit of sound symbolism or phonaesthesia. Related to onomatopoeia, the concept is a contention that certain sounds represent a defined effect or emotion sprung from some mighty instinct.[55] So, the two vowels of "Iä" could "mean" or evoke the celebratory.

"Iä!" accretes to it the exercise of sound as atmosphere. When he wrote that "*Unaussprechlichen* has such a sinister, mouth-filling rhythm" (*A Means to Freedom* 762), his reaction is tilted to the aural. Lovecraft showed a kind of eidetic as well as a poetic ear[56] for speech, which in its unsavory aspects he sporadically dumped in correspondence to ridicule those with ethnic accents.[57] His aural sensitivity was no less proved in his Cthulhuese—tormented idiom from beyond the stars intruding as a notation of eerie sensuousness, where on one level sound does not simply subdue but replace understanding, which is shared with his vocables.

As the fractal corpuscles of Cthulhu reassembled and collapsed back into Its original shape, I cohere, summarize, and fortify erstwhile, separate points into a whole. I began with the reasonable conviction that if "Iä" came from a foreign model, it was Greek—but I wobble seismically, for there is a pretty formidable

---

55. Though I have not looked at it beyond the abstract, see for example Ponsonnet et al.

56. Poet and literary critic Winfield Townley Scott observed, "it seems not unlikely that at one time or another Lovecraft thought of himself first of all as a poet" (316).

57. Rather than call attention to the too frequent examples, I will give one of several where pronunciation is by a national group that HPL admired, the British. See *Letters to J. Vernon Shea* 235–36. For stylistic imitation his talent is also apparent through his Poe evocations in poetry and prose, one example of the former being "Despair" and "The Outsider" for the latter; he even committed a Poe hoax. His popular designation as "the twentieth-century Poe" carries with it shades of irony.

case for Latin as a dominating influencer; or the pedigree may be lost in cloudy bastardy, like the Whateley parentage.

To continue: *Iacche* converts to "shout," and going by its morphology the leading vowels may have fathered Lovecraft's exclamation. Inseparable from the physiological sensation of hot, brutal sound,[58] that name was cried by Dionysian cultists, and (speculatively) as "Iä" was adopted by Lovecraft's Mythos celebrants. With his Apollonian/rational temperament, Lovecraft could willfully read "horror" into the Dionysian/irrational.[59] As an artistic presence the interjection emits different functions, such as an anti-narrative instrument that is joltingly interruptive, and as a suggestion of the flux and reflux of "things fall apart"—physical, mental, and spiritual—which the Mythos beings imprecisely symbolize (if austere symbols of lightless chaos they become allegorical).

When a speaker breaks into the cadence "Iä," he may be revealing its cantankerous dominance over him; or he is adapting to his submission. Either as victims of circumstance or dabblers in the occult, these people are practical examples of the consequences when the Dionysian (the Mythos) overthrows the Apollonian.

Some of the attractiveness of interjections is their rawness, a burst from the depth-dwelling instinct for cacophony. They are the big bang of language, the intermediary from inner emotion to outer meaning. Latin grammarians were onto this, for they saw that "the interjection constituted merely a vocalized expression of a feeling or a state of mind" (Dunn and Aragonés xi). Since then there have been several conjectures about the origin

---

58. In *Paradise Lost* the Apollonian Milton condemned Dionysus (Bacchus) for the *noise* of his presence: "But drive far off the barbarous dissonance / Of Bacchus and his revellers, the race / Of that wild rout . . ." (His masque *Comus* is another example of Dionysian villainy, Comus in Greek mythology being the cup-bearer to Dionysus.)

59. The boon of uninhibited freedom displayed in the worshippers of the Greek god and those of HPL's is testimony to the seductiveness of the irrational for all people. "I propose . . . that during the greater part of our lives we, as human beings, tend to prefer unreason to reason" (Crawshay-Williams 2).

of language and the role of interjections. I am putting my chips on the rudely named "Pooh-Pooh Theory," which proposed "that speech originated from the spontaneous exclamations and interjections of the human animal; cries of fear, surprise, anger, pain, disgust, despair, or joy" (Barnett 47).[60] Behind its implied celebratory reverberance, "Iä" is a throwback to pre-literate emotion, further fixing an impressionistic climate that Lovecraft engineers.

"The Call of Cthulhu" began what I have tagged Cthulhuese. Lovecraft had originated his draft of a new language years before in his contraption of vocables, sounds lacking a fixed meaning. The most prominent early example of Lovecraft flirting with sounds that would unfold into Cthulhuese was the bestial pre-words by the atavistic de la Poer in "The Rats in the Walls."[61] Vocables, combined with the paradigm of Greek, Latin, and other foreign languages, gave way to the makeshift of *"Ph'nglui mglw'nafh Cthulhu . . ."*[62] The interjection "Iä" followed after a while as Lovecraft developed his world-building through the wreck of language.

"Iä" has layers of meaning, part from itself and part borrowed from its context. Of a word, Poe wrote about "the under or mystic current of its meaning," which applies to "Iä," whose impeccable emotional adrenaline arises from its ambiguity. Like the "gods" it so often prefixes, "Iä" seems the speculative product of an occult or mythical empire.

Dreamed up, phantasmagoric words such as "fhtagn" appeared in but two Lovecraft tales for them to gain a hold in the imagination of genre readers, while the tidy, terse, and swaggery "Iä!"—with or without the exclamation point—circulated in a

---

60. I also recognize the competing notion of the "Yo-He-Ho Theory," which has language growing "from reflex vocal utterances—grunts, gasps, glottal contractions—evoked by strenuous physical exertion" (Barnett 47). Barnett shows off more drolly labeled theories in this section.

61. The sounds, by another interpretation, are those of the infant babbling, a riff on "biology recapitulates phylogeny."

62. Scraps from other languages attach to his fiction, as Spanish in "The Transition of Juan Romero."

spread of works, thanks to its versatility and mystique, and soon publicized itself as a shibboleth in his corpus, joining the miserly vocabulary of R'lyeh. As early as 1941 anthologist Phil Stong wrote humorously of "Shub-Niggurath and his [sic] cheering section of five hundred unspeakable abominations, all howling, like football fans, 'Iä!, Iä!, Shub-Niggurath! Hold that line!' Excuse me, that last phrase is not in the text" (329)[63] Like mentions of Cthulhu and the *Necronomicon,* the euphoric "Iä!" is a popular and well-known signifier of the zesty Lovecraftian, evidenced as a fixture in much later fiction of this persuasion,[64] in games, and in the effervescent, if not Dionysian, behavior of fans. A 2024 October book review in the *New York Times* can begin "Iä! Iä! Cthulhu fhtagn!," and the wise reader is prepared for what's coming.[65]

Works Cited

"Ä." *Wikipedia.* en.wikipedia.org/wiki/A

Asimov, Isaac. *Asimov's Guide to the Bible: The Old Testament.* New York: Avon, 1968.

Barnett, Lincoln. *The Treasure of Our Tongue.* New York: New American Library, 1967.

Burgess, Anthony. *Joysprick: An Introduction to the Language of James Joyce.* New York: Harcourt Brace Jovanovich, 1973.

Burleson, Donald R. *H. P. Lovecraft: A Critical Study.* Westport, CT: Greenwood Press, 1983.

Cisco, Michael. "Lovecraft and *The Birth of Tragedy.*" *Crypt of Cthulhu* No. 77 (Eastertide 1991): 3–4.

---

63. The title of Stong's volume has historic heft as "the first important sf anthology. Its twenty-five stories, about half sf and half horror, were mostly from the pulp magazines, not previously regarded as a proper source of material (of sf at least) for respectable hardcover books" (*SF Encyclopedia*).

64. The ä sustains its existence in names by post-Lovecraft writers. Belgian Eddy C. Bertin invented Cyäegha, which has christened a magazine of the same name.

65. The book favorably reviewed is *Nether Station* by Kevin J. Anderson (www.nytimes.com/2024/10/28/books/review/new-horror-books.html?search ResultPosition=1).

Crawshay-Williams, Rupert. *The Comforts of Unreason.* London: Kegan Paul, Trench, Trübner & Co, 1947.

Crystal, David. *The Cambridge Encyclopedia of the English Language.* Cambridge: Cambridge University Press, 1995.

de Camp, L. Sprague. *Lovecraft: A Biography.* Garden City, NY: Doubleday, 1975.

"Dionysus." *Encyclopædia Britannica* (1910). 8.287.

Dodds, E. R. *The Greeks and the Irrational.* Berkeley: University of California Press, 1951.

Dunn, Mark, and Sergio Aragonés. *ZOUNDS! A Browser's Dictionary of Interjections.* New York: St. Martin's Griffin, 2005.

Durant, Will. *The Life of Greece.* New York: Simon & Schuster, 1939.

Eulexis-web. outils.biblissima.fr/en/eulexis-web.

Feder, Lillian. *The Meridian Handbook of Classical Literature.* New York: New American Library, 1986.

Frazier, James George. *The Project Gutenberg eBook of The Golden Bough: A Study of Magic and Religion.* XLIII. "Dionysus."

Funk & Wagnalls Standard Dictionary of Folklore, Mythology and Legend. Ed. Maria Leach. New York: Funk & Wagnalls, 1950.

Godolphin, Francis R. B., ed. *The Latin Poets.* New York: Modern Library, 1949.

Graves, Robert. *The Greek Myths.* Harmondsworth, UK: Penguin, 1960. 2 vols.

———. *The White Goddess.* Amended and enlarged ed. New York: Vintage, 1948.

"Great Vowel Shift." *Wikipedia.* en.wikipedia.org/wiki/Great_Vowel_Shift

The H. P. Lovecraft Archive. www.hplovecraft.com/writings/fiction

Hadas, Moses, ed. *The Greek Poets.* New York: Modern Library, 1953.

Hamilton, Edith. *Mythology.* New York: New American Library, 1942.

Harkey, Joseph H. "A Note on Fortunato's Coughing." *Poe Newsletter* 3, No. 1 (June 1970): 21–22.

"Ia." *Wikipedia.* en.wiktionary.org/wiki/ia

"Iacchus." *Wikipedia.* en.wikipedia.org/wiki/Iacchus

Latdict. www.latin-dictionary.net/search/latin/Io

———. www.latin-dictionary.net/definition/24685/Io

"Latin Phonology and Orthography." *Wikipedia.* en.wikipedia. org/wiki/Latin_phonology_and_orthography

Liddell, Henry George, and Robert Scott. *A Greek-English Lexicon.* 1843. Oxford: Clarendon Press, 1901. archive.org/details/ greekenglishlex00lidduoft

Lovecraft, H. P. *The Complete Works of H. P. Lovecraft.* archive. org/details/TheCompleteWorksOfHPLovecraft_201412

———. *Letters to J. Vernon Shea, Carl F. Strauch, and Lee McBride White.* Ed. S. T. Joshi and David E. Schultz. New York: Hippocampus Press, 2016.

———. *Letters to James F. Morton.* Ed. S. T. Joshi and David E. Schultz. New York: Hippocampus Press, 2011.

———. *Letters to Rheinhart Kleiner and Others.* Ed. S. T. Joshi and David E. Schultz. New York: Hippocampus Press, 2020.

———. *Letters to Woodburn Harris and Others.* Ed. S. T. Joshi and David E. Schultz. New York: Hippocampus Press, 2022.

———. *The New Annotated H. P. Lovecraft.* Ed. Leslie Klinger. New York: Liveright, 2014.

———, and Robert E. Howard. *A Means to Freedom: The Letters of H. P. Lovecraft and Robert E. Howard.* Ed. S. T. Joshi, David E. Schultz, and Rusty Burke. New York: Hippocampus Press, 2009. 2 vols.

———, and Frank Belknap Long. *A Sense of Proportion: The Letters of H. P. Lovecraft and Frank Belknap Long.* Ed. David E. Schultz and S. T. Joshi. New York: Hippocampus Press, 2025.

———, and Clark Ashton Smith. *Dawnward Spire, Lonely Hill: The Letters of H. P. Lovecraft and Clark Ashton Smith.* Ed. David E. Schultz and S. T. Joshi. New York: Hippocampus Press, 2017. 2 vols.

"Medium." *Encyclopædia Britannica* (1910). 18.69.

Nordgren, Lars. *Greek Interjections: Syntax, Semantics and Pragmatics.* Berlin: De Gruyter, 2015.

Oxford English Dictionary. "Alleluia." Oxford University Press, December 2024, doi.org/10.1093/OED/1198220045.

———. "Young." Oxford University Press, December 2024, doi.org/10.1093/OED/1155606815.

Ponsonnet, Maïa, et al. "Vowel Signatures in Emotional Interjections . . ." *Journal of the Acoustical Society of America* (1 November 2024).

"Prayer." *Britannica.* www.britannica.com/topic/prayer

Russell, Jeffrey Burton. *The Prince of Darkness: Radical Evil and the Power of Good in History.* Ithaca, NY: Cornell University Press, 1988.

SF Encyclopedia. sf-encyclopedia.com/entry/stong_phil.

Salonia, John. "Cosmic Maenads and the Music of Madness: Lovecraft's Borrowings from the Greeks." *Lovecraft Annual* No. 5 (2011): 91–101.

Scott, Winfield Townley. "His Own Most Fantastic Creation." In H. P. Lovecraft et al. *Marginalia.* Ed. August Derleth and Donald Wandrei. Sauk City, WI: Arkham House, 1944. 309–31.

Spence, Lewis. *An Encyclopaedia of Occultism.* 1920. New York: University Books, 1960.

Stock, R. D. *The Flutes of Dionysus: Daemonic Enthrallment in Literature.* Lincoln: University of Nebraska Press, 1989.

Stong, Phil, ed. *The Other Worlds: 25 Modern Stories of Mystery and Imagination.* Garden City, NY: Garden City Publishing, 1941.

Versnel, H. S. *Triumphus: An Inquiry into the Origin, Development and Meaning of the Roman Triumph.* Leiden: E. J. Brill, 1970.

Wood, Andrew Paul. "'A Kind of Sophisticated Astarte': On the Nature of Shub-Niggurath." *Lovecraft Annual* No. 17 (2023): 141–62.

The Influence of *Moby-Dick* on H. P. Lovecraft's "The Dunwich Horror"

Peter Cannon

In *Crypt of Cthulhu* No. 49 (Lammas 1987), I published an article entitled "Call Me Wizard Whateley: Echoes of *Moby-Dick* in 'The Dunwich Horror.'" At the time, I had only circumstantial evidence that Lovecraft read *Moby-Dick*. Evidence that he read Melville's masterpiece has since surfaced. In a letter dated 11 April 1925, Lovecraft tells his aunt Lillian Clark: "I shall probably wear my light overcoat, checking it at the Union Station in Washington, where I shall also check the book which is to beguile my hours of idleness—'Moby Dick, or the White Whale', by Herman Melville" (*Letters to Family and Family Friends* 266). In 2017, Lovecraft's copy of *Moby-Dick,* a gift from his bookseller friend George Kirk, was discovered on the shelves of the American Antiquarian Society, as noted in an online essay by rare book dealer Henry Wessells. These developments, capped by my participation on the Lovecraft–Melville panel at the 2024 NecronomiCon, have inspired me to refine my thinking on this case of influence.

Both *Moby-Dick* and "The Dunwich Horror" feature a single-minded fanatic on a doomed quest for the enormous creature of their respective titles, if for opposite ends. Captain Ahab seeks to kill the white whale, while Old Whateley contrives the Dunwich horror's entry into the world with the aim of wiping out all humanity. Note that Old Whateley's grandson, Wilbur, who takes up the quest after his grandfather's death, amounts to the story's true hero, as Donald R. Burleson posits in "The Mythic-Hero Archetype in 'The Dunwich Horror.'" Both Captain Ahab and Old Whateley are married, but their respective wives receive scant mention.

In the first chapter of *Moby-Dick*, Ishmael eloquently explains why he sometimes has an itch to go to sea, that is, to travel. In the first section of "The Dunwich Horror," the omniscient third-person narrator eloquently explains at length why travelers should avoid Dunwich. In the same section, the extract from the Reverend Abijah Hoadley's eighteenth-century sermon signals trouble ahead rather as Father Mapple's sermon on Jonah and the whale does in chapter nine of *Moby-Dick*.

Major shifts of narrative perspective mark each work. Ishmael essentially disappears once Ahab appears on deck, and the white whale takes center stage in the novel's final chapters. In "The Dunwich Horror," Old Whateley is supplanted after his death by his grandson, Wilbur. After Wilbur's death, the focus is on Dr. Henry Armitage of Miskatonic University, but it is the horror itself that dominates the story's conclusion.

Like the whaling ship *Pequod*, Dunwich, Massachusetts, is a self-contained community. Just as Melville shares the voices of the ship's sailors, so does Lovecraft reproduce the backwoods speech of the people of Dunwich, conveying a sense of mundane daily life in the isolated town. These humble folk provide a chorus amid the disturbing doings in Dunwich, just as the ordinary seamen do during the increasingly unsettling voyage of the *Pequod*. Nowhere else in his fiction does Lovecraft take such care to delineate a large cast of supporting characters.

If Melville presents Ahab as a tragic figure of Shakespearean proportions, so Lovecraft apparently nods to Shakespeare in his naming the story's one significant female character, Lavinia. In *Titus Andronicus*, Lavinia is the daughter of Titus, a Roman general. (Incidentally, when "a jocose fish-peddler" [*CF* 2. 428] frightens Lavinia Whateley by trying the locked door to the stairway leading to the horror's lair on the second floor of her family's house, she turns "pale," Lovecraft having forgotten that she's an *albino*.) In Shakespeare's violent revenge play, Lavinia is raped and murdered. Lovecraft's Lavinia, impregnated by the entity Yog-Sothoth in what amounts to cosmic rape, disappears but is probably murdered, a fate shared by the Reverend Abijah Hoadley and Old Whateley's wife. As befits a Jacobean tragedy, "The Dunwich Horror" has an unusually high body count for a mature Lovecraft story, with its multitude of deaths, nearly all of which occur off-stage.

Finally, the climaxes of both works vividly depict a hunt that showcases the respective quarries' unpredictable actions and unforgettable physiognomies. A kind of land whale, the Dunwich horror leaves in its wake a "tarry stickiness" (CF 2. 438) whose viscosity is reminiscent of spermaceti. Over a period of days, the otherworldly monster, capable of near vertical movement, plunges into Cold Spring Glen, then resurfaces, rather as Moby Dick dives below the waves and comes up for air at intervals during the three days covered in the three chase chapters. The Dunwich horror smashes wooden houses just as Moby Dick shatters wooden boats. Armitage and his two colleagues from Miskatonic University, armed with their magical spells, serve the same role as the three harpooners who set out to slay the whale with their earthly weapons. Ahab perishes in a freak accident on a small boat while pursuing a dangerous animal; Wilbur Whateley proves no match for the maddened beast that fatally attacks him in the Miskatonic library, in a no less grotesque death scene.

Of course, Melville's novel is just one of many influences on Lovecraft's powerful tale of supernatural horror. As for any larger meanings or interpretations, I defer to others to make those arguments.

Works Cited

Burleson, Donald R. "The Mythic-Hero Archetype in 'The Dunwich Horror.'" *Lovecraft Studies* No. 4 (Spring, 1981): 3–9.

Lovecraft, H. P. *Letters to Family and Family Friends.* Ed. S. T. Joshi and David E. Schultz. New York: Hippocampus Press, 2020. 2 vols. (numbered consecutively).

Wessells, Henry. "*Moby-Dick* and American Literature of the Fantastic; or, Bound for the South Seas." *The Endless Bookshelf* (19 June 2024). endlessbookshelf.net/2024/06/19/moby-dick-and-american-literature-of-the-fantastic/

Lovecraft and Wales

Felix John Taylor

In September 1927 Lovecraft was visited in Providence by the twenty-three-year-old Wilfred Blanch Talman, whose story "Two Black Bottles" Lovecraft had just revised for the previous month's *Weird Tales*. An enthusiastic genealogist, Talman had encouraged Lovecraft in expanding his maternal line. Hitherto, Lovecraft's understanding of his family history had been based on records compiled by his great-aunt Sarah Allgood, which he had copied out as a teenager in 1905. Talman's visit provoked a reassessment and codification of the Allgood charts, the results of which were reported to Frank Belknap Long in November:

> Well—all this is delightful—but *who is this dame that my great-grandfather William Allgood married in 1817?* Rachel Morris—yes, I knew that before. But where did she come from? *Wales!* O Arthur Machen! O Caerleon! O Second Augustan Legion! O ROMAN MATRON of Isca Silurum! *Racilla Mauritia*, daughter of the propraetor *Publius Mauritius Racillus*, attached to the staff of Cnaeus Julius Agricola, father-in-law of Tacitus. Yes, by St. Paul, a brave Teut. . . . Or *Roman* always makes the best of these things! And that's my great-grandma! (*SP* 453)

Despite the exclamatory tone of the letter, Lovecraft was in fact bored by the whole process, unwilling to interpret the "monotonous reams of heraldic blazonings" (*WBT* 87) that he had found or to put in any further genealogical work after the "Talmanick enthusiasm" (*SP* 452) had worn off. Perhaps this was because of the kind of data his investigations had so far revealed. Lovecraft had apparently uncovered, possibly with some creative guess-work on the part of his great-aunt, the fact that his great-

grandmother had been Welsh. Tracing the Morris line, Lovecraft was led to a Thomas Morris (1777–1817), whose father, Sir
John Morris, had been a baronet from Glamorganshire. From
here ("now out with the worst"), he follows the tree to Owen
Purcell of Llanariba, and to his wife Susanna, daughter of a man
named David Rees (or Rhys), "a Welsh gentlewoman of un-
mixed Celtick blood!" (*SP* 454). His report ends with the wildest
claim of all, that the line of Sir John Morris may go back as far as
Owain ap Gruffudd, a twelfth-century king of Gwynedd: "Full-
blooded Celt! It gives me another sprig or royalty to companion
the 137th King of Erin, but damn the luck that made it *Celtick*
royalty" (*SP* 454).

Ken Faig, Jr. has documented the Irish side of Lovecraft's
family tree, but the true facts about Lovecraft's Welsh ancestry
are so far unproven. Faig's assessment of the Allgood charts—
that they appear to be "largely the creation of the inventor"
(*The Unknown Lovecraft* 20)—turns any speculation into a wild
goose chase. What matters for the present article, however, is
that Lovecraft genuinely seemed to believe in this connection to
Wales. But what did he think of the Welsh? In a letter to Talman following the writer's visit, Lovecraft called his own attitude to Celtic ancestry "ambiguous," saying that he is "for the
Teuton in the last analysis" (a now-outdated term referring to
people of Germanic origin), but that "a Celt or two on the loftier
branches doesn't poison a whole family tree" (*WBT* 87). As early as 1915, he was declaring an unnuanced preference for the
Teutonic peoples as the superior race, evidenced by the fact that
the English are dominant in Britain. According to this view,
Lovecraft saw the Welsh (i.e., non-Teutonic) as being "of little
consequence" (*RK* 47).

Lovecraft's later opinions of the Welsh people, and more
broadly of "Celts" as a racial group (however inaccurate this
term is now considered in modern Celtic studies), was not well
established until the 1930s, when he began his correspondence
with Robert E. Howard; but even then his opinions appear confused. "I have often thought, in surveying the trends of literature
and socio-political organisation today, that the Celtic group is

really the only *young* and unspoiled race left on the planet" (*MF* 74). His letter to Long is further evidence of this inconsistency. On one hand, there is clear indication that his new ancestral find displeased him. He was relieved to note, for example, that "even in the cold light of the crumbling chart granny was not exactly what you'd call one of the Little People" (*SP* 453); in other words, that she was not purely Welsh, but had aristocratic connections. Although veiled in heavy irony, Lovecraft calls his description of his family tree a "terrible chronicle" and a "shocking revelation of hybridism" (*SP* 454), as if, like Arthur Jermyn or the protagonist of "The Shadow over Innsmouth," Lovecraft's discovery has thrown his comfortably Anglophone identity off balance.

On the other hand, unearthing links to Celtic-speaking nations proved a clear source of amusement for Lovecraft, and to be connected with the Anglo-Welsh writer Arthur Machen (1863–1947) even more so. Machen's work had exerted a profound influence on Lovecraft ever since reading *The House of Souls* (1906) in early 1923, a collection of Machen's supernatural tales mostly written in the 1890s. To Lovecraft, Machen was an acceptable Welshman: a weird, English-speaking writer with an interest in the Roman history of his birthplace. Caerleon-on-Usk in the South Wales county of Monmouthshire was once the site of the Roman legionary fortress Isca Silurum (or Isca Augusta), the setting of Machen's first novel, *The Hill of Dreams* (1907). Lovecraft entertains the unlikely theory, based on the name "Machynlleth," the seat of one of Lovecraft's spurious ancestors David Jenkins, that he is distantly related to Machen. "However," he concedes, "I shan't be addressing Arthur M. as 'Cousin Arthur' quite yet!" (*WBT* 87).[1] This game of connecting himself with his literary heroes was extended to Lord Dunsany, whose middle name "Moreton" Lovecraft had discovered on the Fulford family arms, and, in an even further imaginative leap, to Ambrose "Gwinnett" Bierce (though Gwinnett was not

---

1. He was at least correct in this: the etymologies of "Machynlleth," a town in Powys, North Wales, and "Machen" (which Arthur Machen inherited from his Scottish mother), are unconnected.

a family name). "No use talking—all us Machyns and Moretons and Gwynetts [*sic*] jes' nachelly take to imaginative writing," he concludes, tongue firmly in his cheek as he signs off "O'Howard McPhillips ap Lovecraft" (*WBT* 90).

In his later correspondence with Robert E. Howard, Lovecraft revives this point, that "a share of Celt" is a "great asset" for a writer of fantastic literature (*MF* 74). In turn, Howard claimed to detect a "Celtic influence" in Lovecraft's fiction: "You certainly seem to have as much connection with Celtic tradition as Machen!" (*MF* 48–49). Comments of this kind echo the romanticism of the Celtic literary revival in fin-de-siècle Britain; it was fashionable for poets such as W. B. Yeats and Fiona Macleod (female alias of William Sharp) to declare the Celt's superior temperament for writing imaginative literature, compared to the hard-hearted materialistic Saxons, and looked for evidence of Celtic ancestry in well-known English authors. Machen himself violently opposed this idea in an article titled "The All-Pervading Celt" in 1898, a fact that Lovecraft seems to have missed. There is no mention of Wales or the Welsh people in Lovecraft's tales, except a solitary reference to an old ballad "not yet extinct near the Welsh border" in "The Rats in the Walls" (*CF* 1.379), but in "The Horror at Red Hook" the New York detective Malone is said to possess "the Celt's far vision of weird and hidden things" (*CF* 1. 482; see also Sneddon).

As is the case with many of his prejudices, Lovecraft both knew and felt great affection for individuals whose abstract racial and sexual characteristics he privately disliked. Lovecraft maintained a lasting correspondence with amateur journalist Arthur Harris (1893–1966), one of the only genuinely Welsh people that he ever encountered—albeit from a distance. A professional printer by trade, Harris seems to have lived most of his life in Llandudno, a town on the North Wales coast that had become a popular holiday destination since its development in the 1870s. While none of Harris's letters to Lovecraft survive, he edited the long-running magazine *Interesting Items*, copies of which he regularly sent to Lovecraft, and in exchange he received Lovecraft's *Conservative* until its demise in 1923 (*RK* 15).

The pair corresponded mainly about the amateur press scene, but it was from Harris's descriptions of the local area (both in letters and the pages of *Interesting Items*) that Lovecraft began to gain an impression of the "Cambrian scenery & antiquities" (*RK* 260). Harris reported making excursions to Conwy, the river Dee, and Anglesey, and in early 1930 he ascended Snowdon. In March 1931, Lovecraft eventually revealed the facts of his gene-alogical investigations:

> Your visit to Deganwy Castle [in Llandudno] must have been prodigiously interesting, & I keenly enjoyed the newspaper ac-count of the place. I really ought to know more about Welsh antiquities, for one of my lines of ancestry comes from Wales – albeit from Glamorganshire, far to the south of you. Then, too, I am a confirmed devotee of Arthur Machen, & of his strange ta-les of the Gwent region around the Usk. (*RK* 270)

As the correspondence moved into the 1920s, Machen be-came a recurrent point of reference for Lovecraft; he frequently compared Harris's information about North Wales with what he knew about Caerleon, "that noble, forgotten city" (*ET* 31). Ro-man Britain was therefore another topic of mutual interest, and Harris duly forwarded articles on the subject, mostly by the Egyptologist Arthur Weigall (*RK* 289). Lovecraft had also gained fair grounding in the medieval history of South Wales from his reading of Geoffrey of Monmouth (twelfth-century au-thor of *The History of the Kings of Britain*) and Giraldus Cam-brensis (Gerald of Wales). "It appears that the amphitheatre at Caerleon-on-Usk has been found virtually intact beneath the grassy mound that covered it," Lovecraft writes in April 1934, "so that today it forms one of the finest specimens of its kind in the world" (*RK* 289–90). This again was the kind of Wales that Lovecraft deemed tolerable: a land once civilized by Roman oc-cupation, brimming with classical "antiquities" that overshad-owed its barbarian Celtic past.

If Lovecraft received his idea of modern-day Wales solely through a combination of Machen's weird tales and Harris's pic-turesque accounts of local Roman sites, he appears to have gleaned little about its culture or its populace. Revelations about his maternal Welsh ancestry, most likely false, nevertheless provided Lovecraft with a link to Wales (and, along with his Irish family, to the "Celts" in general) that he occasionally used as an explanation for his creative inclinations, and he communicated his findings to friends with mixed disdain and good humor. For Lovecraft, Wales was a fantasy of Roman *civitas* and medieval Welsh kings, "archaic magic & classical heritage" (*ET* 31). But he was also willing to participate in the construction of this fantasy. It was during this late period of ancestral soul-searching that Lovecraft played with the idea of inventing a family tree from himself that connected him to the Romans. "Some day I am going to construct myself a fictitious genealogy linking one of my Welsh lines with the Roman colonists of that region," he writes in a letter to Elizabeth Toldridge in 1929 (*ET* 31). From the Weigall articles sent by Harris, Lovecraft hit upon the theory that there might be "a greater proportion of the blood of Roman Britain," but admitted sadly that by the time the Romans had reached England, they had become "mongrelised" (*ET* 31). "And shall I disown the possibility of harbouring such blood merely because I possess no objective record of it?" he asks (*ET* 31). "Rather shall a reality be made certain by a symbol, & truth live in the aether of a dream."

Lovecraft's relationship with Wales has been brought into renewed focus recently with two collections edited by Mark Howard Jones in 2013 and 2017. Under the title *Cthulhu Cymraeg,* the series showcases Lovecraftian tales by Welsh writers (or writers who have lived in Wales), mostly set in the country itself. Jones observes that at least part of Lovecraft's originality as a fiction writer can be traced back to "Welsh soil," a claim that is rarely made, but given Machen's profound influence on Lovecraft early in his career, it is one that should be taken seriously ("Introduction" to *Cthulhu Cymraeg*, n.p.). The particular windswept, barren hills of Monmouthshire where Machen set his "Little People" tales, the Aklo language from the novella "The White People," and the eruptions of primitive violence all made a deep impression on Lovecraft. His weird fiction owes a clear debt to Machen's portrayal of an enchanted Gwent, and perhaps the reader experiences (albeit vicariously) the same feelings of terror, the same "awe of the forest and the breath of the winding river" ("Preface to 'The Great God Pan' [1916]" 526) that Machen felt as a child at his father's vicarage, translated into Lovecraft's own decaying and witch-haunted New England. Lovecraftian-themed fiction in a British landscape is not a new concept—Ramsey Campbell began writing his Severn Valley tales in 1962, and since 2012 Andrew McGuigan and Andy Paciorek have edited five *Cumbrian Cthulhu* collections—but Wales is a relatively unexplored territory.

An early example of the transposition of Lovecraftian horror to a Welsh setting is the English writer Colin Wilson's "The Return of the Lloigor," first written for Derleth's Arkham House anthology *Tales of the Cthulhu Mythos* (1969). Wilson adopts Lovecraft's method of knitting fabrications into genuine history but goes further to create a blend of conspiracy and mythology to explain the pagan horrors at the core of both Machen and Lovecraft's tales. The Poe scholar Paul Lang discovers the key to the Voynich Manuscript, the actual medieval codex written in an undecipherable language, and concludes that it preserves a fragment of the occult *Necronomicon*. Intrigued by the manuscript's references to the "Khian" language (similar to "Chian" in "The White People") and the hypothesis that Machen "picked up various odd traditions near his birthplace" (368), Lang travels to South Wales to solve the mystery of the *Necronomicon*'s Welsh origins. He meets an English folklorist who lays out his theory (with brief reference to Lewis Spence and Robert Graves, both of whom shaped their own now-discredited theories based on readings of Welsh myth) that the Welsh people are descended from the inhabitants of Mu, an ancient island in the Pacific where human beings once lived side by side with a extraplanetary race known as "Lloigor" (who first in appeared in August Derleth and Mark Schorer's 1932 story "The Lair of the Star-Spawn"). As the story moves forward and Lang eventually tracks down the "Grey Hills" of the Little People, Wilson reworks several scenes from Machen's tales. As a literary detection narrative, "The Return of the Lloigor" proves an effective homage to Machen's world set against a wider framework of Lovecraft's alien horrors, though as a *Welsh* story it achieves little more than reducing the inhabitants to backward, rural stereotypes. "I had always liked the Welsh," remarks Lang, "with their small stature and dark hair and pale skins. Now I found myself looking at them as if they were troglodytes, trying to find evidence of secret vice in their eyes. And the more I looked, the more I saw it" (380).

Is there a danger, then, in setting Lovecraftian tales in a real-world location, especially one with its own national character? The tales in *Cthulhu Cymraeg*, however, find their sources of Lovecraftian horror not in the Welsh populace itself, but rather in its folk traditions, religious culture, and the liminality of its watery landscapes. Far more than "The Return of the Lloigor," the writers featured in Jones's anthologies noticeably try to move away from simply imitating Lovecraft's prose style or Machen's descriptions of empty hillsides. A fruitful theme is the parallel between Lovecraft's R'lyeh and the Welsh legends of a sunken kingdom, sometimes known as "Cantre'r Gwaelod" ("the Lowland Hundred"). In "The Song of Summoning" by Brian Willis, a lake near Caerleon known as Llyn-yr-Eglwys is said to have once been a city, cursed by a bishop to be forever drowned, and in Bob Lock's "The Cawl of Cthulhu" (named for the traditional Welsh stew), the protagonist hears a rumor that Lovecraft himself may have visited the Gower peninsula in 1925 "to see the Kraken," a year before writing "The Call of Cthulhu." Elsewhere, in Rhys Hughes's "How Gangrene Was My Sally," a temple to the Old Ones is rumored to have been built "in ancient times," but its weight and the heavy rain meant that it sank below the surface. Many of Lovecraft's stories are set on the coast (or, like "Dagon," "The Temple," or "The Call of Cthulhu," in the sea itself), using the sinister unknown of the ocean as a backdrop to the action, and a large number of *Cthulhu Cymraeg* tales do the same. Adrian Chamberlin's "Brethren of the Coast," for instance, takes as its starting point a reference in Lovecraft's "The Strange High House in the Mist" to "primal Nodens" riding on the back of dolphins.

Another common thread running through both "The Return of the Lloigor" and *Cthulhu Cymraeg* is the shared "unpronounceability" of the Welsh language and the names of Lovecraftian gods. The obvious example is the familiar double-L digraph found in many Welsh words, used to great effect by Wilson in the word "Lloigor," but Jones also notes in his introduction the difficulty for unfamiliar readers in pronouncing both "Cthulhu" and "Cymraeg" (meaning "Welsh"). In his own story "Pilgrimage" the protagonist thinks that the first half of "Nyarlathotep" sounds Welsh, "but the last part was a bit of a puzzle." Surprisingly, no authors create their own deities using a Welsh tongue-twister, though Liam Davies comes closest with a clever pun on the title of the Dylan Thomas play: "Un-dhu-miluhk would (if he could)." Un-dhu-miluhk slumbers underneath South Wales, his "gaseous head" and mineral-rich body personifying the industrial landscape of miners and "tar-black depths" as he lusts after his fellow Elder God Rhu-thmar-duhk (Ruth Madoc, who appeared in the 1972 television adaptation of *Under Milk Wood*). In Adrian Chamberlin's "Stranger Crossings: Reclaiming the Lost Lands," the track listing of a fictional band's album blends names from Lovecraft's Kadath tales with references to Welsh mythology, such as "The Lament of Y'Ha Nthlei" and "The Sighs of Anwynn." In fact, both *Cthulhu Cymraeg* books burst with puns, black comedy, and word play, proving that the combination of Lovecraftian themes and Wales produces humor in equal measure to existential terror.

Works Cited

Faig, Ken, Jr. "Lovecraft and the Irish." *Lovecraft Annual* No. 15 (2021): 29–45.

―――. *The Unknown Lovecraft.* New York: Hippocampus Press, 2009.

Jones, Mark Howard, ed. *Cthulhu Cymraeg.* Cardiff: Screaming Dreams, 2013. [Includes the stories by Adrian Chamberlin ("Brethren of the Coast"). Liam Davies, Mark Howard Jones, and Bob Lock cited in this article.]

———. *Cthulhu Cymraeg 2*. Cardiff: Fugitive Fiction, 2017. [Includes the stories by Adrian Chamberlin ("Stranger Crossings: Reclaiming the Lost Lands") and Rhys Hughes cited in this article.]

Lovecraft, H. P. *Letters to Elizabeth Toldridge and Anne Tillery Renshaw*. Ed. David E. Schultz and S. T. Joshi. New York: Hippocampus Press, 2014. [*ET*]

———. *Letters to Rheinhart Kleiner and Others*. Ed. S. T. Joshi and David E. Schultz. New York: Hippocampus Press, 2020.

———. *Letters to Wilfred Blanch Talman and Helen V. and Genevieve Sully*. Ed. David E. Schultz and S. T. Joshi. New York: Hippocampus Press, 2019. [*WBT*]

———, and Robert E. Howard. *A Means to Freedom: The Letters of H. P. Lovecraft and Robert E. Howard*. Ed. S. T. Joshi, David E. Schultz, and Rusty Burke. New York: Hippocampus Press, 2009. 2 vols. (numbered consecutively). [*MF*]

———, and Frank Belknap Long. *A Sense of Proportion: The Letters of H. P. Lovecraft and Frank Belknap Long*. Ed. David E. Schultz and S. T. Joshi. New York: Hippocampus Press, 2025. [*SP*]

Machen, Arthur. "Preface to 'The Great God Pan' (1916)." In *Collected Fiction*. Ed. S. T. Joshi. New York: Hippocampus Press, 2018. 1.523–29.

Sneddon, Duncan. "'The Celt's Far Vision of Weird and Hidden Things': H. P. Lovecraft, William Sharp and the Celts." *Horror Studies* 15 (2024): 171–92.

Wilson, Colin. "The Return of the Lloigor." In August Derleth, ed. *Tales of the Cthulhu Mythos*. Sauk City, WI: Arkham House, 1990. 359–409.

The Presence of the Past in *The Case of Charles Dexter Ward* and *The House of the Seven Gables*

Harley Carnell

One of the clearest distinctions between H. P. Lovecraft and Nathaniel Hawthorne is their antipodal relationships with their respective birthplaces. Lovecraft famously adored Providence, his grave adorned with his ecstatic exclamation "I am Providence!" (*JFM* 93), made after returning to his beloved home following his wilderness years in New York. Of this, August Derleth and Donald Wandrei have argued: "The return of an exile has seldom been recorded in such poignant and rapturous detail" (*Selected Letters* 2.xii). Eulogistic paeans to Providence are found throughout Lovecraft's work. Take for example a passage from *The Case of Charles Dexter Ward*:

> His walks were always adventures in antiquity, during which he managed to recapture from the myriad relics of a glamorous old city a vivid and connected picture of the centuries before. His home was a great Georgian mansion atop the well-nigh precipitous hill that rises just east of the river; and from the rear windows of its rambling wings he could look dizzily out over all the clustered spires, domes, roofs, and skyscraper summits of the lower town to the purple hills of the countryside beyond. (CF 2.221)

And of the moment when Ward returns to Providence—"It was twilight, and Charles Dexter Ward had come home" (CF 2.286)— S. T. Joshi has said how "[i]t would be difficult to find a parallel in the whole of Lovecraft's work to the quiet simplicity of this passage" (*The Case of Charles Dexter Ward* 223). In some respects, the greatest tragedy of Lovecraft's life was the loss of his childhood home of 454 Angell Street, which left him feeling suicidal. Lovecraft wrote of how his "Paradise" home had been lost and noted both poignantly and presciently that "Life from that day has held for me but one ambition—to regain the old place & reëstablish its glory—a thing I fear I can never accomplish" (RK 74). Indeed, Ken Faig, Jr. has argued how one of the positives of Lovecraft's premature death was that he was not alive to witness the demolition of the house in 1961 (134). However, it is of no small poignancy that Lovecraft would end his life in rooms at a house on 66 College Street—the setting for his late tale "The Haunter of the Dark"—which was of the colonial design he so adored: "Never had I lived in [a colonial house], yet always did I long to do so. And now, at last, I *am* living in one! Pure luck" (AG 290).

Hawthorne, meanwhile, despised his hometown of Salem, Massachusetts, and more generally the "bleak little world of New England" (*Blithedale Romance* 9–10). In his "Custom House" introduction to *The Scarlet Letter* he speaks, in the third person, of how Salem is "joyless for him; [and] that he is weary of the old wooden houses, the mud and dust, the dead level of site and sentiment, the chill east wind, and the chilliest of social atmospheres" (10).

He once joked to his wife, Sophia, that "all enormous sinners should be sent on a pilgrimage to Salem, and compelled to spend a length of time there, proportioned to the enormity of their offences" (*Letters 1813–1843* 521). Then, in *The House of the Seven Gables*, he is unequivocal in describing New England as a place where "nothing beautiful had ever been developed" (*Novels* 517). This assertion is realized throughout Hawthorne's work, where in "The Prophetic Pictures" we learn that a highly talented artist residing in Boston is in fact from Europe, since Boston is a "perilous abode for artists," and "pictorial skills being so rare in the colonies, the painter became an object of general curiosity" (*Tales and Sketches* 456). Similarly, Alice Vane of "Edward Randolph's Portrait" is only able to flourish when leaving "the rude atmosphere of New England" where "she found few opportunities of gratifying" her artistic talent (*Tales and*

Sketches 642). In *The Scarlet Letter* we also have a passage that the ardent Anglophile Lovecraft, who once spoke of his only fear of traveling to England was that he would never leave and instead "settle there for ever in peace & archaic dignity" (JFM 26), would have appreciated:

> The persons now in the market-place of Boston had not been born to an inheritance of Puritanic gloom. They were native Englishmen, whose fathers had lived in the sunny richness of the Elizabethan epoch; a time when the life of England, viewed as one great mass, would appear to have been as stately, magnificent, and joyous, as the world has ever witnessed. (156)

To seek a deeper explanation for Hawthorne's hostility, we need look no further than his name itself. He was born Nathaniel Hathorne, and from a young age would alternate between the two spellings, before finally alighting on its more familiar iteration (Miller 26). This decision was inspired by his desire to distance himself from his Puritan ancestors, for whose actions he "[took] shame upon [him]self" (*Scarlet Letter* 9). Among these were Major William Hathorne, a brutal Puritan who once ordered a burglar's ear to be amputated and his forehead branded with the letter B (Miller 404), an act that would of course be echoed in *The Scarlet Letter,* where the adulterous Hester Prynne is forced to wear a cloak adorned with the letter A.[1] Major William was also fictionalized in one of Hawthorne's most notable stories, "Young Goodman Brown," where we hear of the titular protagonist's grandfather who, as the town constable, "lashed the Quaker woman so smartly through the streets of Salem" (*Tales and Sketches* 278).

Most prominent among his forebears, however, was the Salem magistrate John Hathorne. Hawthorne described him as being "so conspicuous in the martyrdom of witches, that their

---

1. In "The Custom House," Hawthorne alleges that his inspiration comes from discovering such a cloak in the Salem Custom House where he worked (24–25). However, no such cloak existed, leading his biographer Edwin Haviland Miller to write how this renders Hawthorne's assertion "as much a romance" as the novel itself (279).

blood may fairly be said to have left a stain upon him" (*Scarlet Letter* 9). Hawthorne's shame at his ancestor's role in the trials and other forms of superstitious persecution (what he refers to as New England's[2] "exclusive bigotry" [*Tales and Sketches* 424]), persecuted him throughout his life. Of a frequently morose countenance—his friends jokingly referred to him as "Mr. Noble Melancholy" (*Letters 1813–1843* 73)—Hawthorne was never truly able to dissociate himself from the action of his forbears, and these considerations proliferated throughout his work.

Among the most renowned aspects of Lovecraft's character was his fascination with, and pining for, the past. He wrote longingly of the "Golden 18th century" (*AG* 247) of which he was a self-professed "relic" (*RK* 35). Meanwhile, in "The Tomb," the "dreamer and visionary" (*CF* 1.39) Jervas Dudley slowly becomes fascinated with the titular tomb and becomes embroiled in the world of his eighteenth-century ancestors. In a striking scene, he witnesses the spectral re-emergence of a mansion that had stood on that site, where it "once more reared its stately height to the raptured vision; every window ablaze with the splendour of many candles" (*CF* 1.48). After the house burns down, a tearful Jervas is taken away, begging to "claim [his] heritage of death" (*CF* 1.49), a feeling that is intensified on discovering a miniature in the tomb depicting a man who is identical to him: "I might as well have been studying my mirror" (*CF* 1.50). Jervas is ultimately mollified by his family's promise that he would be buried in the tomb.

Thus, in addition to the dichotomy between their views of their hometowns, Lovecraft and Hawthorne were haunted by the past in directly antipodal ways. It is in this context that I wish to consider *The House of the Seven Gables* (1851) and *The Case of Charles Dexter Ward* (1927), and how they depict the presence of the past.

---

2. Interestingly, Lovecraft's Providence was immune from witchcraft hysteria, in no small part because Rhode Island's founder Roger Williams designated the colony as a sanctuary for people fleeing religious persecution. Such liberality led to the state's branding, by the firebrand Cotton Mather, as "the sewer of New England" (see Stewart 51).

Both *Gables* and *Ward* contain sentiments that could easily stand as representative of the respective authors' entire works and worldviews. In *Ward,* it is Ward's explanation to Willett that he has "brought to life a monstrous abnormality, but I did it for the sake of knowledge" (CF 2.305). In *Gables* it is the moral Hawthorne ascribes to it in his preface, where he speaks of how "the wrong-doing of one generation lives into the successive ones, and, divesting itself of every temporary advantage, becomes a pure and uncontrollable mischief" (352).

Lovecraft's fiction may well be the ultimate exemplary of what could be termed "pure horror"—that is, terror born not from the threat of physical harm, death, etc., but from the very conception of the existence of things outside the accepted spectrum of reality. Take for example "The Shadow out of Time," where the "*merest* mention" (CF 3.363; my emphasis) of the extent of the cosmos and man's "own place in the seething vortex of time" is enough to induce a "paralysing" effect (CF 3.363). While Lovecraft's characters frequently talk of direct threats to the human race, often they become mad simply from contemplating the implications of what their pursuit of knowledge has unearthed. This is most famously iterated in the celebrated opening to "The Call of Cthulhu":

> The most merciful thing in the world, I think, is the inability of the human mind to correlate all its contents. We live on a placid island of ignorance in the midst of black sea of infinity, and it was not meant that we should voyage far. The sciences, each straining in its own direction, have hitherto harmed us little; but some day the piecing together of dissociated knowledge will open up such terrifying vistas of reality, and of our frightful position therein, that we shall either go mad from the revelation or flee from the deadly light into the peace and safety of a new dark age. (CF 2.21–22)

As Lovecraft for the most part eschewed traditional tropes of supernatural horror—believing that weird fiction was "more effective if it avoid[ed] the hackneyed superstitions & popular cult formulae" (DS 83)—he situated his terror in his understanding of the sciences. Lovecraft lived during a period of seismic scientific upheaval, in which conceptions of everything from the age of the Earth to the size of the cosmos to the scope of human history and ancestry was undergoing extensive recalibration. While in the real world this inspired fascination for Lovecraft, it was the instigator for horror in his works of fiction. By thawing the ice of reality, science revealed what incomprehensibilities and, thus, terrors lurked in the margins of existence.

Take, for example, the exemplary *At the Mountains of Madness*. While the premise, and frame, of the story is Dyer's warning to avoid expeditions to Antarctica due to the potential consequences to humanity, the apex of horror in the story is the simple existence of beings in what was previously believed to be an uninhabited place. At one point, for example, Dyer talks of the "*sheer* appalling antiquity" of the place being enough to "overwhelm almost any sensitive person" (CF 3.90; my emphasis). While antiquity alone may not be a source for terror—it may in fact be one of fascination—in Lovecraft it becomes de facto terrifying. Later, Dyer says how it would be "cumbrous to give a detailed, consecutive account of our wanderings inside that cavernous, aeon-dead honeycomb of primal masonry" (CF 3.85) before proceeding to do precisely that. What follows is for the most part a detailed description of architecture. Nothing tangibly terrifying happens, yet the simple fact that such an extensive architecture should exist in the first place creates an uncanny effect. He thus adheres fully to one aspect of Edmund Burke's conception of the sublime, where he talks of "difficulty" being a crucial component. Burke asserts that Stonehenge, which "neither for disposition nor ornament has any thing admirable," simply by its size and the difficulty of conceiving its conception by an ancient people "turns the mind on the immense force necessary for such a work" (63). In *Madness* we read how "[t]he Cyclopean massiveness and giganticism of everything about us became curiously oppressive" (CF 3.86). Similarly, in stories such as "The Shadow out of Time" and "The Rats in the Walls," the horror originates from contemplation of ancientness and physical immensities in subterranean edifices as much as if not more so than the danger the characters may be in.

Like Hawthorne, Charles Dexter Ward had an ancestor, Joseph Curwen, who was prominent in seventeenth-century Salem. In fact, part of the reason Ward was unaware of this was because Curwen's widow, like Hawthorne, resumed her maiden name of Tillinghast, not wishing to be associated with him. We also read how Ward's "mother was not particularly pleased to own an ancestor like Curwen" (CF 2.265). In real life, Jonathan Corwin was one of the witch trial judges, whose ancestor, Samuel Curwen, adopted the new spelling. John Hathorne is also mentioned in the story, as he leads an investigation against Curwen's close friend Edward Hutchinson, known for his interest in the occult.

Of course, the irony of a story like *Ward* is that, in its world, people such as Hutchison and Curwen did in fact commune with evil and so Hathorne et al.'s pursuit of them would have been a noble one.[3] It is through Ward's interest in Curwen that the seeds of his downfall are sown. After declining to attend university to pursue his studies of him, Ward defends his decision by saying how they would "provide him with more avenues toward knowledge and the humanities than any university which the world could boast" (CF 2.277).

Ward's personality gradually becomes subsumed during his studies of Curwen, as his friend Dr. Willett recognizes that "[h]e stumbled on things no mortal ought ever to know, and reached back through the years as no one ever should reach; and something came out of those years to engulf him" (CF 2.362). Willett had previously asked a question that comprises one of the most subtly chilling utterances in Lovecraft's oeuvre: "What had the boy called out of the void, and what had it done to him?" (CF 2.357).

---

3. Although I am speaking somewhat tongue in cheek here, it is also worth noting that one of the more heinous aspects of the Salem witch trials was how, uniquely, nobody who ever confessed to witchcraft was executed, which was largely responsible for the proliferation of nonsensical witchcraft allegations and "confessions" that have so come to define it (see Ray 67). Even if witches had existed in Salem and were genuinely exerting a malign influence, innocent people would still have been killed.

Willett ultimately defeats Curwen by referencing the name of Yog-Sothoth as a culmination of an incantation fired at him. Both due to his atheism and to his non-adherence to traditional supernatural tropes, it was rare for Lovecraft to make reference to traditional Judeo-Christian mythology to combat evil, and it is for this reason that it is only by invoking Yog-Sothoth that Curwen can be defeated. Similarly, when Willett is unnerved earlier in the story, he is not comforted by muttering the Lord's Prayer to himself,[4] but again only soothed when he invokes Yog-Sothoth.

In *Gables*, the living ancestor is Hepzibah Pyncheon, a descendant of Colonel Pyncheon, who had acquired the land by leading a charge of witchcraft against its true owner, Matthew Maule. On the scaffold before his death, Maule cried, "God will give him blood to drink!" (358), which is precisely what accused witch Sarah Good said before her execution during the trials (Boyer and Nissenbaum 7–8). What makes the house so valuable is not the house itself, but the deeds to a large swath of lands in Maine secreted somewhere on the property. Indeed, a descendant of Col. Pyncheon, Gervase, who has traveled through Europe, "look[ed] contemptuously at the House of the Seven Gables" and thought it a "mansion exceedingly inadequate," and is willing to cede it to the grandson of Maule (confusingly also called Matthew) if he can locate the deeds to the land.

Naturally, people believe that the house is cursed. It is here that one of the more interesting aspects of considering Hawthorne's work emerges. Lovecraft described *Gables* as "New England's greatest contribution to weird literature" (*CE* 2.106). However, as with many of Hawthorne's works, the question arises as to what extent it is in fact weird. Throughout the nov-

---

4. Ramsey Campbell has noted how the "jokey Lovecraft set loose in his letters is nowhere to be found in his fiction," which is for the most part true (Campbell, "Grim with a Capital N," in Probert 4). However, this moment gives us a glimpse of superb Lovecraft humor in his fiction, as Willett also attempts to utilize the "mnemonic hodge-podge" of T. S. Eliot's *The Waste Land* when trying to comfort himself, affording Lovecraft an opportunity to interweave his disdain for this Modernist staple seamlessly into the narrative.

el, seemingly supernatural occurrences are problematized by Hawthorne's narratorial interventions. After one putatively supernatural event, Hawthorne interjects: "The fantastic scene, just hinted at, must by no means be considered as forming an actual portion of our story. We were betrayed into this brief extravagance by the quiver of the moonbeams" (593).

The last remnant of Maule on the land is a well he had built there. Shortly after Pyncheon's occupation of the land, its previously safe and reliable drinking water becomes brackish and poisonous, and Holgrave describes it as "water bewitched" (433). In the present day, when looking into the well, Clifford would often see a "constantly shifting phantasmagoria of figures" and various faces in it, one screaming, "The dark face gazes at me!" (484). However, Hawthorne offers an alternative. In the first case, Pyncheon simply dislodged soil when constructing the house, which is responsible for the polluted water. As for Clifford, he has recently been released from institutionalization and, crucially, whenever his relative Phoebe looks into the well, she sees nothing. Hawthorne concludes: "the dark face, that so troubled Clifford, was no more than the shadow, thrown from a branch of one of the damson-trees, and breaking the inner light of Maule's Well" (484). Much like many of the early Gothic novels, particularly those of Ann Radcliffe (1764–1823), where instances of this "explained supernatural" were prevalent, Hawthorne frequently sets up the pins of the supernatural only to knock them down with his explanatory interjections.

It can be difficult, then, to judge the extent to which the novel is in fact weird, and whether Maule's curse is literally being invoked against the Pyncheons. However, for Hawthorne's purposes this is immaterial. In the same way that Lovecraft's gods can be read as much as symbols as tangible beings without distorting the terror of his tales, the existence of Maule's curse is ultimately insignificant when considering what such a curse symbolizes. To explicate, I will take a quick digression to Hawthorne's most celebrated short story, "Young Goodman Brown."

Briefly, in the story Brown wanders through the woods of his native Salem on Halloween.[5] While doing so, he discovers that his whole town is embroiled in a witchcraft conspiracy. When he wakes up the next day, he is unsure whether he merely dreamed the events of the previous night. Following this, he becomes a "stern, a sad, a darkly meditative, a distrustful, if not a desperate man" (*Tales and Sketches* 288). His wife's name is Faith (a recurrent theme of the story sees the pun between her name and spiritual faith). After his dream, he becomes distant from her and thus "shrink[s] from the bosom of Faith" (289). He dies miserable and alone, and his relatives "carved no hopeful verse upon his tomb-stone; for his dying hour was gloom" (289).

Now, whether Brown did uncover a sinister conspiracy in Salem or not, the effect on him is just as deleterious as though he had, due to the oppression he inflicts inward. As Milton's Satan puts it, "The mind is its own place, and in itself / Can make a heaven of hell, a hell of heaven" (*Paradise Lost* 1.254–55). Similarly, the real Salem may not have been overrun with witches in the late seventeenth century, but that did not change the fact that numerous people were executed and imprisoned, and that the aftereffects of what happened during the trials reverberated through the centuries to Hawthorne himself. For Hawthorne, then, it is often the effect of the weird on those who believe they have experienced it, rather than metaphysical concerns as to its existence in the first place, that constitutes his chief interest.[6]

Lovecraft also addresses the problem of the weird in Hawthorne. His definition of what a weird tale is may seem to potentially disqualify works such as *Gables* and "Young Goodman Brown," as he avers that the "true weird tale" requires "a malign

---

5. Compare the story's taking place on a night "of all nights in the year" (*Tales and Sketches* 276) with Poe's "Ulalume," which is set on the "night of all nights in the year" (62). Hawthorne was heavily influenced by Poe's fiction for its "force and originality," although would openly tell Poe that he did not consider him equally impressive as a critic (*Letters 1843–1853* 168).

6. Another potential disqualifying factor for the weird in much of Hawthorne, and especially in "Young Goodman Brown," is what I. B. Johansen has cited as Hawthorne's "spectacularly allegorical cast of mind," which problematizes the existence of the fantastic in his work (89).

and particular suspension or defeat of those fixed laws of Nature" (CE 3.84) and talks of the "true cosmic horror which makes weird literature" (88). However, in the passage below Lovecraft offers a clarification that is uncannily applicable to Hawthorne, even though he is not referencing him directly here:

> We may say, as a general thing, that a weird story whose intent is to teach or produce a social effect, or one in which the horrors are finally explained away by natural means, is not a genuine tale of cosmic fear; but it remains a fact that such narratives often possess, in isolated sections, atmospheric touches which fulfil every condition of true supernatural horror-literature.
>
> Therefore we must judge a weird tale not by the author's intent, or by the mere mechanics of the plot; but by the emotional level which it attains at its least mundane point. (CE 2.84)

Hawthorne is exceeded only by Dickens in his didacticism. When reading one of his works, readers are under no misapprehension who they are supposed to be rooting for. In *The Scarlet Letter*, for instance, Hawthorne's veneration of Hester and loathing of the Puritans who are antagonizing her leaves little room for interpretation. The Puritans are described as "stern and black-browed" (9) and the "most intolerant breed that ever lived" (65); even Puritan children are not spared, as they are designated "sombre little urchins" (71). Meanwhile, another overly Dickensian flavor to Hawthorne's work is his nominative determinism where, for instance, Hester's daughter is called Pearl while one of her chief antagonists is named Dimmesdale. Hawthorne's disgust at the superstitions that led to the witch trials thus makes him reluctant to concede the existence of the supernatural, even within fictional works. It would be very difficult to imagine him writing a story such as "Young Goodman Brown" in which Salem was definitively infested by witches.

It is for this reason that Lovecraft points out how "[s]upernatural horror, then, is never a primary object with Hawthorne; though its impulses were so deeply woven into his personality that he cannot help suggesting it with the force of genius when he calls upon the unreal world to illustrate the pensive sermon he wishes to preach" (CE 2.105). Perhaps, then, the best descriptor of Hawthorne's work can be his own—that it is "somewhere between the real world and fairy-land, where the Actual and Imaginary meet" (*Scarlet Letter* 28). That Lovecraft would categorize such work as weird is also reflective of his considering atmosphere as integral to the construction of the weird. Lovecraft believed that "plot and incident" were secondary considerations, and that a weird tale should instead "[put] all its emphasis on *mood* or *atmosphere*" (*Letters to F. Lee Baldwin* 285). For example, of his own story "The Colour out of Space" Lovecraft wrote that it "must be taken as an atmospheric study rather than a tale" (*DS* 127). Of the *House of the Seven Gables* itself, Lovecraft writes how it typifies

> the dark Puritan age of concealed horror and witch-whispers which preceded the beauty, rationality, and spaciousness of the eighteenth century. Hawthorne saw many in his youth, and knew the black tales connected with some of them. He heard, too, many rumours of a curse upon his own line as the result of his great-grandfather's severity as a witchcraft judge in 1692. (CE 2.106)

Although in his preface to the book Hawthorne enjoins the readers not to locate the book within "any portion of the actual soil of the County of Essex" (353) and states that the story itself is set merely in "one of our New England towns" (355), the basis for the titular house is the Turner-Ingersoll Mansion in Salem. Simply by having this house, with its imposing gabled façade, as a setting for the novel in the first place, Hawthorne is already onto an uncanny foot. Nor is this abnegated too much by many of the tedious interludes—such as the running of the cent shop or the cultivation of the garden—which dilute the atmosphere, and which even Hawthorne seems to recognize as dull: "The author needs great faith in his reader's sympathy; else he must hesitate to give details so minute, and incidents apparently so trifling, as are essential to make up the idea of this garden-life" (481).

In addition, Hawthorne's works situate the presence of the past in the form of a tangible and obtrusive guilt. As he strikingly puts it, "what other dungeon is so dark as one's own heart!

What jailor so inexorable as one's self!" (498). With regard to
Gables, we read how "Matthew Maule, it is to be feared, trode
[*sic*] downward from his own age to a far later one, planting a
heavy footstep, all the way, on the conscience of a Pyncheon"
(368). This guilt extends further than Maule, however. Lovecraft was not alone in lamenting the conclusion of *Gables*, saying
how it was "almost a pity to supply a fairly happy ending" (*CE*
2.106). This putatively happy ending was deliberate on Hawthorne's part. *The Scarlet Letter* was noted for its darkness, with
one reviewer referring to it as indicative of a "malignant Hawthorne" as opposed to the perceived "gentle Hawthorne" of previous works (cited in Miller 300). Indeed, part of the reason
Hawthorne included the "Custom House" introduction was because of his concern that "if the book is made up entirely of 'The
Scarlet Letter,' it will be too sombre. I found it impossible to re-
lieve the shadows of the story with so much light as I would
gladly have thrown in" (*Letters 1843–1853* 307). Herman Melville, who channeled Hawthorne's influence when writing *Moby-
Dick* (which he would dedicate to Hawthorne), wrote to him
saying how with Hawthorne's inspiration he had "written a
wicked book and feel spotless as a lamb" (*Letters* 142), and how
Hawthorne was integral to Melville's imbuing his behemoth
with the "hell-fire in which the whole book is broiled" (*Letters*
133). For an indication of what *Moby-Dick* may have looked like
without Hawthorne's intervention, one need only consider the
interminable whaling and shipping interpolations interspersing
the main narrative. It is also possible that Hawthorne may have
been an influence for the novel's Captain Ahab, of whom Melville writes: "all men tragically great are made so through a certain morbidness" (*Moby-Dick* 82).

As such, Hawthorne was desirous of making *Gables* more
cheerful. Ironically, then, while Melville was attempting to
darken his work, Hawthorne was trying to lighten his. However,
the ending is not quite as happy as it may initially seem. When
the deeds are discovered, Hepzibah—a hermit who up to this
point has been forced into the ignominy of running a cent shop
from the house—is now entitled to great wealth. Throughout

the book we read how "Of [the Pyncheons'] legal tenure, there could be no question," but meanwhile "they were troubled with doubts as to their moral right to hold it" (368). When the deeds are discovered at the end of the book, among the signatories are a number of Native American leaders entitling the Pyncheons to have the land "forever" (624). In the short story "Main Street," Hawthorne talks of the construction of the street and the pathos of the recognition by Native Americans that "The pavements of the Main-street must be laid over the red man's grave" (*Tales and Sketches* 1028). Similarly, at the conclusion of *Gables*, while the Pyncheons have secured the house legally, there remains the figurative yet tangible presence not only of Maule but of the Native Americans. Given how much of Hawthorne's work is predicated on the prevalence of guilt, it is not impossible that Hepzibah's happy ending could later be dissipated and she could find herself subsumed by her conscience.

Hawthorne was far more interested in human psychology than Lovecraft was. Works such as *Ward* demonstrate that Lovecraft was not entirely uninterested in psychology, as both Ward's psychological disintegration following the discovery of Curwen's writings and the aforementioned terror his knowledge inspires work so effectively when compared to his interests at one point being "free from every trace of the morbid" (*CF* 2.225). This has led Joshi to describe it as "one of Lovecraft's few relative triumphs of characterization" (*Ward* 232). But the chief achievement of Lovecraft is his placing horror away from the human and into the vast realms of the cosmos as a result of his "lack of interest in ordinary life" (*Letters to E. Hoffmann Price* 129) and being "not in the least interested" in "ordinary people" (cited in *IAP* 484), whereas in Hawthorne it is in his burrowing to the deepest fathoms of the human psyche.

In addition to the differing receptions to their birthplaces, it is these separate spheres of interest that distinguish the two authors. Indeed, it may initially seem surprising that Lovecraft would write about Salem at all. Speaking somewhat reductively, a Salem narrative will either address the human tragedy of innocent lives being lost due to superstition, or will imagine a world

in which witchcraft in fact exists and then examine the consequences of this ("Young Goodman Brown" is unique in doing
both). Neither of these conceptions seem especially Lovecraftian.

"The Dreams in the Witch House" is Lovecraft's other major
Salem work (which also features Hathorne, who presides over
the trial of the story's witch, Keziah Mason). Although set in
Lovecraft's fictional "changeless, legend-haunted city of Arkham" (CF 3.232), Arkham is of course modeled on Salem[7] and
"Dreams" is inspired by its infamous and extant "Witch House,"
which in fact belonged to Judge Corwin rather than any accused
witch.[8]

Witchcraft is of course a key element to the tale: Lovecraft
not only invents one of the most disturbing fictional familiars in
Brown Jenkin, a rat-human hybrid, but we see arguably the most
gruesome occurrence in any Lovecraft tale, where we read of
how Jenkin burrowed through Gilman's chest and ate his heart.
Yet ultimately the story is about the Witch House's strange angles and interdimensional nature, which allow Mason to "[go]
outside the boundaries of the world of space" (CF 3.235). In
Ward, even though Ward's ancestor comes from Salem, the story is set in Providence and for the most part makes use of Lovecraft's own pseudomythology, forbidden books, etc., rather than
siphoning the lore of Salem and witchcraft to incite horror. Indeed, only Lovecraft could write narratives inspired by the Salem witch trials that have so little to do with traditional
witchcraft. It is perhaps the best example of what Joshi has identified as Lovecraft, where he utilizes traditional tropes, updating
them "so that they can pass aesthetic muster in an age whose
immense strides in scientific knowledge has rendered these concepts virtually unusable because of their reliance on outmoded
religious suppositions" (Unutterable Horror 500).

Similarly, there is very little if any of the cosmic, numinous,
or sublime that is so important to Lovecraft in Hawthorne's
works. Hawthorne would later move to Concord, Massachu-

---

7. See, for instance, Essential Solitude 104.
8. For any "witch-finding" tourists, the closest approximation to a "witch
house" would be the Rebecca Nurse house in neighboring Danvers.

setts, which he adored. After a two-day walking tour with Ralph Waldo Emerson, on returning to his Concord home it was the "first time I ever came home in my life; for I never had a home before" (cited in Miller 215). In Concord he lived in a "paradise" compared to the "Castle Dismal" he resided in at Salem (*Letters 1843–1853* 126, 129). In Concord, he would take long walks in the woods and would fraternize with many of the Transcendentalist writers such as Emerson and Henry David Thoreau. They would gather at Amos Bronson Alcott's Concord School of Philosophy building, located next to Orchard House, the setting of her daughter Louisa May Alcott's *Little Women* (1868–69). With Concord's stunning nature and heartbreakingly beautiful sites such as Walden Pond (in fact a lake), it is no wonder that the Transcendentalist movement should begin in Concord. Indeed, Thoreau himself said of Concord how he was "born into the most estimable place in all the world, and in the nick of time too" (cited in Wilson 3).

With necessary brevity, a key facet of Transcendentalism was its need to ground revelation in people's own personal relation to God—typically achieved through communing with the natural world—in preference to the intermediation of religious authorities. As Emerson wrote, when he was in the woods he "[saw] all. The currents of the Universal Being circulate through me; I am part or particle of God" (13).

Transcendentalism also sought to transcend a limited understanding of reality—to "penetrate the surface of things," in Thoreau's words (*Walden* 65)—so that people may awake from the "divine dream" of life to the "glories and certainties of day" (Emerson 78). Thoreau had a deep appreciation for Eastern and Native American learning, and in particular believed that Native Americans' familiarity with nature lent them "a thousand revelations" that were "still secrets" to white people (*Maine Woods* 247).

Not only did Thoreau and Emerson both take inspiration from the natural landscape of Concord, but Emerson actually wrote *Nature* in the same Old Manse House where Hawthorne had lived, and where his collection *Mosses from an Old Manse*

(1846) was composed. Yet despite existing in these same environs, Hawthorne's complete lack of interest in sublime and cosmic conceptions meant that these considerations never manifested themselves in his fiction. Similarly, even though Lovecraft endured the institutionalization of his father, the mental illness of his mother, and a number of breakdowns that resulted in his own hermitry as a youth, psychological considerations are sidelined in his work.

It is for this exact reason that *The Case of Charles Dexter Ward* and *The House of the Seven Gables,* although both set in New England, both are concerned with the past's impact on the present, and both are reflective of the witch trials, have such wildly divergent executions. Yet while Hawthorne drew inspiration from the cultural, social, and historical realities of New England, and Lovecraft was inspired by its landscape and topography to effect his unique and formative brand of weird fiction, ultimately both their works serve as distinct expressions of how the region of New England is ideally and uniquely situated for the strange, the uncanny, and the terrifying.

Works Cited

Boyer, Paul, and Stephen Nissenbaum. *Salem Possessed: The Social Origins of Witchcraft.* Cambridge, MA: Harvard University Press, 1974.

Burke, Edmund. *A Philosophical Enquiry into the Sublime and the Beautiful.* 1757. Ed. Paul Guyer. Oxford: Oxford University Press, 2015.

Emerson, Ralph Waldo. *Nature.* 1836. Boston: Beacon Press, 1985.

Faig, Ken, Jr. *Lovecraftian People and Places.* New York: Hippocampus Press, 2022.

Hawthorne, Nathaniel. *The Blithedale Romance.* 1852. London: Penguin, 1983.

———. *Centenary Edition of the Works of Nathaniel Hawthorne, Volume XV: Letters 1813–1843.* Ed. Thomas Woodson, L. Neal Smith, and Norman Holmes Pearson. Columbus: Ohio State University Press, 1985.

———. *Centenary Edition of the Works of Nathaniel Hawthorne, Volume XVI: Letters 1843–1853*. Ed. Thomas Woodson, L. Neal Smith, and Norman Holmes Pearson. Columbus: Ohio State University Press, 1984.

———. *Novels*. New York: Library of America, 1983.

———. *The Scarlet Letter*. 1850. New York: W. W. Norton, 1961.

———. *Tales and Sketches*. New York: Library of America, 1982.

Johansen, I. B. *Reflections on the American Fantastic and the American Grotesque from Washington Irving to the Postmodern Era*. Leiden: Brill Ropoldi, 2015.

Joshi, S. T. *Unutterable Horror: A History of Supernatural Fiction*. Hornsea, UK: PS Publishing, 2012. 2 vols.

Lovecraft, H. P. *The Case of Charles Dexter Ward*. Ed. S. T. Joshi. Tampa, FL: University of Tampa Press, 2010.

———. *Letters to Alfred Galpin and Others*. Ed. S. T. Joshi and David E. Schultz. New York: Hippocampus Press, 2020. [AG]

———. *Letters to E. Hoffmann Price and Richard F. Searight*. Ed. S. T. Joshi and David E. Schultz. New York: Hippocampus Press, 2020.

———. *Letters to F. Lee Baldwin, Duane W. Rimel, and Nils Frome*. Ed. David E. Schultz and S. T. Joshi. New York: Hippocampus Press, 2016.

———. *Letters to James F. Morton*. Ed. David E. Schultz S. T. Joshi. New York: Hippocampus Press, 2011. [JFM]

———. *Letters to Rheinhart Kleiner and Others*. Ed. S. T. Joshi and David E. Schultz. New York: Hippocampus Press, 2020. [RK]

———, and August Derleth. *Essential Solitude: The Letters of H. P. Lovecraft and August Derleth*. Ed. David E. Schultz and S. T. Joshi. New York: Hippocampus Press, 2008. 2 vols.

———, and Clark Ashton Smith. *Dawnward Spire, Lonely Hill: The Letters of H. P. Lovecraft and Clark Ashton Smith*. Ed. David E. Schultz and S. T. Joshi. New York: Hippocampus Press, 2017. [DS]

Melville, Herman. *The Letters of Herman Melville*. Ed. Merrell R. Davis and William H Gilman. New Haven, CT: Yale University Press, 1960.

———. *Moby-Dick*. 1851. London: Penguin, 2009.

Miller, Edwin Haviland. *Salem Is My Dwelling Place: A Life of Nathaniel Hawthorne*. Iowa City: University of Iowa Press, 1991.

Milton, John. *Paradise Lost*. 1674. Oxford: Oxford University Press, 2008.

Poe, Edgar Allan. *The Selected Writings*. Ed. G. R. Thompson. New York: W. W. Norton, 2004.

Probert, John Llewellyn. *How Grim Was My Valley*. Alconbury Weston, UK: New Con Press, 2022.

Ray, Benjamin C. *Satan and Salem*. Charlottesville: University of Virginia Press, 2015.

Stewart, Benedict, ed. *The Literary Guide to the United States*. New York: Facts on File, 1981.

Thoreau, Henry David. *The Maine Woods*. 1864. New York: Penguin, 1988.

———. *Walden and Resistance to Civil Government*. 2nd ed. Ed. William Rossi. New York: W. W. Norton, 1992.

Wilson, Leslie Perrin. "Concord." In James S. Finley, ed. *Henry David Thoreau in Context*. Cambridge: Cambridge University Press, 2017. 3–12.

Lovecraft in the Netherlands

Thijmen Zuiderwijk

In discussions of H. P. Lovecraft's reception in Europe, the Netherlands has, thus far, been omitted. This absence has allowed a particular narrative to persist, as introduced by Dutch translators and editors, that Lovecraft was virtually unknown in the Netherlands until well into the 1960s.

However, as early as 1949, Dutch readers encountered Lovecraft's work in translation as part of a high-quality literary anthology, as this article will show. The book *Voor en na middernacht* featured Lovecraft's "The Thing on the Doorstep" ("Het Ding op de drempel") in Dutch and included him alongside such authors as Edgar Allan Poe and William Faulkner. The anthology was edited by Benjamin Jessurun Lobo and published by Elsevier, then, as now, one of the largest publishing houses in the Netherlands. It featured illustrations by J. F. Doeve, who would go on to become one of the most accomplished illustrators in the latter half of the twentieth century. The book sold well and received ample attention in the Dutch national, regional, and local press.

Nearly a decade later, in 1958, a second anthology, *Griezelverhalen* (Creepy Stories), edited by A. de Bruijn and A. Van der Hoek, again featured Lovecraft, this time with "The Rats in the Walls," translated in Dutch simply as "Ratten" (Rats). Despite playing a central role in bringing Lovecraft back to print, De Bruijn publicly stated in multiple interviews that horror fiction was such a niche in the Netherlands that "all its fans could fit into a single car and leave room for a driver" (*Het Vrije Volk* 16).

In the 1960s, the first Dutch writer to contribute to the Cthulhu Mythos, Eddy C. Bertin, made a similar claim, insisting that Lovecraft had only appeared in "two now very rare Dutch horror anthologies," neither of which, in his account, had made much impact (3). I argue that this kind of mythmaking, framing oneself as a lone advocate of a neglected genre, downplayed the fact that Lovecraft had already entered Dutch literary consciousness well before either man arrived on the scene.

Moreover, Lovecraft's visibility was not limited to Dutch translations. English-language anthologies such as Groff Conklin's *The Graveyard Reader* were available in the Netherlands and received coverage in national newspapers. These parallel channels of circulation, through translation, import, and critical reception, further complicate the claim that he was an unknown quantity in the Dutch market.

This article challenges the persistent narrative of obscurity by tracing the contours of Lovecraft's reception in the Netherlands between 1949 and the late 1960s. I argue that Lovecraft was never truly "discovered" by later advocates such as De Bruijn or Eddy C. Bertin; they were entering a conversation that was already in motion. The claim that Lovecraft was virtually unknown in this period has often been repeated, yet it does not hold up against the archival record. By drawing attention to earlier translations, publication data, and press reception, I correct a bibliographic gap and restore a more accurate timeline. The idea of Lovecraft as a fringe or forgotten figure served rhetorical and strategic purposes, allowing these individuals to position themselves as pioneers within a genre that had, in fact, already found an audience, albeit at the margins. This paper argues that such marginality should not be mistaken for invisibility.

When *Voor en na middernacht* was published in 1949, it did not introduce Lovecraft as a central or celebrated figure. Instead, he was presented with a mixture of hesitation and interest. The editor, B. Jessurun Lobo, refers to "The Thing on the Doorstep" as the weakest story in the volume but explains that its ending lingered with him enough to justify its inclusion (xi).

This is not a glowing endorsement, but it is a deliberate decision. In an anthology that also featured Poe, Faulkner, and Dunsany, there was no obligation to include Lovecraft at all. That he was chosen and that Lobo felt the need to explain his choice suggests a degree of self-awareness about Lovecraft's status: not yet canonical, but not entirely unknown either.

The framing becomes more interesting in what Lobo chooses to recommend. Despite his lukewarm evaluation of the story, he advises readers to consult Lovecraft's essay "Supernatural Horror in Literature" (1927). This places Lovecraft in a different category, not just as a writer of horror stories, but as someone who thought seriously about genre. Lobo treats Lovecraft as worth reading, even if the reader remains unconvinced by the particular example on offer. That gesture, however brief, helps complicate later claims that Lovecraft was unknown or fringe: in 1949, he was already being introduced to Dutch readers not just as a fiction writer but as a theorist of the weird.

In the introduction, Lobo highlights two other recent anthologies he enjoyed, particularly Boris Karloff's *And the Darkness Falls* (1946), which also includes "The Thing on the Doorstep" (xi). While Lobo does not name his source, the timing and selection strongly suggest that he encountered the story there. Another influence he explicitly notes, *Great Tales of Terror and the Supernatural* (1944), edited by Herbert A. Wise and Phyllis Fraser, includes "The Rats in the Walls" and "The Dunwich horror." Even if Lobo's endorsement was qualified, his editorial decision reflects a growing awareness of Lovecraft as a figure worthy of literary consideration.

Crucially, *Voor en na middernacht* was not a quiet or marginal publication. It sold more than 2200 copies in 1949 and 1950 alone, a strong figure for a literary anthology in the Netherlands at the time (Van Bel). It continued to sell into 1951, with more than 200 additional copies purchased (Van den Brink). Its visibility was not limited to bookshops. On 24 December 1949, *De Volkskrant* offered the anthology as a prize in its annual Christmas puzzle, a mainstream cultural feature aimed at a broad audience. The book was advertised well into the following year, including in *Nieuwsblad van het Zuiden* in June 1950. Clearly, this was not a book confined to specialist readers or limited print runs; it was actively promoted and remained publicly available for an extended period.

The press coverage was enthusiastic and widespread. *De*

Volkskrant praised the translations twice in the same review and called the volume a delight for genre enthusiasts. The quality of J. F. Doeve's illustrations was singled out for praise in multiple publications, including *De Volkskrant* (7) and *Nijmeegsch Dagblad*, where his drawings were described as "stylish" and "macabre." *De Maasbode* (3) dedicated an entire article to Doeve's artistic ability, noting that his work for the book "reconfirms" he is among the best illustrators in the country.

De Telegraaf (7) described Lobo as "an erudite man with exceptional intellect" and called the stories "fantastic" across the board. *Dagblad de Stem* (6) went further, calling the anthology "an important addition to any bookcase." This was not niche praise from genre magazines but public recognition from major newspapers, writing for general readers.

The book's staying power reinforces this point. In 1958, a deluxe hardcover edition was released nearly a decade after its initial publication, and in 1974, the anthology was reprinted for its twenty-fifth anniversary with an initial run of 8000 copies (Manteau). That reissue came an entire generation after the book's initial appearance, confirming its enduring cultural impact. While Lovecraft was not the central figure of the anthology, his presence in a volume with such reception and longevity undermines any claim that he was invisible or irrelevant in the Dutch literary landscape of the mid-twentieth century. To suggest that Lovecraft was wholly unknown in the Netherlands until the 1960s is to overlook the facts of his publication and the documented enthusiasm with which it was received. The long-term significance of *Voor en na middernacht* is further underscored by its inclusion in the *Letterkundig Lexicon voor de Neerlandistiek,* a major scholarly reference work on Dutch literary history. Lobo's anthology is singled out as one of the few twentieth-century examples of supernatural fiction to have achieved lasting recognition, cited alongside both nineteenth-century predecessors and other postwar contributions to the fantastic tradition (Van Bork et al. 913).

While *Voor en na middernacht* did not present Lovecraft as a central figure, it did not treat him as marginal either. His story was printed under his own name, introduced with commentary (which few of the other stories received), and accompanied by a recommendation to read his critical essay "Supernatural Horror in Literature." The tone may have been cautious, but the inclusion was purposeful. Lovecraft was positioned as someone worth reading, even if not unreservedly celebrated.

In 1958, nearly a decade after *Voor en na middernacht*, Lovecraft reappeared in Dutch translation in *Griezelverhalen*, an anthology of horror stories edited by A. de Bruijn and A. van der Hoek. The volume featured "The Rats in the Walls," translated by W. Wielek-Berg, and once again positioned Lovecraft among prominent authors in the genre. Like its 1949 predecessor, the anthology received ample coverage in the national press. However, despite this continuing pattern of small yet tangible growth, *Griezelverhalen* also marked the beginning of a strategic reframing of Lovecraft's position in the Dutch literary landscape.

That same year, De Bruijn gave a series of interviews, most notably in *Het Vrije Volk* (16) and *De Tijd* (9), two of the most widely read papers in the Netherlands, in which he characterized horror fiction as marginal. He presented himself as an editor and an isolated pioneer working in cultural obscurity. This culminates in a story De Bruijn often told: that he translated Lovecraft using a borrowed copy of "Supernatural Horror in Literature," which he claimed to have transcribed by hand. The anecdote positioned his editorial work as a solitary act of initiative, undertaken without support, tradition, or institutional infrastructure.

This image of the genre as wholly neglected and of Lovecraft as a barely accessible author does not hold up under scrutiny. *Voor en na middernacht*, which had introduced Lovecraft to Dutch readers in 1949, was still in circulation and reissued in 1958 in a deluxe hardcover edition. Far from being forgotten, the book was being celebrated, repackaged, and resold to a new generation of readers. Its original publication had been accompanied by strong sales figures, wide critical praise, and cultural recognition through holiday promotions, newspaper reviews, and sustained visibility in bookstores. The idea that Lovecraft had vanished from public memory by 1958 is incompatible with the reality of a reprint campaign launched by one of the country's most prominent publishing houses. This does not imply that Lovecraft occupied a central position in Dutch literary culture, but that his presence, even in a niche, should not be confused with being invisible.

The contradiction becomes even more pronounced when the nature of De Bruijn's media presence is considered. His remarks did not appear in obscure or specialized outlets but were featured prominently in *Het Vrije Volk* and *De Tijd,* major national papers with broad and diverse readerships. Notably, *Het Vrije Volk* was a democratic-socialist paper, whereas *De Tijd* was a Catholic paper, showcasing a broad cross-cultural appeal.

The fact that a horror anthology could garner such attention from leading newspapers undermines the claim that the genre lacked any meaningful audience or cultural standing. Editors working in genuine obscurity do not typically receive space for interviews in the country's leading publications. That De Bruijn's perspective was deemed worthy of national coverage suggests that the genre's marginality, as he presented it, was at least partially constructed.

Additional evidence of Lovecraft's presence in Dutch discourse can be found in a 1951 article from *Filmfront Filmstudiën* (15). The author briefly references a quotation by August Derleth about Lovecraft's work. Although Lovecraft is not the focus of the piece, the casual inclusion of his name and the assumption that it would carry meaning for the reader reinforce the idea that he was already part of the cultural vocabulary, at least among readers of the literary and cinematic press. This passing reference highlights that Lovecraft was not a forgotten or fringe figure but someone whose name would mean something to a sufficient number of readers to be invoked in a broader discussion of horror aesthetics.

It is worth noting that Lovecraft's visibility in the Netherlands in 1958 extended beyond Dutch-language publications. English-language horror anthologies also reached Dutch readers, including Groff Conklin's *The Graveyard Reader,* which featured "The Outsider" (1921), and the collection *Cry Horror!* (1959)

the following year, as evidenced by reviews in newspapers (*De Haan* 15; *Deventer Dagblad* 9; *Provinciaalse Zeeuwse Courant* 7).

These books, aimed at a mass-market audience, were reviewed and advertised in Dutch newspapers, and their presence in Dutch bookshops demonstrates that Lovecraft's work was accessible through multiple channels, not just literary translation but inexpensive international paperbacks. While the full range of imported material is difficult to reconstruct, it is reasonable to assume that additional English-language editions also reached the Netherlands. For readers with basic English proficiency—and many Dutch readers possessed that—Lovecraft was not a remote or inaccessible figure but an author who could be encountered in mainstream commercial venues.

More broadly, De Bruijn's public statements about the marginal status of horror fiction appear less as neutral observations and more as a form of rhetorical positioning. By emphasizing the absence of readers, texts, and precedent, he could frame his editorial work as an act of rediscovery rather than republication. This move strategically obscures the degree to which Lovecraft's work had already been made available to Dutch readers through earlier efforts. While *Griezelverhalen* undoubtedly contributed to developing horror fiction as a recognizable publishing category in the Netherlands, its significance lies not in its isolation but in its engagement with an already emerging, yet peripheral, and materially visible literary tradition.

Although comprehensive sales records for *Griezelverhalen* have not been preserved, we can infer that the book was successful based on the number of reprints.[1] The anthology reached a fourth printing by 1962, four years after its original release. The continuation of the print run further complicates De Bruijn's narrative of marginality. A genre so limited in audience that "all its fans could fit into a single car" would not typically sustain a commercially successful publishing cycle. The print history thus corroborates what is already suggested by press coverage and import data: Lovecraft's presence in the Dutch liter-

---

1. The publisher's archives have been partially preserved in the KDC in Nijmegen, but I was unable to find any related material there.

ary field was not marked by absence but by a steady, if sometimes understated visibility.

The narrative of obscurity, however, did not end with De Bruijn. In later decades, it was echoed by Eddy C. Bertin, the first Dutch writer to contribute to the Cthulhu Mythos. Reflecting on his early encounters with Lovecraft, Bertin remarked: "I knew Lovecraft from two stories, 'The Rats in the Walls' and 'The Thing on the Doorstep' (published in two now very rare Dutch horror anthologies), neither of which I really liked" (3). The phrasing is instructive. By describing *Voor en na middernacht* (1949) and *Griezelverhalen* (1958) as "very rare," Bertin implies a level of inaccessibility that does not align with the historical record. As discussed above, both anthologies received coverage in national newspapers and were widely distributed. In the case of *Griezelverhalen*, they went through multiple reprintings within a few years. Far from marginal or obscure, they were among the most visible and commercially successful examples of supernatural fiction in the postwar Dutch market. Like De Bruijn's before him, Bertin's framing retrospectively overwrote a context of active publication and reception as one of near-total absence.

This rhetorical move is significant. Bertin implicitly positions himself outside any existing reception infrastructure by suggesting that he had to teach himself English to access Lovecraft. The cultural field he evokes is one of scarcity, in which genre fiction survives not through institutions, publishers, or readerships but through isolated acts of recovery. As with De Bruijn, this emphasis on absence retroactively legitimizes the speaker's role. The individual becomes not just a participant in a tradition but the condition of its possibility.

What makes Bertin's framing particularly revealing is that it appears long after the period it describes. This is not a contemporary account shaped by immediate cultural uncertainty but a retrospective narrative formed in full view of Lovecraft's international canonization. Even decades later, the continued insistence on marginality suggests that the perceived value of such positioning endures. To claim that one encountered Lovecraft despite the cultural conditions of the time, as opposed to because of them, is to reinforce a particular kind of authority: the authority of the discoverer rather than the inheritor.

It is precisely this dynamic that makes Bertin's account so telling. His recollection does not emerge from a vacuum; it repeats, in more personal terms, the same structure of obscurity that earlier editors had already institutionalized. However, unlike De Bruijn, who invoked this narrative to justify an editorial project in real time, Bertin deploys it retrospectively as part of a life story. The myth of obscurity, once introduced, proves remarkably adaptable.

The claim that H. P. Lovecraft was practically unknown in the Netherlands until the 1960s has often been repeated in contemporary statements and later recollections. However, as this paper has shown, those claims say more about the rhetorical needs of the people making them than about Lovecraft's actual reception. From 1949 onward, his work was translated, reviewed, reprinted, and discussed—not widely, but not invisibly either. He occupied a position that was neither prominent nor absent but quietly sustained. To misread that kind of modest visibility as total obscurity is to simplify a far more layered history and, in doing so, to distort it.

Lovecraft's first appearance in Dutch translation, in *Voor en na middernacht* (1949), placed him within a literary context that was anything but marginal. He was published by a major house, alongside canonical authors, and reviewed by leading national newspapers. The anthology enjoyed wide circulation and enduring visibility, culminating in reissues well into the 1970s. A decade later, *Griezelverhalen* (1958) further cemented Lovecraft's presence in Dutch literary culture. Nevertheless, rather than reinforcing a growing recognition narrative, this second wave of publication became the basis for a counterintuitive claim: that Lovecraft had been virtually absent, his readership negligible, and his rediscovering the work of solitary enthusiasts.

This rhetorical reframing, most visibly articulated by A. de Bruijn and later repeated by Eddy C. Bertin, was not merely a matter of personal memory or bibliographic oversight. It constituted a strategic move within the emerging Dutch horror discourse. By positioning Lovecraft as culturally absent, these figures could cast themselves in the role of pioneers rather than participants. The implication was not simply that they admired Lovecraft but that they had rescued him, translated him when others had not, read him when few others could, and brought him into view within a literary field presumed to be inhospitable to the weird and the horrific. The archival evidence tells a different story: Lovecraft was never central but always present. His work was available, reviewed, and reprinted. He was part of the conversation, even if he was not always its focus.

While specific in its details, the Dutch case may not be unique in its structure. Similar rhetorical patterns may have shaped Lovecraft's reception elsewhere in Europe, particularly in countries where genre fiction has historically occupied a marginal position. Future comparative research could productively examine how claims of absence, rediscovery, and pioneering circulate across national contexts and how they interact with the material realities of translation, distribution, and readership.

To reassess Lovecraft's reception in the Netherlands is not to deny that his position was peripheral. It is to insist that peripherality is not the same as invisibility. Lovecraft's Dutch presence was limited, but it was grounded in publications, reviews, and readerships that can be documented. A narrative of total absence obscures this complexity. It replaces a fragmented but traceable reception with a more dramatic, but ultimately less accurate, story of rediscovery.

Works Cited

Bertin, Eddy C. "My European Mythos." *Cyäegha* No. 1 (2008): 3.

Dagblad de Stem. "Romans, Verhalen en Gedichten." *Delpher* (25 February 1950).

De Bruijn, A., and A. Van Der Hoek, ed. *Griezelverhalen*. Utrecht & Antwerp: Prisma-Boeken, 1958.

De Haan, Jacques. "Het Puikje van de Pocketbooks." *Delpher*, Leeuwarder Courant (22 November 1958), resolver.kb.nl /resolve?urn=ddd:010615178:mpeg21:p015.

De Maasbode. "Doeve: Journalistieke Illustrator." *Delpher,* resolver.kb.nl/resolve?urn=MMKB15:000557132:mpeg21:p00003.

De Telegraaf. "Spook—en Griezelverhalen 'VOOR EN NA MIDDERNACHT.'" *Delpher* (3 December 1949), resolver.kb.nl/resolve?urn=ddd:110584751:mpeg21:p007.

De Tijd. "Spoken in de Boekenkast." *Delpher* (31 January 1959), resolver.kb.nl/resolve?urn=ddd:011234758:mpeg21:p009.

De Volkskrant. "Twee griezelboeken." *Delpher* (3 December 1949), resolver.kb.nl/resolve?urn=ABCDDD:010880557:mpeg21:p007.

Deventer Dagblad. "Het Puikje van de Pocketbooks." *Delpher* (22 November 1958), resolver.kb.nl/resolve?urn=MMHCO02:163928072:mpeg21:p00009.

Filmfront Filmstudiën. "Het verdwenen portret." *Delpher* (1951), resolver.kb.nl/resolve?urn=MMUBTB05:253513008:00015.

Het Vrije Volk. "500 griezeldelen in de spookbibliotheek." *Delpher* (1 March 1958), resolver.kb.nl/resolve?urn=ddd:010953133:mpeg21:p016.

Karloff, Boris, ed. *And the Darkness Falls.* Cleveland: World Publishing Co., 1946.

Lobo, B. Jessurun, ed. *Voor en na middernacht.* Antwerp: Elsevier, 1949.

Manteau, Angèle. Letter to R. Jessurun Lobo (11 March 1974). Elsevier Archives, Stadsarchief Amsterdam. archief.amsterdam/inventarissen/details/1103/path/4.1.2.4.1.45.

Provinciaalse Zeeuwse Courant. "Twee boeken over Kathleen Ferrier in één deel herdrukt." *Krantenbank Zeeland* (1958), krantenbankzeeland.nl/issue/pzc/1959-03-19/edition/0/page/9.

Van Bel, P. Letter to B. Jessurun Lobo (5 January 1951). Elsevier Archives, Stadsarchief Amsterdam. archief.amsterdam/inventarissen/details/1103/path/3.2.3.1.10.2

Van Bork, G. J., et al. "Letterkundig Lexicon Voor De Neerlandistiek." *DBNL* (2002), www.dbnl.org/tekst/bork001lett01_01/bork001lett01_01_0020.php.

Van den Brink, R. A. M. Letter to B. Jessurun Lobo (21 April 1952). Elsevier Archives, Stadsarchief Amsterdam. archief.amsterdam/inventarissen/details/1103/path/3.2.3.1.10.2.

Wise, Herbert A., and Phyllis Fraser, ed. *Great Tales of Terror and the Supernatural.* New York: Modern Library, 1944.

Transgression, Trauma, and Transcendence in H. P. Lovecraft's "The Thing on the Doorstep"

James Goho

Although not recognized as one of his best stories,[1] H. P. Lovecraft's "The Thing on the Doorstep" (1937) is a powerful story of parental transgressions that caused enduring trauma for their children. In the story, it is clear that both sets of parents (Ephraim Waite and the Derbys) abused their child in varying ways, but the abuse nevertheless triggered subsequent trauma for their child. Yet it is also a story of a weird transcendence at the end for the characters Asenath Waite and Edward Derby, who suffered that childhood abuse.

The story is noteworthy to some, for example Peter Cannon, because it features a prominent female character, Asenath Waite, the daughter of Ephraim Waite (who is depicted as a notorious dark occultist with unusual powers), which is uncommon in Lovecraft's fiction. But she is a presence and an absence in the work. Her body is present, but her absence haunts the story, as if it were an unheard scream from a child. She is silent because only her body remains. She lived a tragedy. Annie G. Rogers studied the silent language of girls who would not, per-

---

1. HPL wrote the story in 1933, but he refused to submit it anywhere until 1936, when he reluctantly sent it to *Weird Tales*, where it was published in the January 1937 issue. S. T. Joshi calls the story one of HPL's "poorest later efforts" (*IAP* 86). W. H. Pugmire thought the story was "outlandish," but concluded that "Lovecraft's cool narrative tone gives it an air of realism that adds to the effectiveness of the storytelling. It is a tale well told, and one that lingers within our haunted minds" (6).

haps could not, speak about their devastating abuse. The abuse shattered their childhood and caused continuing inner trauma. They endure the unspeakable abuse in silence. Asenath was forever silenced by her father, who killed her in a horrific way. As a conscious person, she is buried in the ashes of the past. Nicolas Abraham argued that all the departed may return. However, some are predestined to haunt, especially those who have taken unspeakable secrets to the grave. That is why Asenath haunts the story as a vanished subject; she is there only in body. As a person, Asenath is a phantom. Abraham contended that the phantom represents "the burial of an unspeakable fact" (289). More so, this phantom suggests that the story itself harbors deeper, unspeakable secrets that remain hidden. What is buried in "The Thing on the Doorstep" is the abuse inflicted on Asenath Waite. One can only imagine the horrors she experienced as a child with such a parent as Ephraim Waite, who probably abused her severely while she was growing up. That is the unspeakable in this story. He was a predatory parent who "did a hideous thing to keep alive" (CF 3.339).

Research has found that childhood abuse has severe, long-term effects on victims, including ongoing trauma. For example, from their research review, Michael D. De Bellis and Abigail Zisk concluded that abuse in childhood is a severe psychosocial and medical problem that has serious long-lasting consequences for those who suffered it. Moreover, in its comprehensive review of the research literature on childhood abuse, the National Academies of Sciences, Engineering, and Medicine concluded: "Child abuse and neglect appear to influence the course of development by altering many elements of biological, cognitive, psychosocial, and behavioral development; in other words, child abuse and neglect have a profound and often lasting impact on development" (154–55). The consequences of abuse are displayed in "The Thing on the Doorstep." But for Asenath, who was silenced by her father, these are unsayable. As Roger B. Salomon argues, horror literature's essential aim is to "remind us of the unspeakable" (15). In this story, the suffering of Asenath is unwritten because it is inexpressible. Ephraim Waite did that by killing her when she was young. In the story, little is said about Asenath's mother, except that she was a veiled, unknown woman whom Ephraim married when he was in his old age. It is apparent that Ephraim, with his occult power of mind exchange, planned early after Asenath's birth to take his daughter's body to house his mind.

Another character who has suffered emotional abuse as a child and into early adulthood is Edward Pickman Derby. It has left him timid, weak, and unsure about himself. Parental overprotection is a behavior when parents excessively monitor and restrict their child's activities and daily lives. This behavior encourages dependence on parents and interferes with the child's autonomy, emotional maturation, and independence (Parker). Linda G. McWhorter et al. found that overprotective or overcontrolling parenting was associated with child emotional/behavioral problems in later life. In addition, Ming Cui et al. (2022) found overwhelmingly negative associations between overparenting and childhood development in psychological, behavioral, social, and relational domains. In general, research has found many negative consequences of overbearing or overcontrolling parents on their children as they grow up. This excessive protective behavior in a child's developmental stage may produce severe social and psychological disorders. It often has lasting effects on children into adulthood.

Daniel Upton narrates the story. He is eight years older than Edward Derby and has known him all his life. He starts the story by telling readers that he has killed Derby, but there are mitigating circumstances that justify his action, which he tells in the rest of the story. He reveals Edward Derby's over-controlling parents and the effects of that control on the actions and non-actions of Edward Derby. In contrast to Asenath Waite, Derby is a complete character in that he has a body and mind, but one that has been deformed by his parents "keeping him closely chained to their side" because of his "organic illnesses," which are never fully explained in the story (CF 3.325). He has not developed a fully independent personality separate from his parents. He has "habits of childish dependence" (CF 3.326). He

exhibits "shyness, inertia" due to excessive "parental protective-
ness," and he develops an "ingrained timidity" (CF 3.328). He
never seems to develop the capacity for independent action or
to assume normal adult responsibilities. When he was thirty-
four, Edward Derby's mother died, and he experienced a "psychological malady," which he appeared to overcome (CF
3.328).[2] Years-long control and domination by a parent stunted
his independent development and left him susceptible to the
wiles of another parent who inhabited Asenath's body. As a
"perennial child," Derby "transferred his dependence from" one
parent to another to his ultimate undoing (CF 3.331).

After his recovery from his psychological collapse, Derby begins to be more outgoing and mingles with a notorious Miskatonic University set. There he meets Asenath Waite when she
appears to be "twenty-three," according to the narrator, Upton
(CF 3.329). Although Edward Derby's fascination is said to be
for Asenath, it is only her "very good-looking" physical being
that remains; she has no mental being (CF 3.329). He is "wildly
taken with her appearance," but is mostly enchanted by her "interests and erudition" (CF 3.330). These latter characteristics
belong to Ephraim, not to Asenath. Moreover, her "overprotu-
berant eyes" blaze at times with the look of Ephraim, and sometimes she looks "fiendishly like him" (CF 3.329). After she
marries Derby, she "aged tremendously" and exuded a "vague,
unplaceable repulsiveness" (CF 3.333), as though Ephraim's personality has begun to show more forcefully on her body. Ephraim
plans to abandon her for Edward Derby, because he prefers a male
body, as he had raged about through Asenath's voice.

The slow, agonizing, and multi-episode transfer of Ephraim's
consciousness to Derby's body probably replicates, in some man-

---

2. Some of these characteristics may apply to HPL during his youth. Maurice
Lévy wrote that he could "recognize Lovecraft in the traits of Edward Derby"
(42). S. T. Joshi also suggests that some elements of HPL's relationship with
his mother might be reflected in the story (IAP 391–92). In a letter to R. H.
Barlow, HPL expressed the mental problems experienced when he was young,
including "hypersensitive nerves" that led to "many different physical illnesses"
and a "breakdown" when he was eighteen (OFF 125).

ner, the agony that Asenath endured. During that time period, Derby, or his body, exhibits characteristics unusual for him, such as blazing eyes and the ability to drive a car. He begins to go through a "metamorphosis" and to look "like old Ephraim Waite" at times (CF 3.334). Confiding to Daniel Upton, Derby says he fears losing his identity. The fragility of self-identity and its loss are underlying themes of the story. Edward fights to maintain his identity throughout the story, yet fails. Ephraim killed Asenath's human identity in her youth. According to Jack Morgan, the "devastation of human identity" is "radically disturbing more than simply 'scary'" (24). A key moment occurs when someone tells Upton's wife (who rarely appears in the story) that she saw a face in a window of Edward Derby's library, a face full of "pain, defeat and wistful hopelessness" (CF 3.335). The face was Asenath Waite's, but the eyes were Derby's. Occasionally, the two traumatized characters merge when Ephraim experiments with mind exchange on Derby.

Some of the episodes that Derby reports to Upton sound like the products of a psychosis. "Psychosis" is defined in *Taber's Medical Dictionary* as "a mental disorder in which there is severe loss of contact with reality, evidenced by delusions, hallucinations, disorganized speech patterns, and bizarre or catatonic behavior." Edward Derby exhibits these characteristics. He states that he traveled to "abysses of knighted secrets," "forbidden places, on other worlds," and had "explorations in remote and forbidden places" (CF 3.336). Later, in a "half-incoherent" frenzy, Edward Derby shouts that he saw a "place of utter blasphemy, the unholy pit where the black realm begins" and other monstrous beings (CF 3.338). Upton fears that Edward has lost "his sanity" (CF 3.335). Ingo Schäfer and Helen L. Fisher found that "longitudinal studies [. . .] suggest a role of childhood trauma in the development of psychosis" (364). In addition, Ioanna Giannopoulou et al. surveyed the current state of knowledge, and it "confirms the relationship between exposure to traumatic experiences in childhood and psychosis" (5). Edward Derby's monstrous travels and dark occult experiments could represent a psychosis caused by the transgressions of his parents. Lovecraft expressed these episodes of "hysteria" in a stream-of-consciousness style that puts the reader into the fragmenting consciousness of Edward Derby (*CF* 3.338). These terrifying experiences also provide an insight into what happened to Asenath under Ephraim's tyranny.

Throughout the story, Derby describes to Upton a torrent of horrific images, events, and strange beings in unbelievable places, as if he had continuous psychotic episodes. These outbursts illustrate Derby's collapsing identity and personality. Upton explains these episodes by suggesting that his lifelong friend appeared as if he had been taken by "some monstrous intrusion from outer space" (*CF* 3.341) or experienced the "intrusion of some sort from the black abyss" (*CF* 3.342). Upton's search for words to explain the condition of Edward Derby expresses the complex and disturbing imagery that people who are diagnosed with a psychosis actually experience. The severity and frequency of these episodes increases over three years, while Ephraim Waite gains more and more control over Derby. That length of time also suggests the minimum time it may have taken for Ephraim to take his daughter's body, a long time to be abused severely by a parent. But at other times, Upton meets a calm and deliberate Derby who dismisses his raving as due to overwork. During his calm episodes, he often stares with a "blaze of his eyes"—the blaze of Ephraim's mind controlling Derby's body (*CF* 3.341). With the passage of time, he looks more and more like "old Ephraim" (*CF* 3.342). As Derby tells of his increasingly bizarre experiences, Upton fears for Derby's sanity and thinks his "mind was in a pitiable state" (*CF* 3.340).

As the story progresses, Derby at times says that Asenath Waite is not alive as a person but is a shell for Ephraim's mind. As if a fragment of Asenath's mind remained, he shrieks at Upton about the *"monster having his trusting, weak-willed* [. . .] *child at his mercy"* (*CF* 3.341). Derby expresses the horror that Asenath experienced as a child. He appears to know that Ephraim had transferred his mind into his daughter's body and sent hers into his aged, poisoned body to die an agonizing death. Indeed, he tells Upton that *"she isn't Asenath at all, but really old*

Ephraim himself" (CF 342).

Asenath's name (57 times), the pronoun "she" (91 times), and the possessive "her" (57 times) and her bodily appearance, in various forms, are frequently invoked in the story, but that character has no consciousness, no separate mind, no sense of her own perspective, and no identity. She is dead. Or is she neither dead nor alive? She is a walking corpse animated by her vicious father, Ephraim Waite. She is a physical shell. She has no functioning independent brain cells, personality, or thoughts. She is called attractive, but her bulging eyes blaze with the evil of her father. All her other attributes, in essence, belong to Ephraim. Asenath is a weird transgender character. She is absent, but also present, in body. She has no individual identity but, in the story, seems to come alive. Asenath confounds two ontological categories and becomes "a spectre," as Julian Wolfreys might suggest, as something "between life and death" (x). She is the extreme weird otherness haunting the story.

Through the rest of the story, Derby becomes ever more lost in an unreal, hallucinatory world. More than distressed and disoriented, he no longer seems able to distinguish the real from the unreal, due to the assaults from Ephraim on his identity and his cognitive ability. In that haze of unreality and despair, Derby keeps using feminine pronouns and Asenath's name throughout the story. This is true even after he has told Upton that she had suffered abuse from her father and that it was Ephraim in Asenath's body. In his final handwritten note to Upton, he writes that "[s]he got me—it's Asenath," and uses "she" several other times. But he hesitates; he thinks that the "soul" might be "Ephraim's" (CF 3.356) in Asenath's body. His continuing use of the feminine pronouns demonstrates the disruption of his mental acuity. The years of Ephraim's mental assaults have eroded his already weakened discernment, intelligence, and decision-making ability from parental over-control. These repeated assaults have destroyed his ability to think and accurately express his own terror. Derby's world becomes a nightmare, described in his hysterical outbursts to Upton. He appears to have lost contact with the world. That is because his reality has changed to a monstrous one. Moreover, Derby experiences what Asenath had experienced when she was much younger. He shares her suffering. He is put in her body on multiple occasions, while Ephraim uses Derby's body to work toward full control. These episodes in her body shatter his sense of self and his sense of identity. He is traumatized, perhaps, beyond rescue. He lives now in a fragmented reality. Perhaps the two abused characters make some weird connection during those periods together. Yet Derby kills Asenath's body. He buries that body in the cellar of their house in an attempt to destroy Ephraim. But Ephraim's powerful consciousness stays alive in the now rotting body of Asenath and later attacks Derby.

Asenath Waite and Edward Derby's traumas teem in Lovecraft's story. Derby experiences the horrors that Ephraim inflicted on Asenath. She lived in fear and trauma most of her short life while being groomed for her father's mind-rape. She experienced an appalling life and death. Asenath is a ghostly presence in the story because what happened to her as a child is unsayable. Derby asks, "Asenath . . . is there such a person?" (CF 3.340). That is the question disturbing the story.

Some scholars contend that "The Thing on the Doorstep" is a subversive exploration of sex. Joel Pace argues that "homoerotic overtones [. . .] are clearly present in the tale" (105). He goes on to suggest that the story implies a "homoerotic link between Edward and Dan as well as Edward and Ephraim" (114). But Dylan Henderson dismisses that idea because "Lovecraft shows no interest in sexual dynamics," hence what he explores was "his sensitivity to—and fascination with—disgust" (29). In his "Excised Passages from 'The Thing on the Doorstep,'" S. T. Joshi discusses a deleted text from Lovecraft's manuscript that hints at sex between Derby and Asenath's body. The section reads that "Asenath has given birth to a stillborn 'monstrosity'" (174). Henderson contends that this demonstrates Lovecraft deliberately expunged "sexuality from his draft" of the story because he did not want it to be about "sex or gender" (28). That text is not part of the finished story. The fascination with finding sexuality in the story misses the abuse perpetrated by Ephraim on his daughter, which may have included sexual assault. The story is about the unspeakable, the unsayable, the abuse of children.

Edward Derby's distinctive knock on Daniel Upton's door at the close of the story signals the union of the two suffering characters. Edward Derby's mind unites with Asenath Waite's body. Ephraim now has firm hold of Derby's body. Asenath's last physical presence in the story is described as that thing on the Uptons' doorstep. She is a "dwarfed, humped figure" and a "foul, stunted parody" of a human being (CF 2.355), ending as a "liquescent horror, [. . .] bones, too—and a crushed-in skull" (CF 3.357). That body exemplifies Julia's Kristeva's notion of "the abject." The abject is the stuff of disgust, while "abjection" is the horror we feel when confronted by the abject—something nauseatingly other, unclean and loathsome (Kristeva 2).[3] But that final image of Asenath may be a composite verbal depiction of the terrors she had gone through during her brief life with Ephraim.

Lovecraft moves the story beyond horror to a transcendent weird experience for the two characters. Edward Derby and Asenath Waite act together to escape Ephraim. In her rotting corpse, Edward and Asenath crawl out of her grave in that cellar on a mission to stop Ephraim. Perhaps Edward was able to achieve this because a shred of Asenath's spirit yet remained in her corpse that urged revenge on her father, and she gave him the will to act forcefully in the last act of his life. In the end, Asenath Waite and Edward Derby share "a single soul" and meet "one common dissolution at the same moment," to borrow a phrase from Lovecraft's "Supernatural Horror in Literature" (CE 2.103). Both have suffered from parental transgressions.

---

3. Asenath's body may also be a "gothic body" or the "abhuman," according to Kelly Hurley. She says she borrowed the term "abhuman" from William Hope Hodgson. For Hurley, the abhuman is typified by a "morphic variability" and is something "in danger of becoming not-itself, becoming other" (7). It refers to something only partially human, or in a process of becoming something monstrous. The concept of the abhuman means becoming the alien other and losing one's identity, which happened to Asenath because of parental abuse.

Asenath's trauma is clouded in silence and only faint echoes or shadows remain. Derby's, at the hands of his mother, is more documented and less severe than Asenath's. But he also re-experiences her abuse. He escaped his mother only to be taken by a father figure dressed as a woman because of what "Mother, Mother!" did to him (CF 3.351). There is no healing in life for them. In death, they transcend the earthly horrors that they had experienced. They gain a freedom they never knew in life—a freedom from parental abuse and trauma. Behind the outward horror, there is an exhilarating release from torment.

Asenath Waite is the specter haunting the story. She is something missing, something lost, something already dead at the beginning of the story. She is a haunting presence of transgression and trauma. Asenath represents the loneliness and terror of children abused by parents. Edward Derby is similar. An overpowering, over-controlling parent stunted his development, leaving him vulnerable to a vicious substitute parent. They die together, but we must imagine them "at peace" in the end (CF 3.356).

In "The Thing on the Doorstep," Lovecraft constructed a compelling weird tale revealing the harmful effects of childhood abuse and trauma. Lovecraft left the trauma inflicted on Asenath by Ephraim as unspeakable, hidden in the story, as happens to so many such tragedies in real life. In many cases of severe childhood abuse, the horrid acts remain buried. They are unspeakable. Underneath the surface horror of the story flows an undertow of sadness, despair, and loss. It is that terrible loneliness of a battered childhood that left one alone and afraid in the world with all its horrors. In Lovecraft's story, that is what the two innocent ones experienced all their lives. A despair flows icily through their world. It is a deep coldness spawned by the ill-treatment of parents and a world consequently populated by monstrous events and things. For the two characters who did not have a genuine childhood, who were weak and suffered torment, there was no healing life for them. But Lovecraft made his two characters united in death, transcending the pain of their lives.

Works Cited

Abraham, Nicolas. Trans. Nicholas Rand. "Notes on the Phantom: A Complement to Freud's Metapsychology." *Critical Inquiry* 13: *The Trial(s) of Psychoanalysis* (Winter 1987): 287–92.

Cannon, Peter. *H. P. Lovecraft*. Boston: Twayne, 1989.

Cui, Ming; Hong, Peipei; and Jiao, Chengfel. "Overparenting and Emerging Adult Development: A Systematic Review." *Emerging Adulthood* 10 (2022): 1076–94.

De Bellis, Michael D., and Abigail Zisk. "The Biological Effects of Childhood Trauma." *Child and Adolescent Psychiatric Clinics of North America* 23 (2014): 185–222.

Giannopoulou, Ioanna, Stelios Georgiades, Maria-Ioanna Stefanou, Demetrios A. Spandidos, and Emmanouil Rizos. "Links between Trauma and Psychosis (Review)." *Experimental and Therapeutic Medicine* 26 (2023): 386. 1–8.

Henderson, Dylan. "The Disgusting Thing on the Doorstep: H. P. Lovecraft's Sexuality and the Science of Revulsion." *Lovecraft Annual* No. 17 (2023): 15–35.

Hurley, Kelly. *The Gothic Body: Sexuality, Materialism and Degeneration at the Fin de Siècle*. Cambridge: Cambridge University Press, 2004.

Joshi, S. T. "Excised Passages from 'The Thing on the Doorstep.'" *Lovecraft Annual* No. 7 (2013): 171–77.

Kristeva, Julia. *Powers of Horror: An Essay on Abjection*. Tr. Leon S. Roudiez. New York: Columbia University Press, 1982.

Lévy, Maurice. *Lovecraft: A Study in the Fantastic*. Tr. S. T. Joshi. Detroit: Wayne State University Press, 1985.

Lovecraft, H. P. *O Fortunate Floridian: H. P. Lovecraft's Letters to R. H. Barlow*. Ed. S. T. Joshi and David E. Schultz. Tampa: University of Tampa Press, 2007. [OFF]

McWhorter, Linda G., et al. "Parental Post-Traumatic Stress, Overprotective Parenting, and Emotional and Behavioural Problems for Children with Critical Congenital Heart Disease." *Cardiology in the Young* 32 (2022): 738–45.

Morgan, Jack. *Joyce's City: History, Politics, and Life in Dubliners*. Columbia: University of Missouri Press, 2015.

National Academies of Sciences, Engineering, and Medicine. *New Directions in Child Abuse and Neglect Research*. Washington, DC: National Academies Press, 2014. doi.org/10.17226/18331. Accessed 18 January 2025.

Pace, Joel. "Queer Tales? Sexuality, Race, and Architecture in 'The Thing on the Doorstep.'" *Lovecraft Annual* No. 2 (2008): 104–37.

Parker, George. "Parental Representations of Patients with Anxiety Neurosis." *Acta Psychiatrica Scandinavica* 63 (1981): 33–36. doi: 10.1111/j.1600-0447.1981.tb00647.x

Pugmire, W. H. "Personal Tragedy in 'The Thing on the Doorstep.'" *Lovecraft Annual* No. 11 (2017): 3–6.

Rogers, Annie G. *The Unsayable: The Hidden Language of Trauma*. New York: Random House, 2006.

Salomon, Roger B. *Mazes of the Serpent*. Ithaca, NY: Cornell University Press, 2002.

Schäfer, Ingo, and Helen L. Fisher. "Childhood Trauma and Psychosis—What Is the Evidence?" *Dialogues Clinical Neuroscience* 13 (2011): 360–65.

Taber's Medical Dictionary Online. www.tabers.com/tabersonline) Accessed 14 January 2025.

Wolfreys, Julian. *Victorian Hauntings: Spectrality, Gothic, the Uncanny and Literature*. New York: Palgrave Macmillan, 2002.

A Few Trees in a Forest: Lovecraft in Pop Culture

Duncan Norris

Howard Phillips Lovecraft inhabits the particularly rarefied air of both acknowledged literary master and pop culture icon. Sufficient time and successive generations have passed to be certain of his secured place in the pantheon of the great figures of horror literature. Yet as with Bram Stoker, Lovecraft's own idol Edgar Allan Poe, or indeed with any much adapted literary figure, this wide dispersion natural inculcates a similar wide diffusion. Such creates interesting results. For example, Stoker is rightly seen as the modern father of the vampire. Yet the popular tropes of the filmic and pop cultural vampire are set as much by the template made in *Nosferatu: A Symphony of Horror* (1922), an illegal knock-off of the novel *Dracula*, as by Stoker's original book. The subsequently famous Bela Lugosi *Dracula* (1931) film adaptation which fully codified the perceptions of the vampire, itself copied *Nosferatu* in places. Thus, despite the immense popularity of Stoker's book, most of those familiar with the character of Dracula have never read the novel. Even seemingly fundamental elements commonly understood as part of the story, such as the old moldering castle and long-lost love, come from the movies and later adaptations.

Allow me to illustrate this osmotic transmission from my own (admittedly Philistinish) perspective. At the random mention of Poe I am immediately as likely to conjure a mental image of the Roger Corman films based upon his work and starring Vincent Price or the inaugural *Simpsons* Treehouse of Horror segment based around "The Raven" as I am of a scene from "The Cask of

Amontillado" or "The Black Cat." Likewise, I have a friend who owns a replica copy of the *Necronomicon* but has never read any Lovecraft. His interest comes solely from the arrogated version used in the *Evil Dead* film series. Lovecraft's own tentacles—the simile one feels is almost mandatory at this point, given the almost intrinsic association of such appendages with the Lovecraftian—have spread farther and wider into pop culture. Indeed, it is intertwined to such an extent that even a brief investigation of all these connections would be doomed to failure by the superficiality of the examination and the larger portion inevitably left out.

Consider *An Exhibition of Unspeakable Things*, which ran from 2007 to 2008 in Yverdon-les-Bains, Switzerland, at the *Masion d'Ailleurs* [House of Elsewhere], commonly known as the Science Fiction Museum. The art exhibited there was niche, even by the standards of the genre, as explicated by the subtitle *Works Inspired by H. P. Lovecraft's Commonplace Book.* The latter is merely a series of notes, quotes, and ideas Lovecraft wrote down as possible story seeds, most of which were never brought to fruition. Even to make brief mention of such art as was produced and displayed would be its own dedicated work.[1] Equally, Lovecraft and his work show up in areas far outside those that might seem his natural remit. A book titled *The Call of Cthulu* [*sic*] is evident on the bookshelf during S2E9 of the Netflix cartoon comedy *Human Resources.* This is an extremely sexualized and adult-oriented creation about the office life of the weird creatures who guide human behaviors, such as Lovebugs, Hormone Monsters, Logic Rocks, Shame Wizards, and Ambition Gremlins. To say it is removed from the Lovecraftian is an enormous understatement. Nor does *The Call of Cthulu* have relevance to a human character in the scene as does *Harry Potter and the Goblet of Fire* beneath it. Other visible titles are very generic, simply *Amadeus* and *Caesar*. The Lovecraft reference is, apparently, just for fun, an Easter egg for sharp-eyed viewers. Such instances abound in the pop cultural landscape. Thus, rather than being encyclopedic, this monograph examines a few, almost randomly

1. The exhibition has its own dedicated book, which is sadly long out of print.

chosen but very specific examples of the interactions of Lovecraft and his creations with modern pop culture. It is hoped that this will provide a useful insight into their relevance, position, and meaning in the twenty-first century.

Highlighting this dissemination of Lovecraft, the initial entrepot to the subject will be connected with two countries that were early adopters of Lovecraft in translation, France and Japan.[2] Lovecraft had a particularly positive relationship with France—insofar as anyone can have a relationship with a place he never visited—and it is widely considered that "The Music of Erich Zann" is set in the winding streets of ancient Paris. As early as 1949, references were made in the French-language *Le Courrier Australien* which juxtapose Lovecraft with Kafka, and it thus seems appropriate that the first complete translation of a Lovecraft book into a foreign language was the 1954 compilation *La Couleur tombée du ciel* [*The Colour out of Space*]. Highlighting the importance of diffusion and the changes ultimately wrought thereby, this collection was curated by Jacques Bergier. He would go on to have a lively career in occultism, UFOs, and pseudoscience, ultimately incorporating Lovecraft's fiction directly into his own supposedly factual work. This would in turn form a fundamental influence on Erich von Däniken and his immensely popular promulgation of the ancient aliens hypothesis in *Chariots of the Gods? Unsolved Mysteries of the Past* (1968).

However this convoluted tale is not the subject of our interest today. Rather it is more modern works—those of the French artists François Baranger and François Launet. Other than the coincidence of their forenames, both men are not simply fringe figures who happen to be French and enjoy Lovecraft, but represent a larger dynamic. S. T. Joshi's two-volume biography of

---

2. To avoid a babble of tongues, I have taken the liberty of translating many works, names, and other aspects here without including the original source language, save when such is particularly illustrative. Translation holds many perils, and curious changes can be wrought therefrom. Consider Junji Ito, discussed herein, and his manga set in a Christian school, "Madonna," from *The Liminal Zone* (2021). The Japanese characters used to form the word ma-do-onna are demon—anger—woman.

Lovecraft was recently translated into French as *Je suis Providence*, demonstrating the vibrant ongoing interest in his work in the Francophone world. This is part of a tradition stretching back even before Bergier and continued generationally with such works as the 1991 debut offering of now famed (and ever controversial) novelist Michel Houellebecq, *H. P. Lovecraft: Against the World, Against Life*. Joshi's work was awarded the Special Jury Prize at the 2020 *Prix Imaginales*, while Baranger's illustrated edition of *At the Mountains of Madness* won in the Best Illustration category, edging out as his competition another adaptation in *The Lovecraft Notebooks* of Armel Gaulme.[3]

Other than their obvious interest in Lovecraft, both artists have worked in the artistic side of creation of major motion pictures. This includes the *Despicable Me* franchise for Launet, and *Harry Potter and the Deathly Hallows, Parts 1 and 2, Clash of the Titans, Percy Jackson: Sea of Monsters*, and 2014 Christophe Gans adaptation of *Beauty and the Beast* for Baranger. Both also are involved in the creation of art for the gaming community, Launet for traditional roleplaying games (RPGs)—naturally including *Call of Cthulhu*, whence he first encountered Lovecraft—and Baranger for video games including *Heavy Rain* and *Beyond: Two Souls*. The two artists even intersect commercially, both having work appearing in the French-language compilation *Lovecraft: At the Heart of the Nightmare* (2017). The work of artists so heavily inspired by Lovecraft being part of the creation of a diverse and diffuse range of modern pop cultural products itself speaks to the oblique nature of Lovecraft's influence. But for the moment let us narrow the focus to two specific offerings from each creator.

Consider Launet's irregularly produced but long-running webcomic, the *Unspeakable Vault (of Doom)*. The format ranges from a single panel to a small series in each strip. As might be expected from the title, it is a comical work, with deliberately simplistic artwork. The pantheon of Lovecraftian entities is portrayed in a recognizable caricature—Cthulhoo, Nyarly, Yogztot, Shubby, etc.—from their common depiction in RPGs. The

---

3. Gaulme would win in 2022 for his illustrations of Rudyard Kipling's *The Man Who Would Be King*.

events of the strips are generally standalone, with the joke frequently revolving about the stupidity of human beings—always
portrayed as faceless creatures of limited importance—trying to
interact with the Great Old Ones, whose main interest is eating
them. The humor is often based deeply in aspects of RPGs, pop
and especially internet culture, the technology sector, heavy
metal bands, archaeology, astronomy, current news, or niche
Lovecraftian minutiae. The latter is present to such an extent
that Launet commonly explains the joke and adds necessary
links under the comic itself to aid in edifying the confused reader. Furthermore, there is often a cross-over with other pop culture icons, and frequently memorial strips done for those having
died with notably Lovecraftian connections. As a scattershot
sampling these former have included references to video game
Splinter Cell, the Cenobites of Clive Barker's *Hellraiser* works,
Marvel's planet-eating Galactus and Pennywise the Clown from
the adaptations of Steven King's *It,* the Watcher in the Water
from Peter Jackson's adaptation of *The Lord of the Rings: The Fel-
lowship of the Ring,* Godzilla, *Moby Dick,* Edwin Abbot Abbot's
Flatland, the Warhammer 40K universe, Sepultura's *Chaos AD*
album, Bear Grylls, *Prometheus,* RPG Delta Green, *Game of
Thrones,* Scooby Doo, *Fallout,* Freddy Krueger, *Ghostbusters,* and
True Detective.

   Memorials—and again this is just a sample—have been done
for figures such as M. C. Escher (the inaugural commemorative
comic featuring a hound of Tindaloo bringing flowers to his
grave), Benoit Mandelbrot, Mœbius, H. R. Giger, Pierre Soulag-
es, Richard Corben, Ray Bradbury, Richard Matheson, Jack
Vance, Terry Pratchett, Ray Harryhausen, Stuart Gordon, Roger Corman, and David Lynch. The fact that so many pop culture
properties are intrinsically or can be so easily linked to Lovecraft's work silently attests to the vitality of Lovecraft in the
wider cultural sphere. Equally importantly, many of the connections just cited are of adaptations of other materials as well,
which adds to the diluting process and makes the associations
less immediately discernible. It is impossible to do justice to The
Vault, as it is known, in its entirety. At the time of writing it

consists of over 700 distinct strips. The fact that its characters have been transposed into their own RPG and have been published as physical books in multiple languages, including Chinese in 2023, should attest to the popularity of the work in a niche part of what is already a niche of fandom.

For the other François, Baranger, let us focus on a very specific image. Over the past few years Baranger has released folio type, stylistically consistent, and fully illustrated editions of Lovecraft's work. These are specifically *At the Mountains of Madness* (in two volumes), *The Call of Cthulhu*, and *The Dunwich Horror*, with *L'Ombre sur Innsmouth illustré* indubitably headed for an English-language version in due course, and others almost certain to follow. The cover of *The Dunwich Horror* is what interests us for the current examination. It is important to understand that this is not a criticism of the work from an aesthetic perspective, or a case of typical fan pedantry. Rather it is to examine the art in a broader context and thus highlight important aspects of Lovecraft and his perception through this specific lens. The image in question is of a dark and looming, fog-shrouded farmhouse framed by a run-down fence, skeletal trees, and a clouded sky, with a single illuminated four-pained window in the upper section of the building. Such colors as are subtly present are extremely subdued, giving an air of the monochromatic at a quick glance, despite a wash of a glacial, almost oceanic sense of blues. It is foreboding, and not just distantly: the menace is palpable. Certainly it is an effective image and representation of the Whateley farmhouse, yet there is an interesting under thread that is worth examining.

It is important to note that while the notorious Whateley property appears in the illustrations inside the book a number of times, the cover image is not from there. It seems to have been separately and specifically drawn for this purpose. To look at the source material, Lovecraft specifically states that the Whateley farmhouse was "a spacious, peaked-roofed affair whose rear end was buried entirely in the rocky hillside" (CF 2.425). This is not exactly how Baranger presents it. Rather, it is a free-standing structure, and other views inside the book proper show an uneven transept design reminiscent of ecclesiastical architecture. This insinuation is augmented by the placement of a small cupola reminiscent of a church belfry visible on the cover image toward the facing roof edge of the house. Such features are thematically fitting. Lovecraft's original tale is filled with a deliberate, and perhaps to some even blasphemous, parody of many key aspects of the Christian tradition, including the miraculous birth of a preternaturally gifted child and the calling out in death throes of such a being to his all-powerful deity father.

Perhaps a more understandable addition is that the building has a gambrel roof. Such a detail is not specifically given in the tale itself, although other buildings in the township are so cited twice, and the implication of the Whateleys' house also being so is highly reasonable. They also reflect reality, and both conscious and unconscious perception. The recent comedy-horror film *The Monkey* (2025) has, shot almost in passing, a gambrel roof barn that could double as a model for that on Baranger's cover, including the sole high-set central window. While shot in British Columbia, the film is set in Maine, per the original short story by that other New England horror titan, Stephen King. Intertextually the gambrel roof is so deeply associated in horror with Lovecraft and his haunted vision of New England that the image is almost a mandatory one. In truth, the lack of a gambrel roof for the nefarious Whateley house might seem odd.

Yet there is another highly likely influence and reason for the design to carry such a distinct look. One of the most famous haunted houses in the world is—or rather was, the number being altered due to the notoriety—112 Ocean Avenue in Amityville, New York, commonly just referred to as the Amityville House. The site's infamy begins with the genuinely shocking mass murder of a family of six in 1974 committed by the eldest son, Ronald DeFeo, Jr. The Lutz family subsequently moved into the property and in turn fled after apparently suffering a series of supernatural events. The ensuing proliferation of paranormal phenomena connected with the locale, both with a pretense to either scholarship or factuality, or purely as fiction, is enormous. *The Amityville Horror* (1977) by Jay Anson, an allegedly true account of the Lutz experiences, was an enormous bestseller and spawned an equally popular film also called *The Amityville Horror* (1979). After eight sequels—although the term here is often liberally designated—there followed a 2005 remake, also inevitably called *The Amityville Horror*. Literally dozens of further film titles draw from the excellent marketability and, being based upon a true events, intellectual property free use of the name Amityville.

The continuity of these films, even when attempted, is bizarre. The first direct sequel, *Amityville II: The Possession* (1982), is actually a prequel based on the work of another psychic investigator, Hans Holzer, *Murder in Amityville* (1979). It elaborates on the extant mythology showing that demonic forces drove Ronald Jr. to his murderous actions.[4] The connection, or more commonly the lack thereof, to the supposed events in many subsequent films was so blatant a trend that in 2022 a movie was realized under the title of *Amityville Gas Chamber*. This satirical comment on the arrogation of Amityville to all and sundry is merely the director reading Anson's original novel and farting.

More seriously, the immensely popular horror film *The Conjuring* (2013), which launched a successful cinematic universe, is but one of many flowing from the Amityville story and formula, with the serial numbers largely filed off, as it were. Demonstrating how fiction, reality, and popular narrative bleed into one another are Ed and Lorraine Warren. The Warrens were real-life husband and wife paranormal investigators, fictionalized as the heroes of the *Conjuring* films. They (in)famously performed a televised séance at the Amityville House in 1976. Lorraine has a cameo in the first *Conjuring* movie and a credit as a consultant in the first two *Conjuring* films; both Warrens were credited as "demonology advisors" on *Amityville II: The Possession*. They are also, again in fictionalized guise, the séance-faking con-artists at the beginning of *Amityville 3-D* (1983), the hero of which is based upon debunker Stephen Kaplan.

Putting aside all such notions for a moment, the physical Amityville House itself is a fine example of Dutch Colonial Re-

4. *Amityville II* also has an infamous motif of incest, which was apparently even more graphic before being heavily excised from the original cut.

vival architecture. Built in 1927, it has a characteristic gambrel
roof and (prior to a 1990 remodel) signature paired quarter-
moon upper windows. The image thus created, especially when
the windows are backlit at night, certainly creates by pareidolia
a credible illusion of a malign face. Such has been ubiquitous in
marketing since the 1979 film. The image has transcended the
horror genre to be a popularly recognized meme and visual met-
onym for a haunted house. For example, the *Simpsons* episode
discussed above includes a haunted house segment in which a
side view of the property is patently this famous view of the Amityville House. As is often the case with early *Simpsons* episodes,
the reference is a deep cut: the prominent view of the property
is actually from the side not the front entrance. Yet with typical
Hollywood vagary, and again illustrating the blending of fact
and fiction so important to the development of paranormal narratives, the house used for the filming of the initial movie is not
actually the Ocean Drive location. It is rather a lookalike house
in Toms River, New Jersey, of which a visible chimney in the
outer wall of the building adds to the pareidolic effect by ap-
proximating the place of a nose. The overall relationship with
Baranger's image, the copula that resembles the chimney placement in the commonly used Amityville House images is too distinct to allow of coincidence.

It is not merely a chance conflation. The circular and often
indirect nature of Lovecraftian influence lurks in the back of the
Amityville House folklore and mythology. Jeb J. Card's *Spooky
Archaeology: Myth and Science of the Past* (2018) states that "The
mix of Puritan, indigenous, and demonic evildoings in 'The
Dunwich Horror' may have influenced the backstory assembled
for the supposedly real *Amityville Horror*, including claims of an
indigenous burial ground and a space for the insane. There are
some strikingly Lovecraftian overtones in the tale" (232). The
most obvious clue is in the parallel names between "The Dunwich Horror" and *The Amityville Horror*, of which George Lutz,
father of the family in the Anson's account, stated in an interview: "I think Anson pulled it from a work done by someone
years earlier called 'The Dunwich Horror'" (Wilson interview).

Consider further the intersection of Lovecraft's story fragments "Of Evil Sorceries Done in New England of Daemons in No Humane Shape," mixing European demonological lore and native America practices, against the lines from Anson' s *The Amityville Horror,* the key original promotion of the haunted Amityville location:

> It seems the Shinnecock Indians used land on the Amityville River as an enclosure for the sick, mad, and dying . . . However, the record noted that the Shinnecocks did not use this tract as a consecrated burial mound because they believed it to be infested with demons. For how many uncounted centuries the Shinnecocks carried on in this manner, no one really knows; but in the late 1600's, white settlers eased the first Americans out of the area, sending them farther out on Long Island. To this day, Shinnecocks still own land, property, and businesses on the eastern tip of the Island. One of the more notorious settlers who came to the newly-named Amityville in those days was a John Catehum or Ketcham who had been forced out of Salem, Massachusetts, for practicing witchcraft. John set up residence within 500 feet of where George now lived, continuing his alleged devil worship. The account also claimed he was buried somewhere on the northeast corner of the property. (81)

Outside of the single factual claim about the Shinnecock Indian Nation, which does indeed still live concentrated on the eastern end of Long Island, all this information is without any validity. Anson's entire account reads like a extract from a Lovecraft pastiche. The implications of using the site as a form of Native American asylum ties in with the great Lovecraftian leitmotif of madness and the perception of his tropes of the insane narrator and asylum inmate. Furthermore, in addition to the black magic and rituals of "The Dunwich Horror," Lovecraft's story fragment offers of the dreaded and unusually shaped building that "'Tis said, one Richard Billington, being instructed partly by evill-Books, and partly by an antient Wonder-Worker amongst the Indian Savages, so fell away from good Christian Practice that he not only lay'd claim to Immortality in the Flesh, but sett up in the Woods a Place of Dagon, namely [a] great Ring of Stones,

inside which he say'd Prayers to the Divell, and sung certain
Rites of Magick abominable by Scripture" (CF 3.516). Others
were obviously influenced by the work as well. Graham Master-
son's bestselling debut novel *The Manitou* (1976) has as its protagonist a malign returned Native American shaman,
Misquamacus, the name of "that same antient Wonder-Worker
of whom *Billington* had learnt some of his Sorceries" (CF 3.516–
17) in Lovecraft's account.

Intersection and interconnection being a key theme of this
examination, the aforementioned Baranger reported with delight to being on the panel *Drawing Lovecraft* at the 2025 Angoulême International Comics Festival with the illustrator who
is our next subject of scrutiny, manga artist Gou Tanabe. His
work in adapting Lovecraft's stories into his native Japan's famous and popular graphic medium has been hugely successful
and widely praised both in his natal land and in translation.
Each successful adaptation has become seemingly a mandatory
nomination for the Will Eisner Comic Industry Awards, the
most prestigious prize in the field. The French-language version
of *The Shadow out of Time*[5] won the 2020 Angoulême International Comics Festival Prize for a Series. There is, as will be
made clear, a seemingly perfect marriage of manga and Lovecraft that goes beyond jokes about Cthulhu and the famous erotic woodblock print of *The Dream of the Fisherman's Wife* by
Katsushika Hokusai from 1814. Tanabe in many ways exemplifies this natural fusion. His style, suggesting many things even as
it fails to give an absolute clarity to overtell and oversell the image, blends seamlessly with Lovecraft's own painting in negative
spaces with words. It would be a significant monograph in itself
to examine all Tanabe's Lovecraftian offerings, and again the
purpose of this work is not to offer a review, as it were. Rather a
brief look at a few important aspects of the 2024 issuing of *H. P.
Lovecraft's The Call of Cthulhu*—the most current English translation as of this writing—should provide some insight into why
Tanabe's adaptations have been so successful.

---

5. The standard French translation of the title is actually the wonderfully
evocative *Dans l'Abîme du temps* [*In the Abyss of Time*].

The attention to the minutiae of detail is probably the most consistent element in Tanabe's work. Such dedication integrates well with Lovecraft's famous dictum about creating his tales "with all the care and verisimilitude of an actual *hoax*" (*Dawnward Spire* 244). For example, "The Call of Cthulhu" opens with an epigraph quoting from Algernon Blackwood. Naturally, Tanabe's manga work includes this, but has also added in the original source in Blackwood's "spiritual autobiography" (*IAP* 610), *The Centaur,* and 1911 publication date. In discussing the merits of the adaptation it is not merely that Tanabe is highly faithful to Lovecraft's original text without being a slavish copy. The acts of translation, first into Japanese for Tanabe to adapt from and then back into English, naturally mean that absolute fidelity is not to be expected. Of course, certain obvious key statements are verbatim, and the close approximations of the original text thread through the entire narrative. It is Tanabe's additions that speak of his devotion to the material and desire to create a worthy homage to Lovecraft's original whilst not making something akin to merely a pastiche in pictures.

To illustrate, in discussing the nocturnal cult activities of the *Alert* crew Lovecraft states that "cable advices from Dunedin report that the *Alert* was well known there as an island trader, and bore an evil reputation along the waterfront. It was owned by a curious group of half-castes whose frequent meetings and night trips to the woods attracted no little curiosity" (CF 2.46–47). Tanabe's take on the same information is highly telling: "the ship had a bizarre and evil reputation—not least because of its curiously tattooed crew, and tale surrounding the habitual torchlit revels on shore leave in Dunedin held in an isolated forest of the Silverpeaks" (143). The inclusion of the tattoos is of course an artistic setup and foreshadowing for their later depiction, wherein bands across their face give them a subtly inhuman aspect that adds to their terrifying appearance. This is very much in accord with Lovecraft's description that "there was some peculiarly abominable quality about them which made their destruction seem almost a duty, and Johansen shews ingenuous wonder at the charge of ruthlessness brought against his party during the proceedings of the court of inquiry" (CF 2.50). Equally important is Tanabe's additional genuine geographic detail of the Silverpeaks. This is a largely uninhabited elevated area of forest and scrub northwest of Dunedin. As with the mention of the South Pacific Gyre in the same section, also absent in Lovecraft but geographically accurate, this detail subtly adds to the credibility of the narrative. A more occult mention is when Tanabe cites the theosophical *Book of Dzyan* in connection with the prominent cult that Lovecraft references multiple times throughout the narrative. Such fits perfectly thematically—theosophists make claims to the work having ultimate extra-terrestrial origins—and adds to the verisimilitude, although Lovecraft himself would not mention this infamous fake tome until "The Haunter of the Dark."

Likewise, "the authorities at Tulane University" (CF 2.51) in Lovecraft's original are fleshed out in Tanabe. Specifically named is George Beyer, a genuine archaeologist of the place and period. Tanabe has Professor Angell, a biologist with a specialty in herpetology, ornithology, and medical entomology, at the 1908 American Archaeological Association meeting state: "George Beyer? I know him. He presented here some time back on the Catahoula mounds" (68) The real Beyer indeed excavated at the area in Catahoula Parish now known as the Troyville earthworks in 1895, whose Great Mound was at one point the second-largest such structure in height in pre-Columbian North America. The implications of ancient secrets, advanced civilizations, and forgotten history connected with these mounds was a popular belief in the nineteenth century. This was often overlaid with ideas of a lost white race of giants, and remains today in variant forms widely promoted in pseudo-archaeological theories. A contemporary headline about Beyer's expedition in the *New York Sun* (6 July 1896) as "Tracing a Bygone Race" and emphasizing their great size speaks patently to these notions. In addition to the sense of genuineness, this mention of Beyer in *The Call of Cthulhu* implies additional layers metatextually in the allusive, subtle, hinting, and vaguely connective manner employed by Lovecraft himself. Such might include the subconscious connection the informed reader might make to Love-craft's ghostwritten "The Mound" or the concluding sentence of section I of "The Dunwich Horror," which states: "Deposits of skulls and bones, found within these circles and around the size-able table-like rock on Sentinel Hill, sustain the popular belief that such spots were once the burial-places of the Pocumtucks; even though many ethnologists, disregarding the absurd improb-ability of such a theory, persist in believing the remains Cauca-sian" (CF 2.421). To this same point of archaeological fascinations one of the sailors, upon arrival at R'lyeh, declares: "I've been to Easter Island ... but this ... doesn't even com-pare" (202). The locale and its famous statues are not men-tioned in "The Call of Cthulhu" but do make a number of direct and oblique references in the total body of Lovecraft's fiction and are definitely germane to the Cthulhu Mythos specifically.

Yet that is not the only occulted reference. In the same American Archaeological Association meeting we are given a small vignette of the excited discussion Lovecraft describes:

> One sight of the thing had been enough to throw the assembled men of science into a state of tense excitement, and they lost no time in crowding around him to gaze at the diminutive figure whose utter strangeness and air of genuinely abysmal antiquity hinted so potently at unopened and archaic vistas. No recog-nised school of sculpture had animated this terrible object, yet centuries and even thousands of years seemed recorded in its dim and greenish surface of unplaceable stone. (CF 2.31)

In Tanabe's adaptation the Chitimacha are mentioned. They are a native people of Louisiana who notably speak—or rather spoke, as the language went extinct in the 1930s, although at-tempts are ongoing to revive it—a language isolate. This is a tongue that has no demonstrable connection to other linguistic families. Again, this hints obliquely at ideas of lost races and civ-ilizations, at least in popular pseudoscience. Lovecraft also notes of the idol: "Totally separate and apart, its very material was a mystery; for the soapy, greenish-black stone with its golden or iridescent flecks and striations resembled nothing familiar to ge-

ology or mineralogy" (CF 2.32). Tanabe has one of the professors speak of dravite, a crystalline silicate of the tourmaline family, and he laments: "I wish we had old Tschermak here" (69).
Gustav Tschermak von Seysenegg was an Austrian mineralogist
and petrographer of international reputation who was the discoverer of dravite. He would have been in his seventy-second
year and officially retired at the time of the conference. Metatextually Tschermak is also an early and important authority on
meteorites. In the original Lovecraft emphasizes the extra-
terrestrial origin by making the point twice in the tale: "I
thought with a shudder of what old Castro had told Legrasse
about the primal Great Ones: 'They had come from the stars,
and had brought Their images with Them'" (CF 2.48). Lovecraft himself is subtly referenced in Tanabe's version of the tale,
with Professor Angell's investigation in dreams of his acquaintances noting "a novelist dreamed of monoliths" (58) who is not
present in Lovecraft's original text.

Art is of course inherently subjective, but the three main characters of the story, Thornton, Wilcox, and Inspector Legrasse,
all—allowing for artistic license—bear enough of a resemblance
to Lovecraft himself to be a deliberate choice. This adds an in-
definable element to the tale and brings it together visually as a
narrative, and has distinct effects in places. The resemblance of
the face of a sacrifice by the Louisiana swamp cultists to our main
characters is an indirect but effective touch. Refreshing by its
absence is any critique of Lovecraft heaped upon him for his al-
leged failings as an author and admittedly often unpleasant racial
views. The story is presented as in its time, and no metatextual
virtue-signaling is awkwardly shoehorned into the text.

Other aspects of the pop-cultural absorption of Lovecraft
make fleeting appearances in Tanabe's work. His full-page image
of a copy of the *Necronomicon* almost certainly can be safely in-
ferred as the one kept under lock and key at Miskatonic University. Akin to the *Evil Dead* version mentioned earlier, it flaunts a
literal and, by implication, genuine human face as the cover.
Again, this is interesting for its metatextuality, both in the input
from secondary sources and the drawing in of a reference to an-

other Lovecraft tale in "The Dunwich Horror" and Lovecraft's universe of the Cthulhu Mythos more broadly.

Perhaps Tanabe's dedication to this work may be more simply illustrated by a gift he gave François Baranger after their panel together. It was a small, handmade model of the Cthulhu statuette from "The Call of Cthulhu," clearly the same image he used as a reference for the drawing in his adaptation. Such devotion pays important dividends. Probably the most famous of the modern horror mangaka, Junji Ito, stated: "I was interested in adapting the works of H. P. Lovecraft but Mr. Gou Tanabe did what I consider the definitive version, so I gave up on that" (ANN interview 2018).

Ito, who as of this writing has four Eisner Awards as but a part of his accolades, is not merely being polite. He has cited Lovecraft consistently as an inspiration. Typical is that Ito offers of the Old Gent that "his expressionism with regard to atmosphere greatly inspires my creative impulse" (Winsby interview). Likewise, Ito's citation of "The Colour out of Space" as particularly scary upon his original reading accords well with Lovecraft claiming it as one of his own favorites (ANN interview 2019). Various of Lovecraft's thematic threads, atmospherics, and literary ideals weave into Ito's work even as it simultaneously retains a consistent distinctiveness of its own. Lovecraft's history in Japan is both extended and obscured, with many adaptations and influenced tales and manga appearing long before formal translations. These stretch at least as far back as Nishio Tadashi's version of "The Statement of Randolph Carter" as "Grave" in 1947. Again Ito's large body of work, and his stimulation arising from Lovecraft being genuine inspiration rather than pastiche or arrogation of familiar names, make it too large a subject for our purposes here. Instead, we will focus on a specific nonfiction work. Ito's *Uncanny: The Origins of Fear* was published in English in 2023 and is an often autobiographical text looking at the art, ideas, techniques, and business of manga creation. At first glance, scrutinizing Lovecraft through a work that mentions him only once might seem hubristic. Yet a deeper examination of Ito and his creative process shows how deeply the Lovecraftian ethos has penetrated into his psyche, and by extension the wider horror community in Japan.

Consider the following intersection. UFOs were a major interest for Ito as a child. The rise of the nascent UFO culture in the post–World War II world and its evolution into ideas of ancient aliens has been definitely shown to have some deep Lovecraftian roots—contemplate for example our friends Jacques Bergier and Erich von Däniken. Ito is himself skeptical of such beliefs now. Yet the sense that "so many mysteries remained in the world" (39) formed a key stimulus upon his young imagination. Like many others of his generation, Ito was enamored of the work of movie stop-motion special effects master Ray Harryhausen. In a distinct echo of Lovecraft's own dictum stated above, Ito observed: "Harryhausen taught me that if you sincerely wish from the bottom of your heart to deceive people, then you must doggedly pursue reality" (54). It has an even clearer parallel with Lovecraft's statement in "Notes on Writing Weird Fiction" that "inconceivable events and conditions have a special handicap to overcome, and this can be accomplished only through the maintenance of a careful realism in every phase of the story *except* that touching on the one given marvel" (CE 2.177). The one marvel is a key Lovecraft diktat. Ito himself likewise strongly advocates such, stating under a heading "Tell Only One Lie": "to be exact, I allow myself one big lie per story . . . to make this nonsense make sense you cannot overlook the details of the story" (192–93). Lovecraft is famous—same might say infamous—for his lack of deep characters and characterization. He focused instead on other aspects in his fiction, perhaps best summed up in the statements that the "mere existence [of the one given marvel] should overshadow the characters and events" and "atmosphere, not action, is the great desideratum of weird fiction" (CE 2.177). Ito is again in close accord, stating that "my priority is the creation of a worldview," "I think it's preferable for characters to have little to no personality," and "characters are not the center of the world (not even the protagonist). They're nothing more than one of many elements in constructing the world" (238–39). Equally, Lovecraft's

work is replete with the negative ending and lack of the traditional triumph of good over evil. Ito offers "a horror manga protagonist must experience unusual worlds and be an anchor to
explain to the reader what's so scary about the situation. In other words they must not overcome the terror" (244).

Ito, in talking of the manga of Hideshi Hino he read as a
child, states that its "cruel depictions . . . contained an energy
and creepiness that stimulated the physiology and instincts in
the darkest recesses of the human mind" (57). Compare this
with the description of the artist's work in "Pickman's Model":
"That's because only a real artist knows the actual anatomy of
the terrible or the physiology of fear—the exact sort of lines and
proportions that connect up with latent instincts or hereditary
memories of fright, and the proper colour contrasts and lighting
effects to stir the dormant sense of strangeness" (CF 2.57). Like
Lovecraft, Ito felt the call of ancient works of art. Probably his
most famous and admired series—Ito himself calls it "my representative work" (Automaton interview)—*Uzumaki* [*Spiral*] has
very much such a genesis. This is in addition to the openly
acknowledged influence of Lovecraft himself. Ito stated that
"the different stages of the spiral were definitely inspired from
the mysterious novels of H. P. Lovecraft" (Winsby) and writes
that "the spiral is also a pattern from ancient times, found on
Jomon pottery from thousands of years ago, and you can really
feel its ubiquity and mystique" (164). Coincidentally or not, the
Jomon pottery figures known as *dogū* (earthen figures) have been
co-opted by von Däniken and his ilk as proof of alien visitors.
Their evidenceless hypothesis is that these are depictions of the
spacesuits of ancient astronauts. Showing further connection to
Lovecraft's own fascinations, Ito stated: "Lost lands and cultures
are a great source of inspiration too" (Winsby). Similarly, Lovecraft offered in a 1923 letter to Clark Ashton Smith that "Atlantis always captivated my fancy" (*Dawnward Spire* 61), and
further comparable references abound in his wider body of correspondence.

As with Tanabe, Lovecraft's influence on Ito is sometimes at
second hand. His *Gyo Ugomeku Bukimi* (*Fish: Ghastly Squirming*),

concerning fish who start walking upon the land, is "quite strong influenced by H. R. Giger, a Swiss artist who did the modelling design for the movie *Alien*" (171). Of course, the stimulus of Lovecraft upon Giger in general and this movie in particular is too well established to require excessive mention here. Influence is a river with many sources. Ito specifically named *Jaws* (1975) as an inspiration for the tale itself. Interconnections are intrinsic to the process of creation and often double back upon themselves. When asked in a 2018 interview about any horror films that have impressed him lately, Ito replied that *Annabelle: Creation* (2017) by David F. Sandberg was "interesting" (*Rue Morgue* interview). It is the fourth film set in the *Conjuring* universe mentioned above.

Unlike the merely written text, manga is equally a visual art form. This adds both immediacy and exactness to a depiction. It also simultaneously hamstrings the depiction of the indescribable that makes up so much of Lovecraft's imagery. Ito's solution is, typically, very Lovecraftian. He declares that "by combining something that does exist with something else that exists, you can create a new thing you've never seen before" (292). Consider in this light Lovecraft's celebrated description of the Cthulhu idol already mentioned: "If I say that my somewhat extravagant imagination yielded simultaneous pictures of an octopus, a dragon, and a human caricature, I shall not be unfaithful to the spirit of the thing. A pulpy, tentacled head surmounted a grotesque and scaly body with rudimentary wings; but it was the general outline of the whole which made it most shockingly frightful" (CF 2.23–24).

Staying with strongly visual media is that of film. Adaptations of Lovecraft, and even more so portions of his work or ideas on screen, continue to be produced at an ever-increasing rate. This is despite a widespread belief, for the reasons cited above having to do with the efficacy of written rather than visual depictions, that Lovecraft has a certain inherent unfilmability. It is an argument not without merit. Yet it equally holds overtones of an elitist perspective that the many terrible adaptations of Lovecraft have tended to reinforce. Again, this is not to be a review of such offerings, but merely a means to discuss Lovecraft, cultural perception, and the depth and diabolism of his penetrations therein. As a random example from one end of the continuum is the crowdfunded release *How to Kill Monsters* (2023). This horror-comedy deals with the aftermath of what in a standard film would be the conclusion of events. The movie beginning with the final girl—the embodiment of the trope of the sole survivor in a horror film—being taking into custody of the police for murder after a summoning of a demonic entity has been defeated. It is a deliberately sanguinary picture and has a number of allusions and homages to the tropes and important films of the Lovecraftian and wider horror genres. A facsimile of Cthulhu itself appears briefly, but the deeper and seriously intended Lovecraftian credentials are deliberately absent. It is more in the vein of Stuart Gordon's seminal schlock cult classic *Re-Animator* (1985) than Huan Vu's very faithful *The Colour out of Space* (2010).

At the opposite end of the spectrum is *The Substance* (2024), an A-list production with a wider theatrical release. It was nominated for the Academy Award for Best Picture, and won for makeup and hairstyling. Although not unfairly billed as a body horror film, *The Substance* uses its grotesquerie and surrealism more in the tradition of extreme excess and taboo breaking of the European arthouse—the director and wider production were French—than in the stomach-turning torture porn of the notorious, and decidedly American, *Terrifier* franchise begun in 2018. That said, *The Substance* wears its influences on its sleeve, as it were. These range from the literary in Oscar Wilde's *The Picture of Dorian Gray* to the cinematic in audio references to notable scores from *Vertigo* (1958) and *2001: A Space Odyssey* (1968). Plot, themes, and scenes are patently derived from *Death Becomes Her* (1992), David Cronenberg's *Videodrome* (1983), and especially his remake of *The Fly* (1986). Notably, there is probably a visual reference to John Carpenter's Lovecraftian remake of *The Thing* (1982) in the mutated form of Monstro Elisasue. Even more germane is the nature of the titular substance itself, which is injected hypodermically to generate the more perfect version of oneself. Its fluorescent green is practically an identity with the reagent used by Herbert West in the previously cited *Re-Animator.* That the typeface used to identify the substance on the label is of a kind with that used in the title of *Re-Animator* demonstrates the deliberateness of the homage.

Moving from tributes and influence to a direct adaptation is *Suitable Flesh* (2023). Directed by Joe Lynch, it is an unabashed and open, albeit ultimately rather loose, adaptation of "The Thing on the Doorstep." It has been described as a spiritual sequel to *Re-Animator,* whose shadow over Lovecraftian cinema looms ever larger. Nor is the comparison just marketing hype or loose referencing. The screenwriter of *Suitable Flesh* is Dennis Paoli, who wrote *Dagon* (2001) and co-wrote *Re-Animator* and *From Beyond* (1986) among other relevant works. The producers of *Suitable Flesh* include Brian Yuzna and Barbara Crampton. Yuzna produced the Paoli-written films and many others including the anthology *Necronomicon* (1993). One of the segments therein, "The Drowned," was the professional debut of the above-mentioned Christophe Gans. Fellow producer Barbara Crampton is famously the lead actress in both *Re-Animator* and *From Beyond* among a larger number of Lovecraftian projects. She also portrays Danielle Derby in *Suitable Flesh.* The deliberateness of the homage in *Suitable Flesh* to *Re-Animator* is patent. The establishing shot of the Miskatonic Medical School Building is the same as used in *Re-Animator. Suitable Flesh* likewise has a morgue very reminiscent of that from Gordon's film. Therein it was a faithful recreation of a genuine locale in Chicago, with *Suitable Flesh* apparently using a genuine mortuary. Key minor moments such as the holding up of a severed head are recreated, while Crampton herself at one point describes an ambulatory body as a "reanimated corpse" and is wearing oversize glasses as does her character in *From Beyond. Suitable Flesh* is dedicated to Stuart Gordon before the end credits.

This diffusion of Lovecraft is vital to understand his place in popular culture. Lovecraft as film is now recognizable as a subgenre of its own, which is often highly divorced from its font. As exemplar, the quixotic *Glorious* (2022) concerns a distraught man who encounters Lovecraft's creation Ghatanothoa in a roadside bathroom. Although darkly comedic in places, it is a far more serious horror film than this brief description would imply. In *Suitable Flesh* such changes to the source material are not merely the gender- and role-swapping of the characters, which the script (interestingly) plays in deliberate contrast to Lovecraft's original. In Lynch's film the body-swapping wizard is actively desiring and particularly enjoying inhabiting a female body. Despite the marketing, including one poster with a deliberately archaizing 1980s vibe, complete with faux-crease lines in the center giving the impression of being folded in quarter, the entire style and tone of the film are far from the cosmic horror and Gothic atmosphere one might reasonably expect from a Lovecraft adaptation. There are some customary accoutrements of the genuine esoteric and occult, both as predictable in the Waite home and less so in the psychiatrist's office, which is decorated with a ceramic phrenology head and a palmistry hand. The overall aesthetic is an interesting presentation of the erotic thriller prevalent in the 1990s, which is then jarringly combined with the brutally visceral bloodshed and Grand Guignol violence that was Gordon's trademark.

Lovecraft's original is followed only in broad strokes: innocent offspring is body-swapped with sorcerous father, to the consternation of a psychiatrist who then becomes the subject of such bodily swapping attempts. Yet as might be expected, given the pedigree of the creators, the distinct and stray Lovecraftian connections are many. The names are all recognizable in the film from the source material, albeit in sometimes different roles and gender-swapped as necessary. Certain moments and vaguely allusive lines, such as the dead body dragging itself off long past the point of death to offer warning, calls for cremation to end the horror, and repeated patterns demonstrating the swapping of personalities, are drawn rather patently from "The Thing on the Doorstep." An unnamed but familiar *Necronomicon,* complete with a face on the cover, is shown multiple times, including with images of Cthulhu. The newspaper covering the door of the Waite house is the *Dunwich Press,* and the house itself is correctly on High Street. (The home of Lovecraft's idol Arthur Machen was, like the house in the film, 33 High Street, but this may be coincidence.) The line "time is just a shadow to me" seems to allude to "The Shadow out of Time."

Most distinctly, Iä! Kamog and *fhtagn* appear in the film—as formulae to body transfer. Here we start to veer again into the absorption of diffused Lovecraftian ideas into the source material. The former two appear in the original story, as does the *Necronomicon*, but the latter term is primarily from "The Call of Cthulhu" and various revisions. Likewise, the perceived tropes of Lovecraft are in abundance. Ephraim Waite is much surrounded by the traditional paraphernalia of the pop culture necromancer. This is an association given an unlikely authenticity by the arrogation of Lovecraft and his creations into genuine occult practices. The story is primarily told as a flashback from an insane asylum. The original Lovecraft tale specifically stated that it was in a police interrogation, but this is not explicit in the story itself and the asylum narrator looms too large in Lovecraftian perception to cast aside easily. The ending of *Suitable Flesh* is unambiguous in having the maleficent force the victor, rather than the ambiguous horror of the unsettled fears and dangers to Daniel Upton in the original.

As we close out our survey, a look forward to an older art form seeing revival bears mentioning. In the wake of the explosion of the popularity of podcasts and the huge rise in audiobook listenership, there has arisen a concurrent interest in radio plays. The three media are rather loosely interconnected, and the blending of formats is common, with a podcast often having additional soundbites or music cues inserted or an audiobook being performed by multiple actors and with sound effects. For the consumer one of the key elements of difference is that listeners are free to perform other actions while they listen. Equally important for the producer of such content, the barrier to entry is remarkably low, especially as compared to other technology media. Lovecraft's work lends itself particularly well to all these formats. Many of his stories have an active chronicler or are told by a omniscient narrator, while the action occasionally dips into the voices of the characters. The outlandish and difficult descriptions already in the original material work far better in aural adaptation than a visual image necessary in other forms. Furthermore, it is almost redundant to state that the use of sound to create atmosphere is long noted for its effectiveness. Even the tendency of Lovecraft's stories to start at the conclusion and work back through the tale is a bonus in an age of short attention spans and the wish for instant gratification. Again, the point here is not to do a survey of the available options. The aforementioned low barrier to entry means there are literally hundreds of examples. These range from single failed backyard attempts through reasonably successful entries up to the BBC Radio 4 production of *The Lovecraft Investigations*. Thus hopefully three paradigms will suffice to give an idea of the whole.

The Atlanta Radio Theatre Company (ARTC) has created ten direct adaptations of Lovecraft's work. These include different live version of recordings, including one originally from 1990 featuring Harlan Ellison playing several characters in *The Rats in the Walls*. (This tale seems perhaps to hold a special appeal. Walter Koenig of *Star Trek* likewise performed readings of it at conventions in the same era.) For the ARTC this Lovecraft output is amidst a wide selection of other genre fare, and several original works in a wider Lovecraftian universe. While many of these are digital creations, others have become physical media, such as *The Dancer in the Dark*. This unfolds the adventures of Cletius Tremaine, Emeritus Professor of Archaeology at Miskatonic University, and is available in addition to a digital download as three CDs or in a novelization. Taking this idea farther are those gentleman at the forefront of Lovecraftian radio, the H. P. Lovecraft Historical Society (HPLHS). In addition to a complete audiobook collection of Lovecraft's entire literary output, including his revisions, and a podcast *Voluminous* focusing on his letters in minute detail, the HPLHS offers Dark Adventure Radio Theatre. In this they recreate not only Lovecraft's tales in the classic radio format but envisioned in the presentation as they might have been in Lovecraft's own lifetime, down to aspects of the time such as hosts and sponsor advertisements. They also come available as physical media, filled with additional props and paraphernalia to enhance the sense of verisimilitude. With the limited well of Lovecraft material having been drunk to the fullest, the HPLHS has taken to adapting related material such as Robert E. Howard's own take on the Cthulhu Myths in *The Black Stone*, prominent RPG modules such as *Masks of Nyarlathotep*, Lovecraft's idol and influence of Poe, and several original adventures.

The podcast *Archive 81* mixes all these ideas together. Beginning in 2016, it ran for three seasons with two miniseries for a total of 35 episodes. Not an adaptation of Lovecraft, it is nonetheless suffused with his energies and conceptions, and deals with the very Lovecraftian motif of a person reconstructing past events of a tragedy and bringing strange fates upon himself by doing so. *Archive 81* gathered an immense popularity and was transformed into a loose adaptation on Netflix in 2022 under the same name, which ran for a season of eight episodes, and wherein the Lovecraftian feel was even more noticeably present. The mixing in of the cult of a powerful seemingly extradimensional entity Kaelego, able to alter laws of space and time, demanding monstrous blood sacrifices during specific celestial timings, and appealed to by chants in an unknown tongue, is very clear as to origins, although it is blended with the trappings of 1920s occultism with their own drawing of theosophy and the dangers of technology as supernatural gateway seen in films such as *The Ring* series. Director of the original *Ringu* (1998) movie and several of the sequels, Hideo Nakata in turn has stated that he "was influenced by the Amityville series of horror films" (Meyer interview), and the cabin in which the cursed videotape is found in the original film with its patent eye windows was chosen for its resemblance to the Amityville House.

All the forgoing is merely a glimpse of some of the many ways in which Lovecraft remains alive and active in popular culture. His time- and place-specific tales seem paradoxically to have a timeless quality, and his locales and interests seem to have an endlessly mutable and transferable quality that is as difficult to define as it is impossible to ignore. Lovecraft in his lifetime refused to conform to markets and adopt the conventions of the genre. It is to our great fortune that his work was of such value that, in time, the genre and conventions have instead adapted to blaze further along the trails and vistas to the dark stars and hidden realms that he first opened.

Works Cited

Anime News Network. *Junji Ito Interview*, www.animenewsnetwork. com/feature/2018-10-31/interview-junji-ito-frankenstein/ .138863 2018.

———. *Junji Ito Interview*, www.animenewsnetwork.com/interview /2019-09-17/horror-manga-mastermind-junji-ito/.151216 2019.

Anson, Jay. *The Amityville Horror.* Englewood Cliffs, NJ: Prentice-Hall, 1977.

Automation. *Junji Ito Interview*, automaton-media.com/en/ interviews/20231115-22359/ 2023.

Card, Jeb J. *Spooky Archaeology. Myth and the Science of the Past.* Albuquerque: University of New Mexico Press, 2018.

Ito, Junji *Uncanny: The Origins of Fear*. Tr. Jocelyne Allen. San Francisco: Viz Media, 2023.

Lovecraft, H. P., and Clark Ashton Smith. *Dawnward Spire, Lonely Hill. The Letters of H. P. Lovecraft and Clark Ashton Smith*. Ed. David E. Schultz and S.T. Joshi. New York: Hippocampus Press, 2017.

Meyer, Joshua. *A Night Alone in 'Ringu' Cabin*, www.dreadcentral. com/editorials/466560/a-night-alone-in-the-ringu-cabin/ 2023.

Rue Morgue Interview: *The Legendary Junji Ito Talks About His New Anime Collection and More*. rue-morgue.com/interview-the-legendary-junji-ito-talks-about-his-new-anime-collection-and-more/ 2018.

Tanabe, Gou. *H. P. Lovecraft's The Call of Cthulhu*. Milwaukie, OR: Dark Horse Comics, 2024.

Wilson, Staci Layne. *Exclusive Interview with George Lutz and Dan Farrands*, horror.com/php/article-763-1.html,2005.

Winsby, Mira Bai. *Into the Spiral: A Conversation with Japanese Horror Maestro Junji Ito*. Tr. Miyako Takano, web.archive. org/web/20141022184345/http://www.78magazine.com/issues /03-01/arts/junji.shtml 2006.

Lovecraft in Mexico: Guillermo Samperio's "Borges, Escher, Lovecraft"

Michael Uhall

Guillermo Samperio (1948–2016) was a Mexican writer, poet, and creative writing instructor based in Mexico City, where he served as the director of the literature program at the National Institute of Fine Arts (INBA) from 1989 to 1992. Before this, he worked as a stained-glass artist, draftsman, and industrial technician at the Mexican Petroleum Institute. Beginning in the late 1960s, Samperio proved extraordinarily prolific, publishing more than fifty books and teaching countless workshops attended by virtually a whole generation of poets and writers in Mexico City. His prose is notable for its experimentalism and metafictional qualities, its subtlety—often blending psychogeographical reflections on the urban landscape of Mexico City with careful, moving, and sly insights into the mysteries of human personality—and its casual intermingling of the fantastic and the real.

Many contemporary Mexican scholars and writers recognize Samperio as a master of the essay, microfiction, and short story forms. In this regard, he might be profitably compared to some strange amalgam of Italo Calvino and Thomas Wiloch, heavily seasoned with the magical realist elements that Samperio, in part, helped to invent. As Mauricio Montiel Figueiras writes, "The evolution of the Mexican short story in the last four decades cannot be explained without the work of Guillermo Samperio." Likewise, Agustín Monsreal recalls, "He is one of the best short story writers of the second half of the 20th century. I met him when he was young, from the very beginning. We were friends. His most memorable work is in short stories and in microfiction, in which he was also able to develop certain capacities of conciseness, precision and accuracy in the handling of the idea of imagination and language."

Samperio remains largely unknown to Anglophone audiences, with only one small collection, *Beetle Dreams and Other Stories* (1994), having been translated. Playfully (and perhaps a little relatably), in a brief interview published by the Smithsonian Institution Scholarly Press (*Out of the Volcano: Portraits of Contemporary Mexican Artists*, 1991), Samperio remarked, "Deep inside, I felt I must be some kind of extraterrestrial."

His self-awareness and wit are perhaps nowhere more evident than in his clever and infinitely reproducible (indeed, perhaps omnipresent) microfiction, "El fantasma" (2009).

Samperio's impressionistic essay "Borges, Escher, Lovecraft" was originally published in the now-defunct journal *Metapolítica* 10, No. 47 (2006): 62–63. A brief history of *Metapolítica* (unrelated to *Metapolítica.news*), founded by a group of political scientists and theorists in 1997 and later transformed into an academic and cultural magazine, can be read in Mónica Cruz's 2004 review article "Metapolítica: Un ejemplo a seguir." Despite Jorge Luis Borges's seminal short story "There Are More Things" (1975), H. P. Lovecraft simply does not have much literary influence in Mexican fiction. Mexican writers who do engage with Lovecraft (or the Lovecraft Circle and its various afterlives) at length or with seriousness include Samperio, represented here, as well as the deeply underrated, profoundly talented Mexican author Emiliano González (1955–2021).

Mejor solo que mal acompañado.

Borges, Escher, Lovecraft (2006)

Like Escher and Lovecraft, Borges built his own labyrinth, a place of no place, of what is and is not, an endless forest without beginning or end. Only by means of an ambush is there an encounter—with the inner gaze, with everything and nothing, with doubt and truth, with the most powerful doubts and the most anguishing truths.

According to Jorge Luis Borges, the literary short story obeys the precise causality of magic, since magic is the overcoming of the nightmare of causality itself, not its contradiction. Howard Phillips Lovecraft stated that one of the reasons he gave his life over to writing fantastic stories was because they brought him closer to the fragmentary sensation of the marvelous.

The central concerns in the tales of Borges and Lovecraft are time and space. They turn time into a geometric figure: the labyrinth. With them, we can postulate that certain spaces are the representation of temporal states. No visual image can be fully described in words; no verbal image can be fully illustrated. Adriana González Mateos, in her book *Borges y Escher: un doble recorrido por el laberinto* [1998], discovers similarities between Borges and Escher that go beyond mere biographical comparisons, that go beyond the denial of time and rejection of realism they share. Instead, she examines the unusual parallels between some of their works—parallels that we also find in Lovecraft's work.

The quest shared by Lovecraft, Borges, and Escher led them to formulate an image of the universe in which conventional ways of understanding space have lost validity, which allows the discovery of other, strangely juxtaposed dimensions. Without disobeying the laws of perspective, Escher creates, in his artwork "Relativity," a disconcerting space where the notions of above and below, inside and outside, left and right are dislocated, causing the viewer to feel disoriented, uncertain of his own ability to comprehend what he is looking at—and perhaps even doubtful of his own spatial location. Likewise, Lovecraft describes the mythical city of R'lyeh in "The Call of Cthulhu" [1926] in the following way:

> The very sun of heaven seemed distorted when viewed through the polarising miasma welling out from this sea-soaked perversion, and twisted menace and suspense lurked leeringly in those crazily elusive angles of carven rock where a second glance shewed concavity after the first shewed convexity.

For Borges, the labyrinth is a symbol of confusion and perplexity, of being lost on the journey of existence. A similar tension can be felt in both Borges's and Escher's labyrinths, namely, the anguish and the vertigo symbolized by a space-time continuum virtually created to disorient its occupants, filled with the echoes of infinity. One of Borges's metaphors is the city of the immortals ["The Immortal" / "El inmortal," 1947], in which architectural elements are combined without discernible order. "Such an architecture had no end" and gives the impression of "interminability," of the "atrocious," the "intricately insane," until an anguished conclusion takes shape: "The gods who built the city were mad."

Borges, Escher, and Lovecraft all favored an abstract representation built more with archetypes, concepts, or generic images than with concrete particulars. Borges himself was interested in the Kabbalah, a current of thought according to which the universe is the result of the combination of the letters of a mystical alphabet. Lovecraft was interested in primitive mythologies and Gnostic philosophies, according to which the universe was created by demons or by some deficient demiurge or broken creator god. As for Escher, his work is a continuation of the arabesque, an abstract form of art created by Islamic artists under the prohibition against the representation of images imitating nature.

Borges and Lovecraft, then, are ironists—or, as Borges expresses it in his story "The Aleph" ["El aleph," 1945]: "Once again, I show my awareness that truly *modern* art demands the balm of laughter, of *scherzo*." Likewise, Lovecraft was actually a staunch materialist who scoffed at his blasphemous entities, and who was able to use them to parody the petty parochialism of our world. These two storytellers questioned the machinery of perception that leads us to give far too much credit to that which calls itself "reality."

Lovecraft and the Horror of Abstraction

Martin Dempsey

This article combines two arguments put forward by S. T. Joshi, that of the "rhetoric of the weird tale," and of Lovecraft's "complex antiquarianism," to propose that Lovecraft's letters and fiction, despite being very different in content, intended audience, and their expression of philosophy and worldview, share a deep-seated "horror of abstraction"—"abstraction" used here as an amalgam of every current definition of the word: dealing with ideas rather than events; freedom from representation; preoccupation; independent of association; removed from context. Once identified, reading his fiction with attention to this "horror of abstraction" reveals interesting nuances and insights into both Lovecraft the man and his writings.

It is, of course, imperative to separate an author from his fiction; but in the case of certain genres of fiction such as science fiction, utopian and dystopian fiction, and several other subgenres, it might be argued that at least part of its aim is to present the reader with philosophical questions. S. T. Joshi argues that this is case with weird fiction: "weird fiction is an inherently philosophical mode in that it forces the reader to confront directly such issues as the nature of the universe and mankind's place in it; in effect, writers of weird fiction are attempting to convince us of their view of the world" (*Decline* 5).

Lovecraft, as displayed in his letters, is fond of debate and of crafting an argument, whereas in his fiction he uses what Joshi has described as the "rhetoric of weird fiction"[1] to simultaneously

---

1. "[I]t appears that logic is customarily the principal method by which 'philosophical' writing (at least in the Anglo-American tradition) seeks to convey its

200

excaudate and simplify his views, to simultaneously distill and amplify, by literally objectifying cosmic indifference through monstrous avatars and placing a reader surrogate character within dramatic moments of epistemic collapse. Again, Joshi asserts: "I believe that Lovecraft's fiction is not merely an outgrowth but an instantiation of his philosophical thought" (*Decline* 10).

Though Lovecraft works within the familiar mechanics of storytelling, his fiction serves as rhetorical advocacy for materialist indifferentism through fanciful scenarios that strip away the anthropocentric veneer of reality. For example, Lovecraft is often criticized for the lack of depth in his characterizations, but when viewed in the light of rhetorical fiction, advocating for a philosophical perspective, his characters are revealed as reader surrogates designed to serve as a lens through which the audience experiences the narrative, providing a neutral or relatable perspective, with their most complex motivation and traits often being an academic background to assure the reader that, were there a rational explanation for the unfolding weird events, they would provide it.[2] This article will attempt to illustrate how a key rhetorical technique in this endeavor is *abstraction* and to imbue this abstraction with a sense of horror.

In *Monstrous Ontologies*, Caterina Nirta and Adriana Pavoni describe Lovecraft in the "default" manner that typifies the reluctant respect he has come to inspire within the "academy": "mainly a dilettante correspondent with a small following among his contemporaries" and the creator "of the subgenre of cosmic horror" (255). While Nirta and Pavoni admirably identify and articulate how monstrosity functions within Lovecraft's fiction, they imply and reinforce the often stated opinion that Lovecraft

---

worldview, while rhetoric (in its widest sense) is the means used in 'literary' writing . . . I believe the distinction—if interpreted with flexibility . . . is sound enough and can be applied to a wide range of writing, including Lovecraft's" (Joshi, *Decline* 6).

2. See S. T. Joshi in *Unutterable Horror* regarding horror authors in general: "It is not that they are uninterested in the portrayal of character or of interpersonal interaction, but that their focus is largely upon the psychology of fear as it affects individuals and groups" (28).

himself is a figure noteworthy for his contribution of the literary philosophy of cosmicism, but that in his personal life he was simply a rather closed-minded, xenophobic, reactionary nostalgic. The assumption is that his artistic contributions should be separated from the man, the art from the artist, and that Lovecraft the man should be reduced to a regrettable footnote to his own corpus. This article seeks to challenge this assumption by approaching Lovecraft's life and writings (fiction, nonfiction, and epistle) holistically, and to build on Joshi's argument that Lovecraft's fiction was a rhetorical expression of his philosophy.

Nirta and Pavoni push back against a view of "the monster" as "pure culture" (as Jeffrey Cohen put it programmatically in 1996), which, they argue, ends up "reducing the monster to an epistemological problem to resolve through deconstruction." Nirta and Pavoni instead assert that "the monstrous is not simply an epistemological construct, but that it has an ontological materiality that is real and that opens up to something else, a more that may be perhaps horrific and yet also productive" and "monsters are not the paradigm shift, rather, they are the paradigm shifting" (18–30). This description of the monstrous is a particularizing of what this article argues is Lovecraft's rhetorical technique of the "horror of abstraction": for Lovecraft "the paradigm" is not independent of that which it epistemologically locates and orients. For Lovecraft "the paradigm shifting" is the gasps of the onlookers, the "actual" shifting that has already occurred, in that the monstrous is the manifestation of the broader phenomena. For Lovecraft, monstrosity is one tool of many he employs in the service of a greater horror: the horror of abstraction *qua* abstraction. This rhetorical use of abstraction itself serves a wider purpose, which is to advocate for indifferentist materialism outside of the fiction.

The Logic of Antiquarianism

Lovecraft is a very difficult person to "pin down" in the precise nature of his views, not just because he tailored his message to his correspondent, but that his output is so voluminous that the emphasis he placed on different principles and topics shifted in line with his moods and experiences. S. T. Joshi notes: "It quickly becomes obvious that Lovecraft adopts different tones and personas in writing to different correspondents" (*Decline* 9), going so far as to warn the reader that "care must be taken in using them [the letters] as evidence for a given view on Lovecraft's part" (*Decline* 9), concluding: "If my tentative distinction between 'philosophical' and 'literary' writing is accepted, then it provides a justification for treating Lovecraft's avowedly philosophical utterances—expressed in letters and essays—separately from the philosophy underlying his fiction and poetry" (*Decline* 8).

Lovecraft expressed a wide range of views in his letters on myriad topics, including aesthetics, politics, ethics, writing, and philosophy. In regard to the themes most closely related to his fiction, in particular the "literary philosophy" of cosmicism of which he is usually attributed as founding, his indifferentist materialism remains a fairly consistent theme within his letters, and Lovecraft reports holding these views from an early age. His materialism, however, appears to have begun as highly pessimistic, transitioning to indifferentist later in life: "By my thirteenth birthday I was thoroughly impressed with man's impermanence and insignificance, and by my seventeenth . . . I had formed in all essential particulars my present pessimistic cosmic views" ("A Confession of Unfaith" [1922]; *CE* 5.147). Further, in a letter to J. Vernon Shea, Lovecraft reveals early suicidal ideation only relieved by his intellectual inquisitiveness: "The one time I seriously thought of suicide was in and after 1904." He overtly cites the love of knowledge as reason to live. In the same letter to Shea he writes: "And yet certain elements—notably scientific curiosity & a sense of world drama—held me back. Much in the universe baffled me . . . the idea of never knowing presented itself, the circumstances of frustrated curiosity became galling to me" (*Letters to J. Vernon Shea* 221–22). Here Lovecraft is describing a period earlier in his life (following the death of his grandfather and the loss of his birthplace in 1904) when he contemplated suicide, particularly by drowning in the Barrington River. He explicitly states that "scientific curiosity" and the frustrating awareness of all the things he *didn't* yet know but *could* learn if he lived were key factors in preventing him from ending his life.

However, it is not *pure* knowledge that seems to justify the frustrations of life for him, as he later argues in a letter written to Maurice W. Moe: "All rationalism tends to minimise the value and importance of life, and to decrease the sum total of human happiness. In many cases the truth may cause suicidal or nearly suicidal depression" (*Letters to Maurice W. Moe* 74). This pessimism is contextualized and often countered by Lovecraft's equally early adoption of a form of "complex antiquarianism": "It is as if in his early years (and by this we mean his life up to as late as 1925) it was aesthetics that was guiding Lovecraft's ethics and politics" (Joshi, *Decline* 19). Thus Lovecraft's pessimistic materialism became buffered by situating his knowledge within a sense of culture, history, and of place and, in Joshi's terms, "began to ebb away and was transmogrified into his celebrated 'indifferentism'" (*Decline* 18), as, it seems, his near (or actually) suicidal pessimism was buffered by a "complex antiquarianism":

> An ethical conception (futility of existence) has impelled, or at least augmented and made conscious, an aesthetic one (antiquarianism) ... Antiquarianism is a very complex notion in Lovecraft; while largely aesthetic (fondness for ancient and eighteenth-century literature and for colonial architecture, writing of archaistic poetry), it can also be ethical (adherence to older standards of conduct) and political (support of monarchism, aristocracy, and the dominance of the British Empire). (Joshi, *Decline* 19)

Adopting Joshi's view, that Lovecraft the letter writer used logical argumentation, whereas Lovecraft the fiction writer used the rhetoric of the weird tail, Lovecraft's philosophical views, when addressing paraxial and practical matters (politics, custom, and so on) might best be described as a form of "complex antiquarianism": "Always partial to antiquity, I allowed myself to originate a sort of one-man cult of retrospective suspiration" ("A Confession of Unfaith"; *CE* 5.147).

Lovecraft's cultural and aesthetic preferences (his antiquarianism) weren't just superficial but formed a comprehensive ethical and political framework: he wished for a culture oriented toward the expansion, preservation, and refinement of its core values and achievements, tied to specific historical standards and structures. Lovecraft's belief that humanity should strive to preserve the past—to be antiquarian—continued throughout his life and takes precedence over his politics. This impulse is mirrored in his correspondence; for instance, in a presumably unsent draft of a letter dated 13 April 1934, Lovecraft defends the New Deal on the grounds that it "values the essence instead of the surface forms of human quality, and tests its appraisals by standards deeper than those of mere convention and recent custom" (CE 5.118). In doing so, the shift in his political views away from championing aristocracy towards more socialist style interventions occurred *because* of his antiquarian values.

Lovecraft's complex antiquarianism aligns with the literary philosophy of cosmicism. In his letters he alludes to antiquarianism as being justified by appeals to nihilism, arguing, paradoxically, that traditions and customs are all that we have, lacking God, virtue, salvation, and afterlife, etc., and therefore they are the only valuable thing.[3] In the essay "The Materialist Today" (1926), Lovecraft echoes Pyrrhonism skepticism, using variations in social customs to undermine the idea that there is a "fixed mode" or "ideal mode" of human behaviour, uniting this skepticism with his own stance of cosmism. As he asserts: "It is most sensible just to accept the universe as it is, and be done with it. All is illusion, hollowness, and nothingness—but what does that matter? Illusions are all we have, so let us pretend to cling to them" (CE 5.76). Lovecraft sees no contraction between his "indifferentist" outlook and his "complex antiquarianism". In a letter to James F. Morton dated 30 October 1929, he pours scorn on the concept of universalism: "those people who maintain the gesture of universalism & cosmopolitanism would—ironically enough—suffer as much loss & bewilderment as the rest if such a chaos were actually to exist. Every one of us

---

3. Trung Nguyen describes cosmicism as a "literary philosophy . . . stating that there is no recognizable divine presence, such as God, in the universe, and that humans are particularly insignificant in the larger scheme of intergalactic existence" (182).

is, unknown to himself, a holder of an illusion fashioned wholly in the manner of his own especial culture" (*Letters to James F. Morton* 191). For Lovecraft the love of one's culture seems biologically or even materially determined (not a choice as such) and one he seems to believe, ironically, would universally benefit all who embrace it.

This initially seems to directly contradict his antiquarianism, but Lovecraft does not just identify with his culture and his customs: for him he and they exist in symbiosis, and he manifests them through praxis. This is seen in his description of his homecoming in a letter to Frank Belknap Long dated 1 May 1926: "There *is* no other place for me. My world is Providence" (*A Sense of Proportion* 71). Lovecraft expresses similar sentiments regarding how embeddedness and enculturation were fundamental aspects of his sense of self in a letter to James F. Morton (16 May 1926): "I am Providence, & Providence is myself— together, indissolubly as one, we stand thro' the ages; a fixt monument set aeternally in the shadow of Durfee's ice-clad peak" (*Letters to James F. Morton* 93). Lovecraft's antiquarianism is the direct opposite of abstraction: it is a simultaneous concretion and specificity, internalization and an absorption into one's culture. Lovecraft is aware that, viewed abstractly, these are illusions, but when cemented within their frame of reference they are for him an effective existential salve. The inverse, the counter, to the revelatory horror that comes with understanding the scale of the material cosmos is to be fully embedded in situ and inculturated: the precise opposite of abstracted.

Lovecraft's weird fiction highlights the ontic, the specific, the grounded, the foundational, and identity itself, as phenomena that can be undermined, and shows the inherent horror that necessarily occurs when they are. For Lovecraft this entails that all which is inimitable to human flourishing is that which undermines the individuated aspects human existence (both good and bad); and all which facilitates human flourishing conserves it; and the means by which these aspects are conserved, for Lovecraft, are *personal* engagement and enculturation into one's traditions, institutions, and customs. It seems, with very board

brush strokes, that Lovecraft's views were that within one's immediate space and time, the solution is "complex antiquarianism," the paraxial preservation and conceptual nostalgia for the
finer (and possibly idealized) aspects of one's past.[4] This is the
stance most commonly advocated for in Lovecraft's letters, and
via revealed preferences, his life. His wider philosophy of materialism, and its more pessimistic implications (which Lovecraft
touched on his letters), is expressed through his fiction. For
Joshi, Lovecraft's letters and his weird tales "are really two facets
of the same thing—they are, in effect, two different ways Lovecraft had of expressing his worldview" (*Decline* 8).

The Rhetoric of Abstraction

As noted above, Lovecraft is most commonly associated, philo-
sophically, with the concept of cosmicism. S. T. Joshi, however
complicates this assertion: "It is, in fact, interesting to see how
closely Lovecraft has followed his predecessors in the enuncia-
tion of his views [on mankind's insignificant place]" (*Decline*
39). Joshi concludes: "We can see, then, that what has traditionally been deemed the 'distinctive' element in Lovecraft's
work—cosmicism—is not especially distinctive as a philosophical conception, but is an inevitable concomitant to the general
materialist worldview" (*Decline* 40). Lovecraft's literary cosmicism is, therefore, his materialism expressed via the rhetoric of
weird fiction.

At first it might be confusing why an avowed materialist
would choose weird fiction as a means to convey these ideas, if
the concept of the rhetoric of weird fiction is correct; but this is
one of the aspects of Lovecraft's work that makes it truly innovative, and one of his main rhetorical techniques was his deployment of abstraction. Lovecraft's fiction conveys two

---

4. It is important to acknowledge that Lovecraft's political views shifted
throughout his life, from an ardent advocate for aristocracy to one of supporting more socialist interventions. This shift, however, seems rooted in his "virtue antiquarianism," as he came to believe that governmental socialist
intervention was the best means by which to preserve those aspects of his culture, environs, and society that he adored. For more see *IAP*.

recurring themes: antiquarianism (not just in the form of objects but also in the cultural and even ethical contexts these objects appear in and the individuals relationship with them) and the horror of abstraction, the undermining and erosion of the former always employed in the service of the latter. Both themes are rhetorical devices to advocate for his materialism, and his increasingly pessimistic conclusions about the nature of human existence he extrapolated from it.

"The Rats in the Walls" is, arguably, Lovecraft's greatest "Poe phase" story. As with many of Edgar Allan Poe's greatest works, the tale is one of obsession and fixation, but in Lovecraft's "twist" on Poe's troupe of protagonists consumed by obsession, Delapore is undone by both obsession and a physical situation—in the sense of location and circumstance. Delapore, led by the desire to reconnect with ancestral roots after the death of his son, renovates his ancestral estate, Exham Priory, and as the project reaches its conclusion he begins to see rats, which he comes to believe live within the walls of the building. Leading a team of investigators, Delapore discovers ancestral secrets and subterranean caverns beneath the estate. The question of whether the description of what is "down there" is "real" or just a projection by the protagonist's fractured mind is then raised as the narration becomes less and less reliable, but what seems clear is that Delapore ultimately attacks his companions and performs acts of cannibalism.

In the climax of "The Rats in the Walls," Delapore's final decent into madness and cannibalism is conveyed language as the narrator, Delapore, breaks down:

> "Curse you, Thornton, I'll teach you to faint at what my family do! . . . 'Sblood, thou stinkard, I'll learn ye how to gust . . . wolde ye swynke me thilke wys? . . . *Magna Mater! Magna Mater!* . . . *Atys . . . Dia ad aghaidh 's ad aodann . . . agus bas dunach ort! Dhonas 's dholas ort, agus leat-sa! . . . Ungl . . . ungl . . . rrrlh . . . chchch . . .*" (CF 1.396)

Breaking down this passage, we see a degeneration of language, and gain the impression of a reverse passage through time:

"'Sblood, thou stinkard, I'll learn ye how to gust": Here "gust" is probably a degenerate version of the Latin "geus," meaning "to taste or choose," and "stinkard" is a term for a pig. Together they may be read: "God's blood, you pig, I'll teach you to savour."

"[W]olde ye swynke me thilke wys?": In Middle English "wolde" is "would," "swynke" is "work," "thilke" is "this," so: "Would you serve me so?"

"Magna Mater! Magna Mater!": A Latin reference to the Goddess, so: "Great Mother! Great Mother!"

"Atys": The mythological figure who castrated the Phrygian king and was castrated in turn. This possibly implies that Delapore is castrating his victim, possibly with his teeth.

"Dia ad aghaidh 's ad aodann": Aghaidh and Aodann are archaic spellings of Aodann—"God against thee and in thy face."[5] Possibly implying Delapore is eating his victim's face.

"[A]gus bas dunach ort!": "May a death of woe be yours."

"Dhonas 's dholas ort, agus leat-sa!": "Evil and sorrow to thee and thine."

As the words themselves break down they reveal, and presumably occur concurrently with, the degeneration of the character physically; indeed, the two are aspects and possibly aspects of one another. The implication is that the narrator is engaged in the act of cannibalism as these lines are spoken or conceived, and therefore it is the process of performing the degenerate physical act that produces the degeneration of the speech act, and they "feed" into one another. The degenerate Delapore's language choice is a material, ontic component on his physical body. His name may be derived from the French *"de la porte"* or "of the gate," implying the body of the narrator is a portal of sorts (note the deliberate misspelling), and it is the narrator's coming to his ancestral home and physically descending under-

---

5. Lovecraft took the Gaelic words from Fiona Macleod's "The Sin-Eater" (1895). Macleod (pseudonym of William Sharp) provides a translation of the words in a footnote. That translation is reproduced here. See Sharp/Macleod 108n. I am grateful to S. T. Joshi for alerting me to Lovecraft's borrowing from this story.

ground that instigate his physical degeneracy.

The title and major theme of the story itself—the rats within the walls—reveals the anxieties embedded within Lovecraft's fealty to antiquarian values. Rats, the archetypal image of sneaking corruption, lie within the walls, the archetypal image of formal structure. When investigated by Delapore they retreat (withdraw) and vanish, yet they remain, and at the end the implication is that they were hallucinations, projections of Delapore's inner capacity for corruption. The "rats" were within Delapore, revealing Lovecraft's subtle implied pun on "house": the building whose walls are infested and the corrupt family lineage.

The manner of the actualization of Delapore's downfall in "The Rats in the Walls" stands in stark contrast to Lovecraft's own antiquarian ways, which are manifested by and therefore *constitute* his own physical being. The interpretation of Lovecraft's philosophy as fundamentally ontic has a cornerstone belief that unless something is physically represented, and often embodied, it has no mode of existence, perhaps even places a new light on his racism. While it neither forgives nor excuses his using slurs and voicing and defending racist ideas, it may be that Lovecraft believed that unless these ideas were spoken and written they had no actual existence. Therefore, on his own terms, his continual raising of them is even more proof of his commitment to them. For Lovecraft, then, there would be no contradiction or even difference between being an Anglophile antiquarian and being a racist; indeed, they would be ways to *be* (not manifest) and thereby *embedded* (the direct inversion of abstracted) in the same principles, ideas, and concepts in the world. "The Rats in the Walls" is a tale of someone attempting to achieve exactly Lovecraft's own solution to the materialist universe, "complex antiquarianism," and the horror is that this solution is inverted to reveal the scale of the problem.

When at his best—and certainly in his works that are most closely associated to his "Yog-Sothothery"—Lovecraft's horror operates not through direct confrontation with the monstrous, but through mediated glimpses. These are artistic renderings, corrupted lineages, and fragmentary accounts: through sculpture

("The Call of Cthulhu"), art ("Pickman's Model"), folklore and engravings ("The Shadow over Innsmouth"), or as hybridized bodies ("The Dunwich Horror," "The Shadow over Innsmouth"). The "mythos" entities themselves are most often described through apophatic language or deferred entirely, "depicted" via their impact on a third-party character. The horror is not the thing itself, but the realization that it exists at all. When the narrator's language attempts to grasp the entities themselves, it becomes apophatic, failing to affirm what they are and instead indicating what they exceed—gesture, scale, comprehension. The result is a horror built not on the entity's presence, or even their effects on the world per se, but in the epistemic collapse their very existence demands.

The sea demons or "Deep Ones" in "The Shadow over Innsmouth" are described in a carving as "half ichthyic and half batrachian in suggestion—which one could not dissociate from a certain haunting and uncomfortable sense of pseudo-memory, as if they called up some image from deep cells and tissues whose retentive functions are wholly primal and awesomely ancestral" (CF 3.168). Note the move here from an engraved image to the sense of epistemological unseating, whereby one's own physiology betrays one's understanding of the world and one's place in it. In "Pickman's Model" it is not so much the physical appearance of the ghouls that unsettles the narrator, as it is the accessing of latent instincts that reorient the narrator from civilized human being to a flighty animal: "only a real artist knows the actual anatomy of the terrible or the physiology of fear—the exact sort of lines and proportions that connect up with latent instincts or hereditary memories of fright" (CF 2.57). In both of these tales (and several others in which Lovecraft touches on the theme of hereditary and genetic inheritance) the threat is to abstract *you*: in the case of the Deep Ones from your culture and identity as raw biology, with the ghouls from your personhood into raw meat.

At the Mountain of Madness is noteworthy as the horror is not just of the revelation of human insignificance within deep time, but one of analogy: despite their alien nature the Elder Things are almost sympathetically described when compared to the manner of their civilization's decline—torn apart by conflict with an still more alien other, and from within by their own means of production. This horror by analogy emphasizes the risks—the horror—inherent in abstraction: the Elder Things abstracted their knowledge to create the abstracted entities of raw production, the shoggoths, which then rose up to destroy them. From an abstract perspective, the Elder Things, despite their technological and social advancement, proved but one among many races (who were alien and beyond treaty or trade); proved insignificant within the context of deep time and cosmic scale; and were ultimately defeated by their own knowledge and technology. Futurist philosopher Nick Land argues that the shoggoths *are* abstract capitalism: "The shoggoths originated as tools—as technology—created by the Old Ones as bionic robots, or construction machinery . . . In the vocabulary of human economic science, we should have no problem describing shoggoth as productive apparatus, that is to say, as capital" (249). The final horror in *At the Mountains of Madness* is unknown even to the narrator: "Danforth refused to tell me what final horror made him scream out so insanely—a horror which, I feel sadly sure, is mainly responsible for his present breakdown" (*CF* 3.156). The Elder Things are abstracted from their own culture via the means of production and by other cultures.

The Old Ones in "The Dunwich Horror" are never encountered, nor is such an encounter apparently possible in any sense that could be conveyed narratively, and, even more importantly, in any authentic, unfiltered manner: "Not in the spaces we know, but between them . . . of Their semblance can no man know, saving only in the features of those They have begotten on mankind" (*CF* 2.434). Thus the Old Ones are noumena in the Kantian sense, and beyond authentic engagement. They are the "abstraction of the abstract," so abstract they need to be recontextualized prior to any engagement.

The structure of "The Call of Cthulhu" is a series for increasingly immediate revelations and the removal of mediation between the narrator(s) and Cthulhu—first through a written account, then in the accounts via artistic representations, oral history, and finally a personal encounter. The structure also serves, in direction contrapuntal inversion, as a series of abstractions. Graham Harman has read Lovecraft's fiction, with direct reference to "The Call of Cthulhu" through the lens of Object Oriented Ontology, highlighting those aspects in Lovecraft's stories that he feels echo his (Harman's) philosophy. For Harman, objects exist independently of human perception and cannot be "reduced" to their interactions with other objects; there is a "real object" aspect to every object that cannot be encountered. Cosmicism, for Harman, is the artistic result of a universe populated by withdrawn, enigmatic objects; the hyper-natural creatures that populate Lovecraft's tales are withdrawn and withdrawing mysterious entities that elude human comprehension; the sublime and awe-inspiring nature of the encounters depicted capture the ultimately unknowable nature of reality. Graham Harman, in *Weird Realism: Lovecraft and Philosophy*, contends that many of Lovecraft's numerous "godlike" entities have a significant physical component which is soon undermined,[6] and their undermining (or, in Harman's terms, "withdrawing") reveals their horrific nature, which Harman reads as testament to and a "bringing to the fore" of the way in which everyday objects withdraw their fundamental "essence" (in a materialist sense—that which makes them "them") and that other objects and human beings may only encounter them on a sensory level.

Harman describes in *Weird Realism* how the idol (the "Horror in Clay") proves a sensory framework to interpret Cthulhu, and he argues that this is a typical part of Lovecraft's style, which "is what I have called the 'vertical' or allusive aspect of Lovecraft's style—the gap he produces between an ungraspable thing and the vaguely relevant descriptions that the narrator is able to attempt" (17). Harman does not press his interpretation beyond this point, but given the title of the segment in which this passage occurs, it seems fair to argue that the "Horror in Clay" is, in

6. So much so that the term "Titan" or "Jötunn" might be a better term than "god." For example, Cthulhu has an awkward physical aspect that seems to shift in and out of reality that "stumbles" and "plops."

an OOO sense, a literal description: the horror is "in" the clay: the "horror" is the clay's withdrawn essence, and this "horror" is, in some sense, *actually* Cthulhu, but that this aspect is hidden under the mere physical artistic rendering in clay of something that cannot be comprehended, let alone depicted. When the OOO reading is extended in this fashion, the clay itself gains a protective quality: *the ontic protects us from the horror bound within it of raw, untethered "ontologicality."*

In terms of the narrative, the function of the idol (the horror in clay) is to emphasize how much Cthulhu is *not* like the idol (despite persistent attempts by pop culture to equate Cthulhu with the idol via plushies, illustrations, and figurines). The idol is an artist's impression, an attempt to provide a formalized chimera to convey some impression of what impressions an encounter with Cthulhu would engender. However, the actual eyewitness accounts reveal: "The Thing cannot be described—there is no language for such abysms of shrieking and immemorial lunacy, such eldritch contradictions of all matter, force, and cosmic order" (CF 2.53). Not only is Cthulhu beyond description, but abstraction surrounds It. Darkness itself, in R'lyeh, is "almost material": "That tenebrousness was indeed a *positive quality;* for it obscured such parts of the inner walls as ought to have been revealed, and actually burst forth like smoke from its aeon-long imprisonment, visibly darkening the sun as it slunk away into the shrunken and gibbous sky on flapping membranous wings" (CF 2.52–53). Geometry itself becomes abstract: "an angle which was acute, but behaved as if it were obtuse" (CF 2.53), and, indeed for Cthulhu "even death may die" (CF 2.40). Cthulhu generates these paradoxes via an infectious abstraction.

H. P. Lovecraft describes the "abnormally chromatic entity" in "The Colour out of Space" in a letter to Elizabeth Toldridge as "only one of the lot I which take any pride in": "Most of my monsters fail altogether to satisfy my sense of the cosmic" (*Letters to Elizabeth Toldridge* 39). In the tale a meteorite lands near a farm and a mysterious Colour starts to tint the surroundings, causing ruination. The Colour spreads, and "suckin' the life out of everything" (CF 2.387), it leaves behind a desolate wasteland. As Lovecraft honed his ideas and craft, the otherworldly entities his protagonists encounter tend to become less and less anthropometric, and crucially for our purposes increasingly abstract, more and more "other," until they are simply "The Colour out of Space," which Lovecraft said of: "I liked that tale myself about as well as any I've written" in a letter to Clark Aston Smith dated 31 January 1928 (*Dawnward Spire* 153).

The "monster" is just a "colour": something that can only be perceived by its slight effects on lighting around objects, resulting in "a colour," a metaphor for the horrors of radiation and pollution. "The Colour out of Space" may be read simply as a story about a radioactive comet, yet via Lovecraft's portrayal the Colour appears to be a force of ontic erosion, and, again crucially, it is the evidence of physical erosion that it causes which is the source of the horror, and as the material erodes so do the ontological components of the lives of its victims: the crops fail and so the farm business fails; the bodies of the victims are compromised and so their minds and their relationships fail; finally, the witnesses are all gone, as is the location—reduced to a "blasted heath" (CF 2.368)—and so the events, too, are lost to the unreliable narration. The Colour's transformative effects on the land and its inhabitants symbolize the breakdown of traditional ontological categories and the dissolution of individual ontic identity. As the Colour spreads and consumes everything in its path, it blurs the distinction between living and non-living, organic and inorganic, human and non-human. "Onticality" itself is eroded. The ontological is rendered chaotic and only second-hand subjectivity and confusion remain.

By the early twentieth century, scientists such as James Clerk Maxwell and others had established that visible light is just one segment of the electromagnetic spectrum, and that color perception is indeed a sensory interpretation of wavelengths, which are cosmic radiation. Lovecraft's interest in science is well documented, and in every sense, "The Colour out of Space" is a story that merges the rhetoric of weird fiction with a pseudo-documentary of radiation sickness. It is not "just" the case that the Colour is highly abstract (it's "just a colour" [CF 2.397]); it is that it's "just" a pseudo-natural phenomena, and just as too much water is toxic, exposure to color (radiation) can be inimicable to human life. The rhetorical point is that reality itself is inimicable to human life within a certain context or dose—when abstracted. At heart, Lovecraft's weird fictional horrors were surrogates (and often thinly veiled ones) for what he viewed as "real" existential threats (from the "threat" of miscegenation and globalism in the case of the Deep Ones to cosmic radiation in "The Colour out of Space"). None of Lovecraft's horrors were, in this sense, fictitious, only their means of delivery: they were rhetorical flourishes for reality viewed at scale. Lovecraft's antiquarianism is a bulwark against this fundamental aspect of reality.

While Harman's interpretation of Lovecraft's weird tales illustrates beautifully both Object Oriented Ontology's key concepts and the depth of Lovecraft's skill in his ability to capturing an arguably fundamental aspect of humanity's phenomenological relations, this reading focuses solely on Lovecraft's fiction and his portrayal of non-human entities and the challenge they pose to anthropocentric views of reality. The suggestion that Lovecraft should be read with an eye to the pervading "horror of abstraction" is not intended to undermine, replace, or compete with Harman's, but to complement the stance that Lovecraft should be "viewed as a writer of gaps between objects and their qualities"—*in effect a writer and philosopher of abstraction presented in the rhetorical style of horror* (Harman 19). Lovecraft's horrors don't just kill you; they take your past, they nullify your teleology (your future and purpose), and they erase your identity (diluting you from a fixed point in a cultural network into a speck on a speck within an uncaring cosmos). For example, the immortal alchemists of *The Case of Charles Dexter Ward* abstract you from your body, by capturing your essential salts, and this process abstracts you from any other sense of essence by removing comforting illusions of a soul, a psyche, or any non-material sense of self, and both Joseph Curwen and Asenath/Ephraim Waite abstract you from your social identity.

Any detailed study of Lovecraft, both the man and the author, will reveal that he was a complex person whose views changed throughout his life and that he would vary the manner and virulence of their expression to fit his audience (just like any other human being). What this article has attempted to do is to lay out the case that for Lovecraft, intentionally or otherwise, abstraction was a vital rhetorical method. The nature and manner of this abstraction varied in regard to whether it was in relation to his personal cultural preferences or as to his deployment of the rhetoric of the weird tale to advocate for his indifferentist materialism. The upturning of materialism within his weird fiction is a rhetorical exercise, but it (materialism) remains "true" in *principle* if not in *fact:* the implications for humanity of "Yog-Sothothery" *and* of materialism are effectively identical (and, in truth, "Yog-Sothothery" is in sense less "pessimistic" in that it offers humanity *more* agency, even if it is an agency that is corrupting and ultimately inimicable to flourishing).

As Lovecraft's influence has become more mainstream, attempts have been made in multiple genres and formats to systematize the world(s) his weird tales occur in and to give taxonomy for the entities and/or phenomena he describes. However, as this article has tried to demonstrate, not only was this not Lovecraft's intention but a closer reading of his stories reveals it to be impossible: we do not know what Cthulhu even looks like; the tales of the Old Ones are the ravings of a madman; we have descriptions of paintings of ghouls, but not even apophatic eyewitness accounts; there are only physical descriptions given by first-hand eyewitness of hybrids; we cannot even conceive of a "new colour," and so on. In possibly Lovecraft's most famous quotation we can note the active terms:

> The most merciful thing in the world, I think, is the inability of the human mind to correlate all its contents . . . some day the piecing together of dissociated knowledge will open up such terrifying vistas of reality, and of our frightful position therein, that we shall either go mad from the revelation or flee from the deadly light into the peace and safety of a new dark age. (CF 2.21–22)

These terms are, of course themselves antinomies of abstraction: *inability;* the *correlation of contents; dissociated* knowledge. Thus it is the *inability* to fully *abstract* these elements which keeps us sane. To conclude: Lovecraft's logic of materialism and the inherent implications of scale were portrayed rhetorically via his weird fiction, and one of his most potent tools for this was abstraction.

Works Cited

Harman, Graham. Weird Realism: Lovecraft and Philosophy. Winchester: Zerobooks, 2012.

Joshi, S. T. *H. P. Lovecraft: The Decline of the West.* 1990. Berkeley Heights: Wildside Press, 2000.

———. *Unutterable Horror: A History of Supernatural Fiction.* New York: Hippocampus Press, 2014.

Land, Nick. *A Nick Land Reader: Selected Writings.* eBook, Anonymous, 2017.

Lovecraft, H. P. *Letters to Elizabeth Toldridge and Anne Tillery Renshaw.* Ed. David E. Schultz and S. T. Joshi. New York: Hippocampus Press, 2014.

———. *Letters to J. Vernon Shea, Carl F. Strauch, and Lee McBride White.* Ed. S. T. Joshi and David E. Schultz. New York: Hippocampus Press, 2016.

———. *Letters to James F. Morton.* Ed. David E. Schultz and S. T. Joshi. New York: Hippocampus Press, 2011.

———. *Letters to Maurice W. Moe and Others.* Ed. David E. Schultz and S. T. Joshi. New York: Hippocampus Press, 2018.

———, and Frank Belknap Long. *A Sense of Proportion: The Letters of H. P. Lovecraft and Frank Belknap Long.* Ed. David E. Schultz and S. T. Joshi. New York: Hippocampus Press, 2025.

———, and Clark Ashton Smith. *Dawnward Spire, Lonely Hill: The Letters of H. P. Lovecraft and Clark Ashton Smith.* Ed. David E. Schultz and S. T. Joshi. New York: Hippocampus Press, 2017.

Nguyen, Trung. History of Humans. (*Is There a God?, Book* 3.) n.p.: EnCognitive, 2016.

Nirta, Caterina, and Adriana Pavoni. "Introduction." In Monstrous Ontologies: Politics Ethics Materiality, ed. Caterina
Nirta and Adriana Pavoni. Wilmington, DE: Vernon Press,
2021. 18–30.
Sharp, William (and Fiona Macleod). *The Sin-Eater and Other
Weird Stories.* Ed. S. T. Joshi. New York: Hippocampus Press,
2025.

Briefly Noted

With publication of *A Sense of Proportion: The Letters of H. P.
Lovecraft and Frank Belknap Long,* the effort to publish Lovecraft's letters has come to a close (although "Letters to the *Providence Journal*" herein shows that fugitive letters may continue to
emerge from time to time). But readers seeking Lovecraft's letters may be find solace in *Hail Stylites!*—a collection of letters *to*
Lovecraft to be published by Hippocampus Press in 2025. Ernest
A. Edkins, an old-time amateur journalist, corresponded with
Lovecraft for the last four years of the latter's life, during which
time, thanks to Lovecraft, Edkins resumed activity in the National Amateur Press Association. (This parallels the events
chronicled in *Letters to Hyman Bradofsky and Others.*) As such,
the book represents the "flip side of the coin"—a correspondent's response to letters Lovecraft wrote to him. The discussion
is lively, and the elder statesman pulls no punches in friendly
debates with Lovecraft on myriad topics. A related collection
soon to be available is *Letters to R. H. Barlow,* a familiar name to
readers of *Lovecraft Annual.* The letters afford insight into the
various "careers" of Lovecraft's most devoted disciple—
including letters, from Edkins and E. Hoffmann Price, urging
Barlow not to aspire to be a mini-Lovecraft, but to seek his own
path. And this Barlow did. The book complements *Eyes of the
God* which collects Barlow's creative writing over those various
"careers" leading to his ultimate career as a Meso-American an-
thropologist.

How To Read Lovecraft

A Column by Steven J. Mariconda

Part 8: Extra-Cosmic Consciousness

Picture an average, unsuspecting reader—one who likes Stephen King, or J. K. Rowling, or perhaps Lemony Snicket, and who played a Cthulhu role-playing game years ago. On the online social media platform where they spend hours each day, posters are up voting somebody named H. P. Lovecraft. Our reader, finally convinced by noticing their sister's Cthulhu plushie slippers, stops by Barnes & Noble and finds Penguin's *The Thing on the Doorstep and Other Weird Stories* (2001). Settled in back at home, they pick up the book and open to the first item. Hmm, story about a tomb it says here. They likely expect to read something like this.

> I'm confined in an insane asylum. My narrative will be doubted.

In other words, something that reads like a text message. Instead, they meet this:

> In relating the circumstances which have led to my confinement within this refuge for the demented, I am aware that my present position will create a natural doubt of the authenticity of my narrative. (CF 1.38)

The first reaction of our unprepared reader might be: "What?" Now, consider that this reaction is one that Lovecraft is *soliciting on purpose*. It is *not* evidence of his verbal incompetence.

We have arrived at the topic central to understanding Lovecraft: his prose style. It remains a stubborn "truism" in popular accounts that Lovecraft's style was an embarrassment. But the single most important thing in here is to recognize that his style was *thoughtfully crafted* to create atmosphere. Surely he was quite capable of writing linear sentences without ornamentation. But this didn't suit his purpose: to convey a mood. Neither did it *amuse* him to write in the standard idiom expected in a short story. In our discussion of play and humor in Lovecraft we have seen that for him "nothing in existence is more important than elegant amusement" (3 September 1929; *Letters to Elizabeth Toldridge* 99).[1]

Dirk W. Mosig, one of Lovecraft's most astute critics, suggested as early as 1978 that he is *sui generis* and thus is most profitably read as such.

> Lovecraft's works defy classification. They are not science fiction, for they do not involve extrapolation to possible futures or alternative universes . . . They are not fantasy tales, in the sense in which J. R. R. Tolkien's are. They are not ghost stories, nor mysteries, nor do they fit into any of the other traditional categories. . . . They are simply imaginative stories . . . European critics, who in general do not seem to suffer of as severe a case of classificatory compulsiveness as their American counterparts, have been able to treat Lovecraft as a writer (rather than as a writer of science fiction, fantasy, or what not), which perhaps explains in part their more positive reaction to his work. (16–17)

The most constructive way to read Lovecraft, then, is not as a genre writer or even as an American short story writer. He is a category unto himself. The vast number of authors attempting to write in his style, and failing, are attestations to this. These writers use the apparatus rather than the approach.

The misunderstanding of this writer's style is, in part, because of the common image of him a periwigged eighteenth-century gentleman (or an antiquated crank). Readers may be wary in advance of opening a book of what they anticipate to be "old-fashioned" writing. Little do they know that Lovecraft took as much from Modernist fiction as he did from Swift, Johnson, and Addison. Arriving at the same place as the Moderns by a different route, he said of the latter:

---

1. See this space, *Lovecraft Annual* No. 14 (2020): 77–82.

Modern art does not emulate photography, but tries to incorporate some essence of the subjective—some hint of the inward & unreal perspective through which the artist individually & uniquely views his subject. . . . Modern art tries to shew what an artist sees when he looks at a thing. It is not, except nominally, a portrait of the object. Essentially it is a diagram of the artist's *mood.* (23 October 1931; *Letters to J. Vernon Shea* 67–68)

This is congruent with Lovecraft's program as a creative writer. In "Notes on Writing Weird Fiction," he states: "usually I start with *a mood* . . . which I wish to express, and revolve it in my mind until I can think of a good way of embodying it in some chain of dramatic occurrences capable of being recorded in concrete terms" (*CE* 2.176; my emphasis). In July 1923, the nominally traditional fiction writer made a starling pronouncement to his amateur journalist colleagues, from the lofty perch of "In the Editor's Study" in the *Conservative:*

What is art but a matter of impressions, of pictures, emotions, and symmetrical sensations? It must have poignancy and beauty, but nothing else counts. *It may or may not have coherence.* If concerned with large externals or simple fancies, or produced in a simple age, it is likely to be of a clear and continuous pattern; but if concerned with individual reactions to life in a complex and analytical age, as most modern art is, *it tends to break up into detached transcripts of hidden sensation* and offer a loosely joined fabric which *demands from the spectator a discriminating duplication of the artist's mood.* The Philistine clamour for a literature of plain statement and superficial theme loses force when we assign to literature—especially poetry—its proper place in aesthetics, and compare it to such modes of expression as music and architecture, which do not speak in the language of primers. . . . Traces of this tendency, whereby *pictorial methods are used, and words and images employed without conventional connexions to excite sensations,* may be found throughout literature; especially in Keats, William Blake, and the French symbolists. This broader conception of art does not outrage any external tradition, but honours all creations of the past or present which can shew *genuine ecstatic fire* and a glamour not tawdrily founded on utterly commonplace emotions. (*CE* 2.71; my emphasis)

Lovecraft places demands upon us—reading that is reflective and recursive, with a sensitivity to word connotations and rhythm.

Aside from an emphasis on mood and hatred of Victorianism artificiality, the fundamental commonality between Lovecraft and the Moderns was an intense interest in *subjective states of consciousness.* In July 1932 he wrote:

> We realise in this age as never before the *confused, irrelevant hodge-podge of complexities which constitutes our real inner cerebral life* behind the mask of conventional simplicity and *coherence. . . .* We have a right to object to the deliberate suppression or wilful neglect of links between a primary image and any *comprehensible* "reality" which the poet may himself envisage as the source of the image. But we must not forget that in many cases a powerful and clear-cut primary image may exist without being referable to any single source in reality. In such cases, the want of a concrete interpretation ought not to chain the poet down to silence. Perhaps his readers can interpret what he cannot—and perhaps there are as many possible (and equally valid) interpretations as there are different persons in the world. (12 July 1932; *Letters to Maurice W. Moe* 291; my emphasis)

The statement that "[p]erhaps his readers can interpret what he cannot—and perhaps there are as many possible (and equally valid) interpretations as there are different persons in the world" has the flavor of reader-response criticism. Lovecraft cares less what the materials are, and more that the reader feels the emotions he is attempting to evoke. Reader-response criticism also emphasizes how readers react to literary works, rather than treating the works as self-contained objects with fixed meanings. Any individual's freedom of interpretation is constrained in advance by his or her life experience, psychological constitution, education, and other circumstances. What we have been discussing in this column is the reader's opportunity to modify learned ways of reading and discovering new strategies for enjoying and appreciating this unique author (Baldick, *Criticism and Literary Theory* 171; *Oxford Dictionary of Literary Terms* 212).

So each of us arrives at Lovecraft with a unique set of skills and expectations. The experience of reading Lovecraft is inimi-table and comes as something of a jolt to the unsuspecting. Some may be familiar with Poe, who set the example, but Love-craft is far more radical. He expands upon Poe's innovative em-phasis on the consciousness of the narrator by factorial increasing the use of a sophisticated set of narratological modes—strategies for presenting *consciousness in the text.*

Commentators have noted "The Outsider" could pass for a lost tale of Poe. On the contrary, the story's differences from Poe illustrate just how "modern" is Lovecraft. Foremost is the con-cern we see in "The Outsider" with *the Self* and its alienation from wholeness and from the world. Malcolm Bradbury says a Modernist work typically exhibits "node[s] of linguistic energy" (50). One can find at least one such "node" in most of Love-craft's tales.

> I did not shriek, but all the fiendish ghouls that ride the night-wind shrieked for me as in that same second there crashed down upon my mind a single and fleeting avalanche of soul-annihilating memory. . . . Now I ride with the mocking and friendly ghouls on the night-wind, and play by day amongst the catacombs of Nephren-Ka in the sealed and unknown valley of Hadoth by the Nile. I know that light is not for me, save that of the moon over the rock tombs of Neb, nor any gaiety save the unnamed feasts of Nitokris beneath the Great Pyramid; yet in my new wildness and freedom I almost welcome the bitterness of alienage. (CF 1.271–72)

Similar are the denouements of "The Dunwich Horror," "The Rats in the Walls," *At the Mountains of Madness,* "The Haunter of the Dark," and many others. The unconventional method serves not only to heighten the emotional impact during the reading, but also to cement the feeling-tone in the memory upon closing the book. Lovecraft is endlessly re-readable because we want to re-experience that feeling, and try again in a more mindful fashion closely attending to one's reactions.

Lovecraft's Soliloquy of the Mind

Lovecraft's horror has two poles. The first, of course, is the notion that mankind does not have a unique and exalted place in the universe, but is subject to indifferent natural law—it is the least of many beings in the universe and even on earth. Man is "a buffoon" who may have been created "as a jest or mistake" (*CF* 3.100, 41). The second source stems from the perils of existing inside a human mind, one that is vulnerable and ill-adapted. It is unfit to accommodate the revelation of the indifferent cosmos. Further, the demarcation between reason and unreason is fragile and permeable; human cognition, emotion, morality, and personality are the thinnest façade protecting us from atavism and madness.

In Lovecraft's most effective and characteristic tales, not much horror actually occurs in the physical world. The most important action occurs *within in the narrator's mind*—thus the need for a radical approach to first-person narration. In "The Shadow over Innsmouth" the narrator sees a lot of very creepy people and has a bad experience with his travel accommodations; what matters, however, is *his realization* that a race of fish-frog-men are standing by to take over the world and then—worse—the "shock of recognition" that he is one of the fish-frog-men.[2] Albert Wilmarth, narrator of "The Whisperer in Darkness," urges the reader in very first sentence to "[b]ear in mind closely that I did not see any actual visual horror at the end" (*CF* 2.467). He gets odd letters from an eccentric rustic, sees a black stone, hears buzzing voices on a primitive recording. He doesn't see anything horrible happen in exterior reality. The final straw is observing a

---

2. The kind of deliberate dumbing-down of Lovecraft's plots as a way of razzing the author goes back to Edmund Wilson's famous comment in "Tales of the Marvellous and the Ridiculous." He says "The Shadow out of Time" is unworthy because it is "about" an "invisible whistling octopus" (*Classics and Commercials* 288). Of course, the story is actually "about" realizing that "hope [is] impossible" (*CF* 3.280). But the comment goes to show how Lovecraft, with his concepts but without his prose style, is not Lovecraft. Wilson, once regarded as among leading American literary critics of the twentieth century, demonstrably misses the point.

kind of prosthetic hands and mask lying on a chair, which pre-
cipitates a total interior collapse. He flees in a hijacked car: "I
actually managed to get out of that room and that house without making any further noise, to drag myself and my belongings
safely into the old Ford in the shed, and to set that archaic vehicle in motion toward some unknown point of safety in the black,
moonless night. The ride that followed was a piece of delirium
out of Poe or Rimbaud or the drawings of Doré, but finally I
reached Townshend" (CF 2.538).[3] This "delirium" (cognitive
state) is what Lovecraft has built the story around, rather than
such things as the disagreeable lunch offered by his host. The
narrator reinforces that the horror here was not in the things he
saw: "The trouble was in what they led one to infer" (CF 2.538).
The only way to express this type of horror is to document the
narrator's mental state—that is, to use Lovecraft's style. Even
when there are disturbing events in the real world, the horror
remains mostly cognitive. The nominal action in "The Call of
Cthulhu" consists of the narrator reading various papers, examining a bas-relief, and talking to various people. The real action
the narrator's consciousness in the process of "correlat[ing] all
its contents" (CF 2.21). The exterior events of "The Shadow
out of Time" has the narrator recovering from a psychotic break.
But the forms of the verbs "feel," "think," and "know" occur
more than 300 times, sharpening focus on "certain impressions"
in the mind; "*notions* of the cosmos, and of [man's] place in the
seething vortex of time, whose merest mention is paralyzing"
(CF 3.362–63; my emphasis).

Before leaving the example from "Whisperer," we should
note that here again is a first sentence whose ambiguity tips off
the narrator's unreliable state of consciousness. The phrase "see
any visual horror" seems to be a solecism. (It is analogous to saying something like, "I see with my eyes.") But the unusual expression reinforces how horror is not outside (visible) but inside
(within the narrator's consciousness).

The intentional substitution of one grammatical form (per-

---

3. A less successful example of Lovecraft delineating an internal state, more
evocative of a Mack Sennett car chase.

son, case, gender, number, or tense) for another, violating the rules of syntax, is called *enallage*. It is another method to directly convey an unhinged psyche. Lovecraft, an ever-vigilant rhetorician who spilled a tremendous amount of ink flogging the grammar of inexpert amateur journalists (see the "Department of Public Criticism" columns in the *United Amateur*), was familiar with the concept.[4] He blithely cautions the great unwashed that "the use of enallage in prose is at best highly questionable" (*CE* 1.19). Writing anonymously and dissecting his own poem "Phaeton" (1918), he even admonishes himself: "as a purist we must protest against the rhetorical enallage whereby the adverb or preposition *beyond* is made to serve as a noun" (*CE* 1.211).[5] In the fiction he had no such qualms.

Finnish literary critic Liisa Dhal, a specialist in Modernist literature with especial reference to narrative strategy, proposed that "stylistic study is based on the principle that *a mental tension differing from the normal* is represented by a corresponding unusual literary expression. The subject-matter leaves its mark on the style" (441; my emphasis). Lovecraft was operating upon a set of premises dissimilar to other authors—not so much *to tell an accessible story* but *to create mental tension.*

> . . . [No] matter how prosaic the language of a weird tale may seem, it must always be carefully managed with a view to atmospheric effect. Effective weird-fictional language through rhythm & associative word-values, must always have a certain undercurrent of *menacing tensity*. . . . Very, very few things in

4. There are 21 installments of the column from November 1914 to May 1919, amounting to something like 81,000 words. In them, Lovecraft reviewed recent submissions to the United Amateur Press Association, identifying defects and offering advice to improve members' poetry and prose composition. Membership around this time numbered approximately 250 ("United Amateur Press Association," *The Fossils*, thefossils.org/horvat/aj/organizations/uapa.htm. Accessed 28 May 2025.)

5. The lines under consideration are: "Why should I fret in microscopic bonds / That chafe the spirit, and the mind repress / When thro' the clouds gleam *beckoning beyonds* / Whose shining vistas mock man's littleness?" (*AT* 429; my emphasis).

W.T. ever achieve the desired degree of atmospheric menace.
(7 November 1930; *Dawnward Spire* 261)[6]

Tensity as a fictional objective stands with "atmospheric effectiveness" and "weird mood" (December 1936?–February? 1937;
Letters to James F. Morton 399; to Duane W. Rimel, 28 September 1935; *Letters to F. Lee Baldwin* 286) as critical concepts important his understanding.

Lovecraft's reliance on first-person narration has been widely
noted. Indeed, first-person narration is the keystone to his success; his expert and varied use of it in the creation of atmosphere is what most makes his work captivating. Poe's
innovations in first-person technique suggested the idea to
Lovecraft.[7] The latter made it his own, varying it in innovative
ways no writer has done before or since in the service of mood.[8]
It provides a canvas for the unique effects we call Lovecraftian.

Lovecraft is all about the soliloquy of the mind—the mind of eccentric, unbalanced individuals suffering with terrifying circumstances. Relative to this idea, Dahl says:

The presentation of the stream-of-consciousness in fiction dif-

---

6. Relative to the importance of internal monologue in Lovecraft, it is useful to
note how Clark Ashton Smith (one of the few writers whom Lovecraft deemed
as expressing a cosmic sensibility) worked (like most if not all other weird fic-
tionists) in a different mode. While he made heavy use of rhetorical devices
and exotic vocabulary to convey otherworldly vistas, he rarely used stream-of-
consciousness and similar techniques.

7. "The Tell-tale Heart," of course, is the outstanding example of this ground-
breaking technique in Poe.

8. It is difficult to identify other writers who have used first-person narration
specifically as tool to create mood as well as to convey a state of consciousness
instrumental to the work. Of the latter the leading exponents are Joyce, Virginia Woolf, Beckett, and Gertrude Stein. Oddly, Jack Kerouac is another author who worked in this vein, directly "from the mind to the voice" ("On the
Road [song]," *Jack Kerouac Reads On the Road,* Rykodisc, 1999, CD, RCD
10474). Kerouac took the formula to its limit; he claimed never to revise his
first (typewriter) drafts. Nick Mamatas's *Move under Ground* (2004) picks up
on the very tangential commonality, attempting to meld the "mind-styles" of
Kerouac and Lovecraft.

fers from all other psychological writing in that it is concerned with those levels of consciousness that are less developed than rational verbalization. . . . In the psychological novel an attempt is made to reproduce series of associations as they are experienced at the moment at which they originate in the mind, i.e. consciousness at the pre-speech level. It is . . . partly under the influence of the subconscious. Because interior monologue illustrates associations following each other in the order that they develop in the mind it is free from many of the restrictions characteristic of ordinary literary expression. It proceeds with the rhythm of psychic life. Associations sometimes develop consistently, so that each separate fragment contributes to the general impression. In some cases, however, associations follow each other abruptly, seeming to change from the original concept to a completely different or even directly opposed one, if studied superficially. These "leaps" are, however, always in harmony with the psychological background [in Lovecraft, a mood of atmospheric *tensity*]. (440)

She identifies several types of sentences found in internal monologue. The *rounded impressionistic sentence* is a hybrid of traditional and experimental form—impressionistic but with occasional anchoring to the starting point. Sentences with *attributive structure* are even more "loose": additions and modifiers attach freely without strict subordination. *Impressionistic sentences* are merely a chain of loosely connected components with no central focus. Of the latter, Dahl cites critic Luise Thon, who suggests the defining feature of an impressionistic sentence is "paratactic succession" (of which more later).

In some Lovecraft sentences, the starting point seems to fade from awareness as new elements are added. This is due to his heavy use of *addition* in the form of clauses and phrases.[9] Hence

9. A future installment will examine Lovecraft's most characteristic use of clauses (a group of words that contains a subject and a verb; may be adverbial, relative [adjectival], noun), coordinate, non-finite, elliptical) and of phrases (does not contain both a subject and a verb but acts as a single part of speech; noun, verb, adjectival, adverbial, infinitive, participial, gerund, absolute, and most often in Lovecraft, prepositional).

the opening of "Beyond the Wall of Sleep": "I have frequently wondered if the majority of mankind ever pause to reflect upon the occasionally titanic significance of dreams, and of the obscure world to which they belong" (CF 1.171). The contorted diction conveys the narrator's psychological unease from the outset, even before he relates the tangible events he experienced. He has repeatedly wondered (past) and still wonders (present): the focus is on the *act of wondering* itself, as if suspended in time. The sentence is subordinate-heavy, with nested clauses.

Main Clause: "I have frequently wondered"
└── *Dependent Clause (noun clause as object):* "if the majority . . . ever pause to reflect [upon] . . ."
    └── *Object 1:* "the occasionally titanic significance of dreams"
    └── *Object 2 (elliptical):* "[the significance] of the obscure world"
        └── *Relative Clause:* "to which they belong"

The reader has to deal with multiple elements in a single sentence.

- the narrator ("I")
- the majority of mankind
- the act of wondering
- the act of pausing
- the act of reflecting
- the act of belonging dreams
- the significance of dreams
- the obscure world [physical realm] to which [significant dreams] belong

The ensuing story will focus on the "obscure world"—the semiphysical environment of Slater's dreams, experienced in the narrator's mind as journeys impelled by an "active intellect of cosmic entity" (CF 1.71).

The sentence seems to wander around, furthering the sense of dissociation. Then the terse first sentence of the second paragraph snaps us back to reality: "It was from a youthful reverie filled with speculations of this sort that I arose one afternoon in the winter of 1900–1901" (CF 1.72). This example uses "cleft" construction (a form which emphasizes a specific part of a sentence by splitting it into two clauses) to emphasize the source or state from which the narrator (and reader) has emerged—that of "a youthful reverie." Rather than saying in S-V-O form that "I arose from a youthful reverie . . . ," the cleft again shifts focus *to the reverie*. Lovecraft cues us that the winding grammar of the first sentence indicates a specific and important non-rational mental state.

Lovecraft as always chooses words for connotation as much as denotation: "*reverie*" is from the (Old French *resver*, to dream, wander, be delirious). The first paragraph reflects the narrator's mind in that deportment. The subject of the story, an intellectually disabled backwoodsman under the influence of an intergalactic entity, will be shown as one who *wanders* through the cosmos. The connotations of *reverie* foreshadow the narrator's description of these travels: "in a kind of semi-uncorporeal dream life Slater *wandered* or floated through resplendent and prodigious valleys, meadows, gardens, cities, and palaces of light; in a region unbounded and unknown to man." Similarly, Slater "*raved* of things he did not understand and could not interpret" (*CF* 1.77, 76).

The story is keyed to the concept that although Slater experiences incredible things, his internal narrative is too feeble to convey the full import of this to the reader. His most expressive stream-of-consciousness "ravings" under the influence of the cosmic entity tell of a "'big, big cabin with brightness in the roof and walls and floor, . . . the loud queer music far away . . . [and a] thing that shines and shakes and laughs'" (*CF* 1.74). Put another way, his mind-style is inadequate in terms of affecting the reader. The utterances are strange, but not in a way that can create fear or wonder.

To mentally perceive Slater's experiences, the narrator constructs a "cosmic radio"; and (as again prefigured by the first sentence of the story) ends up perceptually *roving* the cosmos. The device works, and we get a more impactful stream-of-consciousness rendering of the visions in question—this time not in the "debased patois" (*CF* 1.73) of the backwoodsman but in a far more effective idiom:

> Chords, vibrations, and harmonic ecstasies echoed passionately on every hand; while on my ravished sight burst the stupendous spectacle of ultimate beauty. Walls, columns, and architraves of

living fire blazed effulgently around the spot where I seemed to
float in air; extending upward to an infinitely high vaulted dome
of indescribable splendour. Blending with this display of palatial
magnificence, or rather, supplanting it at times in kaleidoscopic
rotation, were glimpses of wide plains and graceful valleys, high
mountains and inviting grottoes; covered with every lovely attribute of scenery which my delighted eye could conceive of, yet
formed wholly of some glowing, ethereal, plastic entity, which in
consistency partook as much of spirit as of matter. As I gazed, I
perceived that my own brain held the key to these enchanting
metamorphoses; for each vista which appeared to me, was the
one my changing mind most wished to behold. Amidst this ely-
sian realm I dwelt not as a stranger, for each sight and sound
was familiar to me; just as it had been for uncounted aeons of
eternity before, and would be for like eternities to come. (CF
1.80–81)

The passage serves as one apex of the gripping atmosphere of
the first-person story. Relative to the subject-object phrases of
Slater, the structure, rhythm, and word choice here provide the
characteristic Lovecraft magic. The "big, big house" more com-
pellingly consists of "walls, columns, and architraves of living
fire." The "loud, queer music" is now strikingly described as
"[c]hords, vibrations, and harmonic ecstasies [which] echoed
passionately."

Lovecraft here and elsewhere enhances atmospheric impact
not merely by relating his narrator's internal narrative but also
by complementing or contrasting it with the stream-of-
consciousness of a character who is less articulate or under du-
ress. His most remarkable accomplishment in this vein is in
"The Colour out of Space"—Ammi Pierce's monologue, which
is the most truly terrifying scene he ever wrote. In sheer cosmic
horror it exceeds even the story's climatic scene as experienced
by the narrator, which powerfully conveys the "eruptive cata-
clysm" of the Colour's departure from earth.

Fiendish Violations of Known Natural Law

The debate about how best to define prose style is perennial and too complex to take up here. One instructive idea is to consider how the writing in question differs from "plain English." For this perspective, prose style can be considered *the departure from an expected norm.* We are taught to compose sentences in specific form—subject-verb-object (SVO) or subject-object-verb (SOV). When we use complex sentence forms, we deviate from an implied norm or baseline of formal expectations. Readers notice and are affected by this.

Lovecraft, in the guise of his "18th century senex"[10] persona told a correspondent that "there's no excuse for barking out . . . Hemingway machine-gun fire" (26 March 1932; *MWM* 284). Hemingway's style can stand in as a baseline to show by instructive contrast how Lovecraft works. The former embodies the use of forthright sentences in S-O-V and S-V-O mode. (This is the method of *exclusion* in contrast to Lovecraft's *addition*.) A representative example of Hemingway is "Big Two-Hearted River: Part I." The protagonist has recently returned from World War I, physically and psychically wounded. The story is a first-person narrative, told by an omniscient third-person. The narrative voice gives the effect of a person alienated from the Self: "Nick looked down into the pool from the bridge. It was deep and clear. He saw the trout in the sandy shallows. They were steady in the current. He watched them. They floated motionless. They were not disturbed. He was happy" (151). The style is terse, but not meant to convey mood.

This plain-spoken sentence construction is what readers are conditioned to expect, both by instruction and by their experiences picking up a "typical" book. It is easy to spot the divergent item among the following examples.

---

10. For a discussion of this, see this space in *Lovecraft Annual* No. 13 (2019): 204–14.

Author	Story	Pub. Date	First Sentence
Stephen Crane	"The Price of the Harness"	1898	"Twenty-five men were making a road out of a path up the hillside." (1)
Ring Lardner	"Harmony"	1915	"Even a baseball writer must sometimes work." (571)
Sherwood Anderson	"Death in the Woods"	1924	"She was an old woman and lived on a farm near the town in which I lived." (3)
Seabury Quinn	"The Devil's Rosary"	1929	"My friend Jules De Grandin was in a seasonably sentimental mood." (437)
Lovecraft	"Hypnos"	1923	"May the merciful gods, if indeed there be such, guard those hours when no power of the will, or drug that the cunning of man devises, can keep me from the chasm of sleep." (CF 1.325)[11]

Lovecraft is an outlier relative to expectations, even in the context of a pulp fiction milieu.

One amusing way to further illustrate the point is to contrast Lovecraft's style with an unadorned style. Take as an example a random paragraph from "The Colour out of Space":

By September all the vegetation was fast crumbling to a greyish powder, and Nahum feared that the trees would die before the poison was out of the soil. His wife now had spells of terrific screaming, and he and the boys were in a constant state of nervous tension. They shunned people now, and when school opened the boys did not go. But it was Ammi, on one of his rare visits, who first realised that the well water was no longer good. It had an evil taste that was not exactly foetid nor exactly salty, and Ammi advised his friend to dig another well on higher

---

11. I hope I may be forgiven for (obviously) slanting the examples here to reinforce my point. Such are the charms of writing a column and not an academic paper.

ground to use till the soil was good again. Nahum, however, ignored the warning, for he had by that time become calloused to
strange and unpleasant things. He and the boys continued to
use the tainted supply, drinking it as listlessly and mechanically
as they ate their meagre and ill-cooked meals and did their
thankless and monotonous chores through the aimless days.
There was something of stolid resignation about them all, as if
they walked half in another world between lines of nameless
guards to a certain and familiar doom. (CF 2.381)

By way of contrasting how much this departs from an S-O-V or
S-V-O baseline, here is a rewrite of the passage.

It was September. The plants turned to powder. Nahum worried
the trees would die. He thought the poison would stay in the
ground. His wife screamed. Nahum and the boys heard her.
They all felt fear. They turned away from people. School
opened. The boys stayed home. Ammi came to the house. He
drank the water. The taste had changed. Ammi told this to Nahum. He said dig a new well. Nahum ignored him. He and the
boys drank the water anyway. They ate the tainted food. They
worked aimlessly. They sleepwalked through the days. They
waited for the end.[12]

The plain (non-Lovecraft) manner is less likely to move us,
less likely to stay with us, and less likely compel us to return to it
again and again. Go back to the original and observe exactly
how Lovecraft deviates from a standard point of departure.

Having been reminded that Lovecraft is manipulating our
consciousness with narrative technique, we begin to notice the
varied and powerful methods he used. While using traditional
onomatopoeia for effect, he advances by sometimes impounding
it into the textual structure itself.

---

12. I initially attempted to use Artificial Intelligence (ChatGPT) to convert
Lovecraft's original text into "plain-speak." (Readers are encouraged to try this
amusing exercise themselves using choice passages from the fiction.) The AI
performed so poorly I had to do it myself. It is now *de rigueur* to note that no
other AI is used here or elsewhere.

> West of Arkham the hills rise wild, and there are
> valleys with deep woods that no axe
> has ever
> **cut.**
>
> (CF 2.367)

"Rise" and "wild" contain the same complex vowel sound (/aɪ/) that begins with one open vowel and glides to another within the same syllable. In this gliding we metaphorically ascend with the hills. Conversely, "deep woods" (/iː/ /ʊ/) are simple vowel sounds which lend a sense of release and descent. The vowel articulation of "rise," "wild," and "deep" are tense and seem to denote rising motion. The vowel articulation of "woods" and "cut" (/ʌ/) are lax, metaphorically letting us down. The sound of "cut" punctuates the end with a thud, as an abruptly landing on the forest floor.

Lovecraft uses a similar rhetorical gambit is during Wilmarth's auto journey into the unknown: "After that we cast off all allegiance to immediate, tangible, and time-touched things, and entered a fantastic world of hushed unreality in which the narrow, ribbon-like road rose and fell and curved with an almost sentient and purposeful caprice amidst the tenantless green peaks and half-deserted valleys" (CF 2.510). Up, down, around, it is almost enough to make one carsick as well as uneasy. It is an illustration of Lovecraft's idea that "the inner rhythms of the prose structure must be carefully fitted to the incidents as they march along" (24 March 1931; WBT 162). Except here we are driving rather than marching.

Lovecraft's additive style, initially confounding readers expecting the S-V-O or S-O-V sentence structure, eventually becomes its own baseline in its sonorous musical effects and escalating periods. That is, after time spent reading and re-reading Lovecraft, his unique manner of expression becomes accommodated or normalized. It effectively becomes the new reference point.

Knowing this, Lovecraft doubles back and reverses the reversal, so to speak. At critical narrative junctures, he will switch out of usual complex sentence mode and go to a simple S-V-O or S-O-V form. There are numerous memorable examples.

- I'm coming down! (CF 1.138)
- You can't understand! (CF 1.138)
- You see them? (CF 1.199)
- But that was not all. (CF 2.386)
- I hear him! (CF 1.162)
- We must go! (CF 1.162)
- That came from Yuggoth. (CF 2.518)
- My brain! My brain! (CF 3.349)
- [M]y head's no good. (CF 2.389)

In the context of the established point of departure (e.g., Lovecraft's characteristic idiom), these simple sentences become increasingly impactful and linger long in the memory.

So when the narrative effect called for it, Lovecraft was not above using a bit of staccato "machine-gun fire," though always in service of the interior monologue of the narrator or character. Note the diary entries of Robert Blake: "The lights must not go"; "It knows where I am"; "I must destroy it"; and . . ."Lights out— God help me" (CF 3.472–73). This is stream-of-consciousness using what Thon called "paratactic succession." Another example is the radio transmission from *At the Mountains of Madness:* "They cannot stand the things. . . . Papers must get this right. . . . Spread wings have serrated edges. . . . Flexibility surprising despite vast toughness" (CF 3.37–39). Lovecraft's sentences thus need not be complex to create a sense of disorientation. Later in his career he found ways to evoke a mood of fear using more compact sentence forms. *At the Mountains of Madness* is told in the first-person by geology professor William Dyer. While not exactly straightforward in grammatical form, the opening does not pile on clauses as elsewhere in Lovecraft: "I am forced into speech because men of science have refused to follow my advice without knowing why" (CF 3.11). As with "The Tomb" and "Beyond the Wall of Sleep" but in a different manner, we are instantly thrown off balance. Dyer says scientists refuse to follow his advice "without knowing why." Did the scientists refuse to follow his advice, without knowing *why they refused to follow his advice?* Or did the scientists refuse to follow his advice, without knowing *why he gave them the advice?*

Possibly both, or neither. Perhaps the narrator is just out of his mind. Again, to suggest that this anomaly is mere incompetence on the part of the author is ridiculous. This is Lovecraft having written for two decades, in a story widely acknowledged to represent him at the apex of his powers. There is no possibility an author with such a "keenly developed sense of the niceties of English usage"[13] would neglect to revise for clarity the very first sentence of a novella of some 1,400 or so sentences.

Critic Louise Rosenblatt blended elements of reader-response criticism and close reading to formulate a "transactional" model of reading. The informed reader and the text continuously act and are acted upon by one another. She contrasted *efferent reading* (the way we approach non-fiction) with *aesthetic reading*.[14] Of the latter Rosenblatt states, "In aesthetic reading, the reader's attention is centered directly on what he is living through during his relationship with that particular text." Further, the "'thinking and feeling and seeing' during the reading is both the purpose of aesthetic reading and the essence of the aesthetic experience" (Rosenblatt, *The Reader, the Text, the Poem* 25; "What Facts" 287). So too with how to read Lovecraft.

In the next installment, we examine Lovecraft's work in light of cognitive poetics—how language reflects and shapes our thought processes. A related concept is that of entrainment, the psychology of how consciousness can become synchronized with external rhythmic stimuli.

Works Cited

Anderson, Sherwood. *Death in the Woods and Other Stories*. New York: Liveright, 1933.

---

13. This priceless locution, used here solely through a lack of restraint, is from a "Situations Wanted" classified ad Lovecraft placed in the *New York Times* in August 1924 (reprinted in *IAP* 509). The ad prompted a response from an employment agency, who apparently sensed that here was a job-seeker in dire need of help. Look for appropriate situations to try it out on colleagues.

14. Rosenblatt coined the term "efferent" from the Latin *efferre* ("to carry away").

Baldick, Chris. *Criticism and Literary Theory: 1890 to the Present*. New York: Routledge, 1996.

———. *The Oxford Dictionary of Literary Terms*. New York: Oxford University Press, 2015.

Bradbury, Malcolm, and James McFarlane, ed. *Modernism: 1890–1930*. Harmondsworth, UK: Penguin, 1976.

Crane, Stephen. *Wounds in the Rain: War Stories*. New York: Frederick A. Stokes Co., 1900.

Dahl, Liisa. "The Attributive Sentence Structure in the Stream-of-Consciousness Technique: With Special Reference to the Interior Monologue Used by Virginia Woolf, James Joyce and Eugene O'Neill." *Neuphilologische Mitteilungen* 68 (1967): 440–54.

Hemingway, Ernest. *In Our Time*. New York: Scribner, 1996.

Lardner, Ring. "Harmony." In *The Portable Ring Lardner*. Ed. Gilbert Seldes. New York: Viking Press, 1946.

Lovecraft, H. P. *Letters to Elizabeth Toldridge and Anne Tillery Renshaw*. Ed. David E. Schultz and S. T. Joshi. New York: Hippocampus Press, 2014.

———. *Letters to F. Lee Baldwin, Duane W. Rimel, and Nils Frome*. Ed. David E. Schultz and S. T. Joshi. New York: Hippocampus Press, 2016.

———. *Letters to J. Vernon Shea, Carl F. Strauch, and Lee McBride White*. Ed. S. T. Joshi and David E. Schultz. New York: Hippocampus Press, 2016.

———. *Letters to James F. Morton*. Ed. David E. Schultz and S. T. Joshi. New York: Hippocampus Press, 2011.

———. *Letters to Maurice W. Moe and Others*. Ed. David E. Schultz and S. T. Joshi. New York: Hippocampus Press, 2018.

———, and Clark Ashton Smith. *Dawnward Spire, Lonely Hill: The Letters of H. P. Lovecraft and Clark Ashton Smith*. Ed. David E. Schultz and S. T. Joshi. New York: Hippocampus Press, 2017.

Mosig, Dirk W. *Mosig at Last: A Psychologist Looks at Lovecraft*. West Warwick, RI: Necronomicon Press, 1997.

Quinn, Seabury. "The Devil's Rosary." *Weird Tales* 13, No. 4 (April 1929): 427–54, 567–72.

Rosenblatt, Louise M. *The Reader, the Text, the Poem: The Transactional Theory of the Literary Work*. Carbondale: Southern Illinois University Press, 1978.

————. "'What Facts Does This Poem Teach You?'" *Language Arts* 57 (1980): 386–94.

Wilson, Edmund. "Tales of the Marvellous and the Ridiculous" (1945). In *Classics and Commercials: A Literary Chronicle of the Forties.* New York: Farrar, Straus & Giroux, 1950. 286–90.

Briefly Noted

August Derleth's *Sac Prairie Journal* for 1938, just published by the August Derleth Society, contains intriguing discussions of Derleth's attempts to secure the book publication of Lovecraft's tales. In a trip to New York that Derleth made in September 1938, he stopped in at the office of Charles Scribner's Sons (which had just published his Sac Prairie novel *Wind over Wisconsin*). A laconic entry for September 12 reads: "Some discussion of the Lovecraft omnibus of short stories." This is clearly what became *The Outsider and Others.* Later that day Derleth met Donald Wandrei and others in a Kalem Club meeting, noting: "Don Wandrei and I made our report, carrying news of Scribners interest, and suggesting that a selection of his work published thusly [*sic*] would greatly aid the cause rather than our holding out for an omnibus at this time. To that everyone was agreed." Derleth provides brief portraits of the Kalem members who showed up at Frank Long's apartment on that September evening: "Most of the Kalem Club had already assembled; I met them in rapid succession—Herman Koenig, a tall; towheaded young man in his early thirties, a quiet, assured person; venerable Dr. James F. Morton; white-headed and white of moustache, stout of body, and very thoroughly a gentleman; Rheinhardt [*sic*] Kleiner, a thin, thin-faced, big-eared and big-eyed man of middle age, nondescript in brown; Arthur Leeds, an aging man betraying all the marks of faded gentility, with tired eyes, a well-trimmed moustache, iron grey hair standing out against his dark skin, an odd little old-fashioned wing collar contrasting his black coat, his neatly combed hair with the aspect of wetness and cleanliness; Claire Beck, a red-headed youth, a little raw, coatless and somewhat shy with the general air of a knight of the road; Kenneth Sterling, a young Hebrew of obviously marked intelligence, dark of hair and eyes, reserved and with an air of listening; Miss [Margaret] Sylvester, a slight, dark-eyed Jewess, who professed her eagerness to do what she could to perpetuate HPL's memory by typing his letters as we edited them; Donald Wollheim, a quiet attendant, who had little to say; Samuel Loveman, wide-eyed, eager for debate, always ready for discussion about anything, accompanied by a young ballet dancer, who argued that Masters was through, he was done, he had no social consciousness, which I stepped hard upon and silenced. Finally, there was Mrs. Long, who was preparing some welsh rarebit for the assembled friends of Lovecraft: a stout woman, with a motherly interest in the entire gathering."

Contributors

Peter Cannon has been publishing works related to H. P. Lovecraft, both nonfiction and fiction, since 1978. His latest book is *Long Memories and Other Writings* (Hippocampus Press, 2022).

Harley Carnell lives and writes in London. His fiction, which has been nominated for the Pushcart Prize, appears in *Confrontation, Litro, Shooter Literary*, and *Riptide Journal*, among others. His critical work appears in the *Lovecraft Annual, Gamut, L'Espirit Literary*, and *Aurealis*. A lifelong devotee of weird fiction, he counts Lovecraft, Thomas Ligotti, and Shirley Jackson among his influences.

Martin Dempsey received his Ph.D. from the University of Westminster and holds a master's degree from the University of Exeter. He writes TTRPG scenarios rooted in Lovecraft's Mythos for Xipe Totec Press and served as narrative designer for *Lovecraft's Untold Stories* 1 & 2. His fascination with cosmic horror began at fourteen with "Pickman's Model" and has evolved into a lifelong philosophical and narrative engagement with cosmicism across academic and gaming platforms.

Ken Faig, Jr. has been studying Lovecraft's life and work for more than fifty years. He is the author of *The Parents of Howard Phillips Lovecraft* (1990), *The Unknown Lovecraft* (2009), and *Lovecraftian People and Places* (2009), and *More Lovecraftian People and Places* (2025), among many other books and articles.

James Goho is a researcher and writer with many publications on dark fiction. In 2014, Rowman & Littlefield published his *Journeys into Darkness: Critical Essays on Gothic Horror*. McFarland published his *Caitlín R. Kiernan: A Critical Study of Her*

Dark Fiction in 2020. His higher education research is found in academic journals, and his infrequent short stories appear in literary magazines. He lives in Winnipeg, Canada.

Pietro Guarriello is an Italian collector and scholar of weird literature. Through his amateur press he edits and publishes three journals: *Studi Lovecraftiani, Zothique,* and *Weird*—the last dedicated to discovering and translating rare classics of the fantastic. He has written numerous articles and essays and has edited books by William Hope Hodgson, Clark Ashton Smith, Arthur Machen, H. P. Lovecraft, Stefan Grabinski, and others. His most recent work is *Canti dall'Altrove* (2025), a study and translation of Lovecraft's poetry.

Dylan Henderson is a fifth-year doctoral student at Purdue University, where he studies English literature, specializing in weird fiction, H. P. Lovecraft, and pulp magazines. Before returning to graduate school, he worked for many years in public libraries, having additional degrees in history and library science. Born in rural Oklahoma, he now lives with his wife and two small children outside of Battle Ground, Indiana.

Rebecca Kunkel is a reference librarian at Rutgers Law Library in Newark, New Jersey, where she also works on developing and expanding the library's collection of free online legal resources. In previous versions of herself she clerked for the U.S. Court of Appeals for the Armed Forces and worked for the State of Maryland as an assistant public defender. In her spare time she enjoys searching for the symbols of the divine in the trash stratum.

Steven J. Mariconda has been writing on H. P. Lovecraft since 1983. His work was collected in *H. P. Lovecraft: Art, Artifact, and Reality* (Hippocampus Press, 2013). He was the Scholar Guest of Honor at NecronomiCon Providence 2017. A 10,000-word essay, "To Thrill and Agitate: Complex Figuration in Emerson and Lovecraft," will appear in the forthcoming *Father of the American Mind: The Influence and Continuing Relevance of Emerson's Philosophy on Culture and Society* (Routledge Studies in

American Philosophy), edited by Emile Alexandrov and Steve Stakland.

Duncan Norris is a resident of Brisbane, Australia, who has haunted strange, far places including an overgrown city in Africa, ruined monasteries in Asia, and archaeological digs for vampires in nightmare countries. His book *Things I Want to Say to Joe: A Conversation about Aliens, Atlantis, and Archaeology* is now available via Amazon.

Felix John Taylor is a writer living in Oxfordshire, England. His literary history of the Order of the Golden Dawn will be published in 2026, and he is now working on a book about Arthur Machen.

Michael Uhall is an academic, author, and translator currently based in the United States. His academic and nonfiction work has appeared in *3:AM Magazine, the Ancillary Review of Books, Contemporary Political Theory, DIFFRACTIONS, Gothic Nature Journal, Limina, Nature and Culture, Rhizomes, SYNTHETIC ZERØ, Utopia District,* and *Vault of Culture,* as well as various academic and university presses. His fiction has appeared in publications from Grimscribe Press, Hedera Felix, Moth Hovel Games, Mount Abraxas Press, Pseudopod, Raphus Press, and Ulthar Press.

A retired academic librarian, **Steve Walker** has had an enthrallment with Lovecraft since the mid-1960s, and most relevantly this came down into his joining in 1986 the Lovecraft amateur press association the Esoteric Order of Dagon, for which he turns out a fanzine, *The Criticaster*. He has talked about him at various conferences.

Thijmen Zuiderwijk is a freelance writer and translator. He holds an M.A. in North American Studies from Leiden University. He lives in The Hague.